SUPERVISING

SUPERVISING
a guide for all levels

Paul O. Radde

Distributed by
UNIVERSITY ASSOCIATES

SUPERVISING:
A Guide for All Levels

Library of Congress Catalog Card Number: 81-1827
ISBN 0-89384-053-X
Printed in the United States of America

Learning Concepts
Austin, Texas

Distributed by University Associates, Inc.
8517 Production Avenue
P.O. Box 26240
San Diego, California 92126

To Geraldine, Mercedes, and Angela Morris, my parents, who
  supervised my health, safety, and upbringing;
To Walter Langford, friend and project director, who tolerated my
  early attempts at supervising live employees;
To Albert Shapero, professor and friend, who inspires me with his
  zest for life and empirical data;
To Benjamin Franklin Purdy, colleague and friend, who made me
  aware that supervising is different from "doing the work";
To Larry Nolan Davis, friend, colleague, mentor, who first
  suggested this book and guided it to completion.

CONTENTS

Read it all

I. What It Means to Choose to Supervise: The Supervisory Role

II. Supervising When It's All Happening at Once

Read it all

III. Supervising in the Human Dimension

Dramatic vs. effective supervision—Critical incidents—
Fear is the motivator—Catastrophizing—The survival
mentality—You can get from "trying" to doing—
Heroics!—Perfectionism is an inhuman demand—"I never
ask more of you than I ask of myself"—"My door
is always open"—Don't "should" on yourself—Because
you are human—Dealing with your "shoulds"

List of Figures

List of Tables

Preface

Can you use one of the following benefits from reading this book?

_____ "I want to know what supervising is all about. I especially want to know if I am doing everything that is expected of me as a supervisor." Supervisory responsibilities are covered thoroughly.

_____ "Employees can demand a lot from me, but what can I legitimately demand from them? What power and what rights do I have as a supervisor?" Supervisory power is described at some length, and you are encouraged to exercise your rights with employees and management.

_____ "I've heard of employee suits—directly against their supervisors for negligence in duties—that resulted in damage to career advancement and loss of income just from mismanagement. What do I have to do to cover my rear end?" Supervisory conferences, documentation, evaluation, and feedback are just a few of the items covered in the learning modules in Part II.

_____ "I need a good desk-top reference I can go to for advice when I run into trouble with an employee." The learning modules cover a range of topics from hiring through termination, the full range of the supervisory cycle.

_____ "I don't want to read some moldy manuscript on supervising or some ivory tower textbook with highfalutin' theories and language." Most of the material for the book came from supervisory training sessions of new and seasoned supervisors from a wide spectrum of organizations. It is written to be both informative and easy reading.

_____ "Is is possible to enjoy supervising? I've heard so many different opinions. I know I will have to work harder to learn how at first. But then, I want to enjoy myself." Part I will help you through your transition from employee to supervisor, while the learning modules are available on specific topics when you need to refer to them, and Part III, "Supervising in the Human Dimension," should give supervisors some sound basis for enjoying the job.

_____ "I see supervising as just a first step up the line to upper management. I want to advance rapidly, but I don't want to get overextended, so that I suddenly find myself in a position in which my skills don't apply any more." The supervisory issues and skills are treated in a generic way—equally applicable to first-line supervisors and mid-level and upper managers who also supervise. You can take this book with you when you move up the line.

Your needs and concerns will determine how useful this guide will be in supervising. Whether your incentive for reading and using it is job security, preventing a possible future law suit, increasing productivity, or learning the "joy of supervision," I hope that you will also improve your supervisory practices.

Supervisors have a lot of concerns about their position. Many do not spend sufficient time in training (if indeed they get any formal supervisory training at all) to incorporate sound supervisory practice into their daily work with employees. So many of us who supervise tend to think that because we have a college or graduate degree, we have some innate or natural ability to supervise. Our employees would tell us otherwise. To supervise correctly requires understanding, skill, and commitment. I have attempted to provide some of that understanding and some skill in the following pages. You will have to provide the commitment.

How can one book provide all these things to the new and seasoned supervisor?

The first part provides an *initiation* and an *orientation* to supervising. The second part provides a *smorgasbord of supervisory topics and issues* in distinct learning modules, which you can sample at your leisure. The final part provides a narrative establishing a new *perspective* and possibly a different attitude for confronting supervisory responsibilities, activities, and interactions.

Part I—What It Means to Choose to Supervise: The Supervisory Role

To elaborate, *Supervising: A Guide for All Levels* is written to benefit the brand new and the seasoned supervisor. The new supervisor can use it to guide his transition into the new role with its attendant responsibilities.

The book can help the new supervisor find and use the support of some of the power vested in the supervisory position, once he knows about it. He may be resistant to even taking on the role due to wide-ranging myths about what supervisors should not do. The new and the seasoned supervisor may both have encountered impediments to assuming their position fully. All these issues are addressed in Part I. New supervisors especially will benefit.

Part II—Supervising When It's All Happening at Once

The seasoned supervisor, especially, will find the nineteen distinct learning modules in Part II useful for quick reference and consultation. With topics ranging from the "selection process" to "playing the system the way it is" and from "personal feelings" to "shaping up or shipping out the employee," this part of the guide provides a convenient, desk-top reference for planning supervisory conferences, problem solving, and taking personnel actions—and it allows for short-course study in just about any topic of your choosing. You may select any single module at random and read it, for each module stands on its own (except Module 8, which requires a reading of Module 7 first).

Part III—Supervising in the Human Dimension

Finally, Part III provides a fresh and humane perspective on "supervising in the human dimension" that rises above the turmoil and stress of the work place and seeks to resettle supervisory activity at a manageable and supportive level. In Part III, you will be able to pose some essential questions for yourself, such as "Do you want to be effective or dramatic?" and acknowledge some observations tempered by reality, such as "Perfectionism is an inhuman demand." You will have the opportunity to explore your "survival mentality," "heroics," and illusions about "critical incidents" in supervising.

So—while Part I assists you in taking on your supervisory responsibility through confronting internal and external resistance and Part II provides you with a reference library of short courses on supervising elements and issues—Part III is designed to help you reduce the physical and emotional wear and tear of supervising. You may even learn to enjoy your work.

PART I

WHAT IT MEANS TO CHOOSE TO SUPERVISE: THE SUPERVISORY ROLE

Introduction

Surprisingly, this part of the book is for both new and seasoned supervisors. The surprise may come for seasoned supervisors—especially the supervisors who long ago thought they had worked through the issues of their transition from employee to supervisor. Yet many supervisors who have made the outward transition still feel some resistance to the role.

Sources of resistance to supervising are numerous. And even though you may have been in a supervisory position for some years, you may have had difficulty capturing some sense of your own resistance. There is nothing automatic about accepting supervisory responsibility even though you may have initially sought the job.

Many employees move into supervisory positions without freely or deliberately choosing or accepting the responsibilities of the position. For some, it seems like an automatic thing to do—"Others have done it. I guess I will too." "After you're here so long on the line, you become a supervisor." There is little thought given to what constitutes supervision, little differentiation between the supervisory position and the prior position. Without a clear delineation of the responsibilities of supervision, it is possible for an employee to enter that position and appear to carry it out. Yet, he or she never really accepts the position, partly because the differences in responsibilities are never acknowledged.

Supervision is sometimes seen as somewhere between a "rock and a hard place" on the organization chart. The supervisor is the last member of management to deal with policy, procedures, and objectives—which often are formulated several levels above or in a central office far from the supervisor's input and realities. It can be a lonely position indeed.

Reluctance to fully accept supervisory responsibilities also emerges in some highly regulated work sites. The supervisor may be vulnerable to the wrath of employees when the organization does not maintain health and safety regulations. In some cases, employees have to leave the union when they take a supervisory position. They are then seen as management and subtle references may be made to slashing their tires if they try to carry out their supervisory responsibilities.

Some of the resistance to the position is more subtle—even the supervisor may not necessarily realize he is resisting. He may hold fewer supervisory conferences or unit meetings than necessary to keep employees current, or fail to document deficient performance because he sees it as unnecessary "paperwork." In fact, only the supervisor himself can tell just how it is that he projects the image of supervising, carrying out the responsibilities of the role and yet resisting the role.

Part I is intended to jar your awareness of some of these issues, to assist you in completing your transition from employee to supervisor— even if you have been supervising for some time. Chapter 1 looks at the functions of the supervisor by considering the power inherent in the supervisory position itself. Chapter 2 elaborates on the supervisory role, separating fact from fantasy. In Chapter 3, you will have a chance to review your actual transition from employee to supervisor and then consider some additional factors that may continue to restrict your effectiveness within the unit. Chapter 4 is a brisk walk through the ongoing cycle of supervisory activities. It provides an overview of your job responsibilities as a supervisor as it defines and distinguishes the important milestones in the entire cycle of your interaction with employees—from hiring to termination.

So, Part I helps you "get into it" more fully...by exposing you to the foundations of solid supervisory practices and encouraging you to look at how you accept and execute the supervisory role.

Becoming one of "them"—management—means taking on a wider mantle of authority than just your own individual productivity within the organization. You now stand in the line of authority to effect the total production of your unit. You are also immensely important in both the job development and the career development of the employees within your unit. So, the choice to become a supervisor and to work in that position directly affects the organization and your employees.

Throughout your supervisory career, it is important for you to be aware of the resistance you encounter in yourself to performing your supervisory functions and activities. Your choice to supervise did not stop with your acceptance of the promotion. You have a continuing choice to remove yourself from that responsibility. Or you have a duty to go beyond your initial acceptance of the position—to choose to deal with the organizational and interactional issues that will continue to arise throughout your career in supervision.

Be aware of this continuing choice and the additional daily choices implicit in your remaining in the supervisory position. The job is active, not passive or automatic. You have to make some effort to assimilate and activate all your responsibilities. Not only does your career depend upon how well you learn your position, but your employees will benefit or be deprived, as will the organization, by the way you perform the supervisory role.

Your career can probably survive your subtle resistance and inaction. But why risk it? On the other hand, your career can thrive if you provide yourself with a solid grounding in sound supervisory practices. If you choose to remain in supervision, a wide range of job opportunities are open to you beyond the position you hold now. You place yourself on a career track with multiple opportunities ahead.

1

The Strong Suit For Supervision

In many ways supervising can be a piece of cake. You need not agonize over all of the decisions and interactions that drain off the energy of an uninformed supervisor. You simply have to *know what inherent vested powers you have going for you as a supervisor.* There are many safeguards and bargaining points built into a supervisory position. That is why it makes so much sense to know both the full range of responsibilities of the position and also how others properly relate to you in that position. The position is choreographed so that you and your employees can work together. In many respects you have it made to begin with. You only need discover how you have it made, how it all fits together. Without this knowledge it is possible that your assumptions alone could keep you from exercising your position activities productively. So, here are some key points that can lighten your supervisory tasks.

YOUR EMPLOYEES ARE CONSENTING ADULTS

Each employee in your unit was once outside the organization that employs you—working somewhere else, walking the streets, going to school. And at some time, each individual heard about a job opening in your organization.

Each individual became an employee through a series of choices. He or she chose to inquire about the job, chose to interview for the job, chose to stay in contention through the selection process, and chose to accept the job when it was offered. At that choice point, once the job offer was made, each individual became an employee of your organization through his or her own choice and consent.

> ## *Major Point About Supervising*
> Your employees are consenting adults. Each employee chose to take the job and stay. It is not your job to "make" your employees work.

5

YOUR EMPLOYEES PRESENTED THEMSELVES AS CAPABLE ADULTS

When people present themselves to interview for employment, it is their responsibility to approach some job position for which they have *a reasonable and timely possibility* of fulfilling the requirements. It is the responsibility of the applicant to make up for deficits in job capability and job performance early. It is important for the applicant to understand those deficits and the job requirements in order to fill the gaps, for it can be damaging to the employee's career as well as a setback for the unit if others have to continue to fill in for the new employee's shortfalls in production.

The interviewer also has the responsibility for determining whether the potential employee is capable of the job performance. An interviewer generally attempts to meet or match job requirements with an able applicant. If the position to be filled requires immediate performance and the work is essential to the production of the unit, the interviewer will look for someone who can match the job position. *Match* means the new employee can step into the position and perform with a minimum of adaptation to the job. The employee is ready to go without further training. *Meet* means that the new employee has the basic background and skill to perform the job but may require some time to develop full capability for the job requirements, perhaps with further orientation or training.

Unfortunately, applicants too often do their best at "image management," accepting the interview as a challenge to be overcome. Applicants often bluff, just to get chosen, paying little attention to whether they can, or even care to, perform the actual job activities. The interviewer-supervisor often feels stuck when he or she selects a promising applicant and later finds the employee lacking.

And unfortunately the interviewer sometimes bluffs a bit also—to present the most favorable impression of the job and of the organization. In that attempt, the interviewer can become seductive by overselling the organization, promising more than the job can deliver. When the interviewer sells, rather than attempting to select an employee whose qualifications meet or match the job requirements, the supervisor may be left to "kiss a frog," relying on magic to turn the person selected into a capable employee. Luckily, the selection process extends through the probationary period for the new employee and for the supervisor.

Major Point About Supervising

Employee responsibility to the organization begins with the hiring interview. *Both* the interviewer and the applicant have a responsibility to match real ability, potential, and willingness to learn with the actual requirements of the job.

YOUR EMPLOYEE HAS A CONTRACT

Once an applicant accepts a job offer, he or she enters into a contractual relationship with the organization.

In signing on with the organization, the new employee receives information on the tasks to be performed (job description), the general function of the job, and other specifics such as salary range, vacation, and absence policy. In choosing to become an employee, the individual agrees to perform the essential duties set forth in the job description and in the interview. For a reasonable performance of these duties, the employee receives a salary and other benefits.

Supervisors often operate under the mistaken belief that employees perform job duties out of loyalty or love for the supervisor. Even if this were the employee's rationale for actually doing the work, this belief ignores the reality of the employee's contractual relationship with the organization. The organization can still expect and exact specific performance from the employee or replace the employee.

Furthermore, if you as supervisor think that employees are there solely due to your personal charm, try not paying them for a few weeks and see how long they continue to show up to work for you. Don't flatter yourself.

Major Point About Supervising

Your employees are under contract with the organization. By contract they are entitled to remuneration and benefits *in return for* the specific performance of job activities and responsibilities assigned to their position.

PERSON + (EMPLOYMENT CONTRACT + JOB POSITION + ORGANIZATION) = PERSONNEL

Once you sign on with an organization, you are no longer just a person to that organization. You are an employee, and as an employee you are "personnel." You now have specific tasks and activities to perform, and you are paid for what you do. That is one distinguishing feature between individuals outside the organization and those of you who are employees on the payroll...you have a contract.

Part of your supervisory responsibility as an agent or representative of the organization is to make this contract explicit. Before your employees can meet objectives, you have to communicate clearly and specifically what they are to do.

Nothing befuddles work relationships more than not having an initial clear understanding of one's duties as an employee. Excessive emphasis on the personal aspects of supervisor-employee relationships— "motivating" employees and relating to them as "people"—may obscure the working relationship that is the basis for supervisor-employee inter- action. Ignoring the basis for this working relationship—the tasks that must be done—jeopardizes productivity. Lack of productivity can threaten the very continuation of the organization, and employees are the first to feel the high stress of that situation when they question their own continuity with the organization. Therefore, the work relationship necessarily comes first.

Establishing and maintaining humane, high quality work relation- ships depends first and foremost upon meeting the main objectives of the organization. Organizational productivity guarantees a continuing environment in which employees can perform with increasing skill and satisfaction. The work relationship is essential, involving all the exchanges of information, support, supplies, and agreements required to get the job done.

Major Point About Supervision

When you enter an organization under employment contract you become "personnel." The focus or basis for the supervisor-employee relationship is the work, which must continue to be held primary and foremost to sustain the mission of the organization and the organization itself.

EMPLOYMENT: A CHOICE TO PERFORM UNDER CONTRACT

Your employees have a position in the organization independent of you. They are not "your people." While you are supervising their work unit, they are the personnel you work through. However, when you are on vacation, absent, promoted, or transferred, they continue to be employees of the organization and to perform in their distinct capacities. Their contract is with the organization.

Employment is a contractual proposition. It transcends specific personal relationships and has a legal character to it. The organization extends beyond your involvement, so know the responsible limits of your involvement with employees and with the organization.

Your employees have a contract with the organization to perform the tasks set out in their job descriptions. They are accountable for this performance. As the agent for the organization, you are there to help them keep on track with their performance and stay focused on their outcomes. You do this by providing resources, support, and guidance so they can reach their objectives. But remember, employees will continue to have specific performance requirements and objectives under their contract with the organization whether you are the supervisor or someone else is. Your employees have a contract that says they take responsibility for being in the organization. They are therefore accountable for fulfilling their side of the contract through satisfactory performance.

Major Point About Supervision

In most cases you will supervise intact, physically and mentally competent human beings who are capable of performing job tasks and learning new skills. They chose to work in their positions, and, by virtue of their employment contract, they assume responsibility to carry out the majority of the tasks assigned them within your unit.

SOME EMPLOYEES WILL NOT MAKE IT

Some employees are hired on the basis of their perceived potential, their developed skills, and their initiative to reduce their deficiencies. One of your responsibilities as a supervisor is to help them develop their capabilities. However, you are not expected to work miracles. Attempts to make a skilled technician out of a klutz only exercise one's desire to be heroic, to be all-powerful and godlike. You have to have the basic raw material, some fundamental competence to work with. Fortunately, most adult employees will possess some developed capabilities as well as some perceived potential for development.

You may have interviewed and selected a new employee, someone who cannot perform. If you did, you know that you made a poor selection. Learn from your mistakes.

However, you may not have had a major role in interviewing, or you may not have had the final say. Yet you have this employee to work with.

Now you have to decide whether the employee is capable or not. And you may not be able to determine that without considerable interaction, support, guidance, and assessment. The employee's responsibility extends beyond just taking the job. It extends to learning the job, and that may require employee initiative in seeking information, guidance, on-the-job training, and practice—taking active steps to meet the full requirements of the job . . . both present and future.

If you "inherited" the employee and determine the employee is *not* capable and *not* trainable, then, no matter who did the hiring, either shift the employee into a job that meets his abilities or terminate him. The employee may even request a transfer if he is concerned about his career. With luck, you will discover the employee's major shortcomings during the probationary period of employment and take appropriate action.

Major Point About Supervising

Your employees share responsibility for choosing, learning, and performing their job activities . . . and if some employee is unsalvageable, you are not his or her keeper.

YOU'RE NOT ASKING ANY FAVORS . . .

. . . when you ask an employee to do his job. From one perspective, it is in the employee's best interest to perform these tasks. If he does not, his job will be vulnerable. Someone else will be brought in to fill his position.

Many supervisors think that requesting an employee to work depends on the supervisor's leadership ability and charisma. Hogwash! The work is the employee's contractual obligation.

Here are a few phrases that help to distinguish work requests from personal or social requests. Generally, the focus of work requests is on the tasks, activities, and resources required to get the expected results. The focus on tasks is reflected in the language you use.

Work		Personal
"Part of your job includes your doing _____."	*rather than*	"I want you to _____ _____."

Work		Personal
"In order for you to accomplish _____, you will have to get a clearance on _____, negotiate with _____, etc."	*rather than*	"Do the following: _____" or "You should _____"

You clarify and guide the employee in what is required, but doing the work is up to the employee.

Work		Personal
"Our overall unit objective is _____ (number) 'gastors,' of which your portion would range from an average of ____ to _____ per hour."	*rather than*	"I need for you to produce an average of _____ (number) 'gastors' per day over the next few weeks to total _____ per week."

Communicate clear, specific, detailed objectives as the guiding factors rather than your personal "needs" or "wants."

Although these requests are placed on a job-related basis, rather than on a personal, friendship basis, they may not seem natural in all settings. Think of them, rather, as clarifying fall-back statements to use when the lines get blurred between your employees and yourself, when there is a lack of firmness in establishing the tasks to be accomplished. In some settings you would alienate your employees by reverting to the more task-oriented statements. In other settings, you will have to use these more task-oriented statements to regain perspective within the work unit. Then you can return to the more personally based requests . . . if your employees respond more favorably to them.

Here are some additional examples of work-based versus personal requests.

Work		Personal
"The work of this unit requires that you _____."	*rather than*	"Would you please _____?"

Work		Personal
"The type of tasks for which your position was created include the following: _____"	*rather than*	"There's something I want you to do."

Work		Personal
"Our overall unit objective is _____ optional drafts, for which you are expected to deliver one every ten days."	*rather than*	"Here's what I need for you to do in the next ten days."

Make your requests job-related, rather than relying on a personal, charismatic leadership style. Charisma, personal power, and personal relationships may be useful over and above appropriate supervisory practices, but by no means are they essential to get the job done. You ought to begin with a solid base of supervisory procedures and practices. One part of solid supervisory procedure is to make instructions work-related and task-specific, rather than expressions of personal wants and wishes.

> ## Major Point About Supervising
>
> A supervisor supervises task performance to get results. Task performance is the basis for the supervisor-employee relationship on the job. Know what the job requires and the results for which you are responsible as supervisor. Know also the resources (skills, activities, tasks, materials, and support) required to get those results. Communicate resources and objectives clearly to employees.

SUPERVISING IS . . .

Some supervisors see themselves more as puppeteer than as guide and supporter of employee performance. Some of this over involved puppeteer behavior can be traced to a strong need to control or a sense of covering one's rear end by not allowing employees any discretion or latitude.

Some supervisors are puppeteers out of a distorted sense of what their jobs require. This approach is exhausting!

When a supervisor behaves like a puppeteer, he is operating on the belief that he himself is responsible for "doing" the activities for which individual employees are responsible, instead of believing he is responsible for the overall output of the unit. . .which in fact he is.

Remember each employee has certain specific tasks for which he or she is responsible; the supervisor is responsible for the overall results. As a supervisor you delegate tasks. You do not directly *do* the work activity yourself; rather, you get that work, service, delivery, or production accomplished *through an employee* . . . the employee does it. Once you have delegated the task, you are responsible for seeing that the results are obtained. But you can no longer be *directly, personally,* and *immediately* responsible for doing that delegated task.

For a supervisor to literally assume responsibility for the tasks of his employees would require him, for example, to intervene in the employee's activities to the point of taking the employee's hand and writing a memo with both of them holding the pen.

Supervisors cannot supervise those tasks that they take upon themselves. The purpose of supervising is to distribute the responsibility for tasks and results equitably among appropriate employees in order to increase overall effectiveness in meeting objectives. Supervisors rely on the knowledge that their employees are consenting, capable adults under contract to do the work.

Usually, employees have specific job activities; however, there are some exceptions. In a labor shortage, during periods of high absenteeism, or during a production crunch, for example, supervisors and employees will fill in for each other and other employees by doing a broader range of tasks. However, this is not the usual rule for good supervision on a daily basis. Normally, your employees are required to know their specific tasks and stick to them.

The lines may blur for some supervisors when they act like player-coaches: they are both directly involved in producing goods or delivering services and, at the same time, they supervise some of the same people with whom they do the work. For these worker-supervisors it is *even more important* to know the specific responsibilities of supervising in order to be able to make that distinction and separation in roles when it is required on the job.

For most supervisors, other people are clearly responsible for getting the work done, and the supervisor's work is to schedule, guide, provide support, and follow up on progress to help individual employees meet their responsibilities.

So, you may breathe a sigh of relief. Even though you are responsible for the outcome, you are *not* responsible for doing all the work of the unit. That is why you have employees. Employees do the pieces of work. Your part is to plan with them, guide them, provide support when required, and—with them—assess the quality of their performance and their production. That is supervising.

Major Point About Supervising

If you try to be directly responsible for a delegated task, you have not really delegated. Rather, you have retained primary responsibility for doing that task. Your job is to delineate employee responsibility for tasks and to direct them to the desired results.

FORGET MOTIVATION!

When I conduct supervisory training programs I invariably encounter supervisors who are preoccupied with "motivating" employees. Certainly there are times when morale could use a boost—available incentives are sparse, and they want to lift spirits. Too often, however, the discussion about motivation sounds more like a search for the "buttons." They ask, "How can we make them productive when they won't work?" "How can I control employees in my unit?" It sounds as though the employee is seen as some type of robot to be remotely controlled by this supervisory gizmo called "motivation." The entire approach strikes me as both patronizing and demeaning to the employee, as well as draining for the supervisor.

If you are willing to grant that the employees—

- are on the job out of personal choice,
- have the capability to perform the major job functions; and
- understand the specific performance and results that are spelled out,

then there should be less preoccupation with how to "make" employees work and more emphasis on how to assist employees to become more fully aware and capable of handling their job responsibilities.

When I presume that my main supervisory responsibility is to "motivate" an employee, I take on a truly superior and dominant position in the work relationship. In order to preserve that position of superiority, I may have to manipulate the facts and the employee. By accepting the position of "motivator," I somehow imply that I am the essential element in his or her performance—the missing link. I can assume that the employee is slothful or resistant to work and conclude that by some show of stealth and cunning I will engage that employee in doing something he or she does not want to do. The power struggle is on.

Supervisors and employees have an extensive series of games arranged around this "dominance" relationship; some of them are games brought directly from prior relationships such as child to parent and student to teacher. As soon as the supervisor takes on responsibility for making the employee perform, the employee can push the supervisor into a win-lose situation as to who is going to get the upper hand in the game. (Transactional analysis states that generally the lower member in the dominance relationship—in this case the employee—wins.) A subtle renegotiation of the work contract accompanies this dominance game— the rules change from the original contract, and there is no explicit agreement about who is really responsible for what.

In such a power struggle, the employee may begin an evasive ploy of nonperformance—getting by with as little productive work as possible. The supervisor then begins to search for some magic buttons to stimulate this inert human mass. Little does the supervisor realize that this same employee chose to get up this morning, get dressed, and get to work and only now is doing what is termed "nonperformance."

However, the supervisor often gets so engrossed in the imagined or assumed responsibility for getting the work out and getting the employee to be productive that he tends to view the employee narrowly. The employee is perceived as a machine with a low battery that has to be "jump started" by the supervisor—hence, the search for the right motivators or "juice."

In this view, the employee is considered incapable of self-generating activity. So, the supervisor takes on the employee's responsibility, ignores the employee's contractual basis for being on the job, and becomes vulnerable to hidden agendas—all in all, a failure to share responsibility with the employee. The imbalance is not fruitful. While productivity hangs in the balance, the supervisor becomes increasingly desperate for a remedy. Much of the remedy could be a change in the supervisor's perspective that the employee is not a responsible individual.

You do *not* motivate employees in a direct, linear, cause-and-effect relationship between what you do and the employee's immediate action. Your relationship is not the same as the croquet mallet's to the croquet ball. At best you provide one major impetus in any supervisor-employee transaction. You may provide some incentives and create a humane work climate that facilitates the employee's performing work tasks and activities. *But the basic energy, drive, motivation, and choice to act belong to the employee.* It is the height of grandiosity to think that you, all by yourself, can pump up your employees like hot-air balloons—and make them go.

Even if you initially think you are succeeding with this kind of direct "pep-rally" effect, you will soon exhaust yourself or create employee dependency on you and your energy. Using yourself as a short-term stimulus or goad does not foster the employee's self-reliance, reliability, independence, or autonomy, which are required for long-term job performance.

Some organizations hold employee "motivation sessions," which often serve the same purpose as putting sugar in the bloodstream. Listlessness may lead to popping in some sugar. When it hits the bloodstream and raises the glucose level, there will be a temporary "high." Then the sugar level drops and you feel even more depleted, for the sugar has added no lasting nourishment to your system, nor has it addressed your boredom or some other more central reason for your listlessness. The temporary "high" can feel like a "motivator" in the short term, but the sugar is a depressant in the long term.

Employees have to find for themselves some personal payoff or satisfaction for doing their job activities. You may provide employees, at varying levels of job tenure, additional incentives for some tasks or incentives to increase their job satisfaction. You can also develop an environment with your employees in which they recognize their work responsibilities whether you are present or absent. However, once you have done what is within your realm to do, then it is up to the employee to continue to choose whether the job payoff is adequate—to make the decision to stay and perform—or split.

Every employee has "downers," situations that require concern from fellow employees and the supervisor. That is part of living. However, when those downers become repetitive or establish an unproductive pattern, the attention you pay the employee may reinforce his depression rather than move the employee toward performance. Compassion has limits.

Consider the employee activities you pay attention to. You may be rewarding unproductive activity by focusing on it.

Major Point About Supervising

The supervisor has the responsibility of maintaining responsible job performance of each employee within the unit. *The actual energy, stimulus, and choice to perform the work comes from the employee.* When the employee refuses to fulfill the requirements of the job position, it is the supervisor's responsibility to fill that job position with a responsible employee.

The major points presented so far about supervising have centered on the relationship of the employee to the organization and with the supervisor. The last part of this chapter deals with two important things to do in supervising, as well as in life, to improve one's power and effectiveness: (1) establish and maintain a common data base as an essential element of communication, and (2) attend to reality as it is, in order to cooperate and collaborate more fully.

A COMMON DATA BASE WORKS WONDERS

The major points about supervising so far have punctuated the knowledge that communication (not motivation) is a key part of supervising. In any organization, supervision requires tapping into sources of information as well as sharing information (being a source). A *common data base* is the combined data gathered from all the available sources in an organization. *It is an essential tool for solid supervisory practice.*

A common data base is one of the central building blocks of productive, clear communication. Information that is withheld or not available to share is not held in common. Missing data then increases the probability of inaccurate speculation, unfounded interpretation, and plain guessing to fill in the information gaps.

Establishing a common data base involves intentionally disclosing information to individuals so that they can both understand and make decisions. It is essential for anyone to know how to elicit information from others to build one's own data base. Most employees, however, have little idea that they also have a responsibility to communicate upward with their supervisor—whether asked to or not. That supervisors do not often ask for or listen to information from employees is more a commentary on the deplorable state of supervision and management in many organizations than it is on its appropriateness as an employee responsibility.

The importance of the common data base within the work unit is underscored by the story of the four blind men and the elephant. Here it is.

> Four blind men often walked together through the city. One day as they were tapping their canes along a sidewalk, they passed a circus train unloading and an elephant tethered near the sidewalk. One blind man wandered off the sidewalk slightly and bumped into the elephant's trunk, which he promptly took hold of and began to describe to his friends. "I have found some sort of spigot or hose. It feels a lot like the chute of a grain truck at an elevator," he said.
>
> The second blind man ran his hands around the elephant's leg, which he said felt like a tree trunk. The third man bumped his nose on the broad side of the elephant. At first he thought he had run into an overhanging limb. But upon further checking, feeling the rough, rounded broadside of the elephant, he described it as a "weather-beaten kiosk." The last blind man, meanwhile, found himself at the elephant's tail, which he promptly dubbed a "radiator brush."

Establishing a common data base sometimes requires getting beyond the early, limited, or preconceived experiences and notions of others in the organization. You face the same problems of reconciling incomplete and discrepant descriptions, each person's piece of the truth. Sometimes this can be done simply by gathering all the bits of information available. Other times it requires dealing with egos, personal investment, values, and beliefs.

Most of us do not have all the information all of the time. (That prerogative and ability is usually reserved for God, an entity not currently on the personnel roll of most organizations.) We have opinions, conjectures, suspicions, limited information, correct and incorrect information, perceptions, distortions, projections, interpretations. However, unless we can compile more information, it can be difficult to fully grasp what we are dealing with.

Organizations and individual careers can grow or fail as a result of the formal and informal ways employees establish their data bases.

In organizations, there is a need to know what each position provides and requires. Until employees get together with one another and with their supervisors to clarify their roles, they may act quite like the blind men, each one thinking that he alone has the only real, true, and important piece of the organization's work, and so miss the connection between their mutual responsibilities. Yet organizations require interdependent activity among employees, which in turn requires an established and updated common data base.

Major Point About Supervising

Because we do not know all things, we must rely on each other to provide additional information or data. All the available facts, information, and data regarding the organization that is held in common between employees constitutes the common data base, an essential element in communication and supervising.

Some Particular Data That Needs To Be Common

Few employees have a clear idea of what a supervisor's responsibility is, sometimes even after they get promoted themselves. Meanwhile, the supervisor faces resistance and indignation. Employees exclaim, "My supervisor doesn't do a damn thing! And she makes more money than I do. Why should I break my neck when she doesn't do any of the work?" The supervisor is perceived as "not working" when in fact she is doing her job—getting the work done through others.

Employees can be informed about supervisory responsibility—be given some brief in-service training so that they might understand other levels of the organization. Employees would benefit from having temporary supervisory responsibilities (say, as acting supervisor) to see what it's like.

Establishing a common data base requires an openness to exploring new developments or at least to remaining open to new information. As with all dynamic entities, the description of the total unit or organization, or a particular supervisor-employee relationship, will require a continuing update to remain current. At the bare minimum each individual has to be open to receiving this new information.

Information is power. Not only is it important to establishing a common data base throughout, it is essential in the supervisor-employee relationship. Specific steps and action need to be taken to maintain that data base with complete, comprehensive, and current information.

In the supervisory relationship with the employee, the common data base begins with the hiring interview and with the job description. It progresses with a shared and updated understanding of organizational purpose, objectives, and rationale for objectives; policies and procedures; and the employment contract. It continues with feedback in supervisory conferences and two-way communication throughout the employment cycle (Table 1).

The common data base can get you past the "brier-patch syndrome" in supervision, in which you think all the issues are sticky and thorny and

Table 1. Contributions to the Common Data Base

Supervisor Provides	Employee Provides
Job announcement	
Hiring Interview:	
Job description	Applicant experience, skills
Organizational procedures, policy, budget, etc.	Desire for job, references
Orientation:	
Introductions of personnel	Employment data, demographics
Organizational benefits, etc.	
Supervisory Conference:	
Job requirements	Resources required
Objectives	Task understanding
Policy interpretation	Client information
Procedure explanation	Production information
	Support needs
Unit Meetings:	
Goals, quotas, outcomes sought	Work place and teamwork issues
Information exchange	New ideas, suggestions, plans
Problem solving, decision making, planning	Priorities

yours to handle alone. Establishing a common data base ensures that *you share information and responsibility with employees on their specific job responsibilities from the beginning.* The common data base is a tool, a means of getting information straight, for getting responsibilities clarified with your employee.

There need be little difference between the emotional loads you carry in handing out paychecks (usually seen as an agreeable supervisory activity) versus explaining potentially unpopular policy mandates at a meeting (usually seen as a disagreeable supervisory activity). In many cases you are simply a conveyor of information. That is part of your job responsibility. (We will deal with your advocate role later.) And you need not be dumped on or abused for carrying out that responsibility.

As a supervisor, you can prevent numerous stresses and abrasions by knowing and sharing information on the limitations and responsibilities of your own job. By clarifying *your* role responsibilities with your employees, you also begin to clarify *their* role responsibilities. You then begin to build a shared understanding of what you expect from one another—that is, what is their responsibility and what is yours.

Much of your work through the supervisory cycle will involve a continuing update of organizational realities that affect your work relationships and unit productivity. This includes updating job descriptions, policies, and procedures, together with keeping current on the local scuttlebutt. A great deal of your energy will be devoted to establishing and maintaining a common data base of ongoing work of the employees in your unit. That is a requirement of your supervisory position.

Major Point About Supervising

Establishing and maintaining a common data base of work-related issues and information with employees are a major supervisory responsibility and a major employee responsibility. The common data base provides an important way to reduce stress by sharing available, accurate, and current information on work responsibilities and organizational realities. The common data base is a vital and continuing communication practice for meeting organizational goals.

REALITY: ANOTHER POWER BASE FOR THE SUPERVISOR

Supervising is not completely dependent on the personal characteristics of the supervisor. Although the skills and personality of the supervisor certainly will affect the degree to which the supervisor communicates and gets results, the supervisory position carries with it several reality "reference points" that buttress and support supervisory activity. Some of these are:

- The employee's contractual relationship with the organization
- Objectives, rationale, and outcomes sought (unit productivity or output quotas)
- Delineation and guidelines for work activity
- Recognized and clarified roles and responsibilities

Of major importance, aside from any of the particulars mentioned up to this point, is a truth that applies to supervising and to life.

Major Point About Supervising

Reality never lets you down. Only your own expectations, distortions, and demands on reality let you down.

Learn to put your supervisory tasks in the perspective of your position power rather than letting them overwhelm you. Supervising is a humane, feasible, and satisfying activity, and there is sufficient legitimate power in the supervisory position to support you all along the way.

Myths Versus Realities About the Role

How is it some people become burned out or negative in supervisory positions? Some supervisors think they have to pay a great price to maintain their jobs. Others sometimes shrink from their employees, thinking they will be sucked dry and consequently will have nothing further to offer their employees or the organization. Many employees who become supervisors carry with them a variety of supervisory myths. Some of those myths are spelled out below. A number of them are about supervision in general, others concern the transition from employee to supervisor.

Myth: **"I can't remain friends with my subordinates and still be effective on the job." "Can I socialize with my employees and still retain their respect?" "Won't I lose my authority if I get too friendly?" "How can I hope to enforce some unpopular policy?" "Everyone will be trying for favors."**

The myth here is that you must remain aloof, distant—even isolated—from your subordinates in order to get them to do their jobs. Distance is supposed to act as leverage (perhaps like a big stick). What is overlooked is the fact that you can deal with employees who are friends and still function effectively as a supervisor *as long as you have a clear idea of what is required of them and from you in your work relationship.* If you are not clear about your respective roles and job performance requirements, distance and isolation will not provide any further supervisory power.

Myth: **"I like to be aboveboard in my dealings with employees. Yet, I know that top management sometimes withholds information or requires silence from supervisors. We are expected to get employee cooperation or compliance without an explanation. How can I be open about my job when the company puts these restrictions on me?"**

Sometimes you may have to withhold information or maintain confidentiality simply because that was a condition placed on you when you were given the information. However, there is a myth about deceptiveness here—that you are being dishonest by not disclosing every bit of information you have. Try thinking about it this way: your employment agreement charges you not to disclose the information. You may, however, let your employees know that you are currently bound to tell them only so much and that you will fill them in on the withheld information as soon as you are able.

Occasionally you may get caught in a situation in which employees have already figured out what is going on even without your information. In that case, use your sense of humor and tell higher-ups that the grapevine is better informed than the organizational hierarchy.

►**Myth:**   **"I hate to be manipulative, but sometimes I am handed assignments that cannot be handled during a forty-hour week. Not only that, but we have no overtime or compensatory time for some employees, so that anyone working late is donating effort. I don't feel right about getting work out of employees that is beyond their responsibility and resources, especially when the company has the resources but won't turn them loose to accomplish the objectives."**

There are times when extra effort will be called for. Remember that your employees still have a choice. At the same time, however, if you are frequently asking for uncompensated work from employees, you may be fostering the continuation of low budgeting. You need to look at the consequences of the extra effort—for yourself, your unit, and individual employees. You may want to communicate the consequences of being underbudgeted to your boss. You can also tell employees about their responsibilities and rights under the circumstances. You do have a responsibility of advocacy for them and for the unit.

Sometimes you may find yourself playing into the very situations you consider most unbearable. But you have options. You are not required to (and should not) make up for major organizational deficiencies through your heroic efforts. If you do try heroics, the organization probably will not allocate resources where they are truly required. By making up the deficit you can create an unrealistic picture about what employees can actually accomplish and what resources are actually required. You will also invite some costly production gaps due to illness or turnover in your unit if you allow continuing exploitation of your employees.

➤**Myth:** "I know that sometimes I get into it with my friends here on the assembly line, but I just can't see taking a supervisory job where I would have to confront this gang constantly."

Some people see their supervisory tasks as daily confrontations with subordinates. Once again, assuming that employees have to be "forced" to work and meet performance standards is a myth. Actually, supervisory confrontation ought to be only on specific job-related activities. Focusing on the job takes confrontation out of the personal arena and makes it more objective. If you have clear role distinctions, performance guides and standards for employees, and a common data base, confrontations of this sort will help employees improve their job performance and will not be a personally exhausting and alienating activity for you as supervisor.

MYTHS VERSUS REALITIES IN YOUR TRANSITION

Not all of the difficulties in making the transition from worker to supervisor have to do with relationships with new subordinates. Some of the most limiting or restrictive difficulties may emerge from within your own mind. You may create some of your greatest problems. Here are some of the myths I've heard from new supervisors.

➤**Myth:** "You have to like the people you work with."

Bunk! You simply have to be able to *work* with them. Compatibility is essential in a work relationship. But compatibility means that individuals will find a way of working together effectively to get the results required. "Liking" is a personal matter. And there is no guarantee that just because people like each other they will work together more effectively. Morale may be temporarily higher, but getting results involves performing job-related tasks. As long as those tasks are clearly spelled out and employees know what is expected of them—and what they can expect of each other—the work can get done.

Most of us would prefer to work with people we like. But the *main* responsibility in working is to accomplish organizational objectives, not to fulfill your social needs. So, while friendliness and closeness may be a personal preference, the minimum required of any work relationship with colleagues or subordinates is compatibility—you are required to work together to get the job done.

➤**Myth:** "I must appear competent, even when I don't know what I am doing."

Your need to be or appear competent may be a major obstacle in the early steps of your transition from employee to supervisor. In our culture, one of the worst things you can say about someone is that he or she is incompetent. You can tell Joe he is ineffective, and he will probably shrug his shoulders and walk off. But telling him he's incompetent—them's fightin' words!

The *appearance* of competence is a major objective of most individuals in this society, and much energy is placed on "image management." Often, the demand for performance calls for appearing to be near perfect. So we tend to stress appearances. But remember, your self-demands for supervisory competence may be premature and excessive. You need not be nor appear perfect.

For example, on Wednesday afternoon at 3:00 P.M. George is called into his boss's office and informed of his promotion. George is to take over a unit the next morning, and the old supervisor will be there to introduce the employees. Suddenly, like Clark Kent stepping out of a phone booth, George is supposed to emerge a *super-visor!* One day a worker, the next "boss." For some individuals that change of roles portends magical, if not miraculous, changes: the employee becomes the all-knowing supervisor. Most of us realize the impossibility of such massive, rapid change. But the new supervisor keeps the pressure on himself to look totally competent and in charge.

The real internal questions in your transition should be: "Now what do I do? How can I handle all of this? What was it my old supervisor did? I wish I had paid close attention." However, the external behavior (the way the new supervisor wants to come across) may involve a big disguise. And often employees will get caught up in that bluff and "protect" the supervisor from appearing incompetent or out of control. But the new supervisor who appears to know it all starts out "out of control." There is no way anyone can make such a switch instantaneously. Just familiarizing yourself with the unit history and individual positions and activities requires time. By meeting the situation the way it is—new and unfamiliar—you can gain a much greater long-term advantage toward supervising.

A supervisory situation gets out of control when the supervisor strikes an authoritative pose, making it difficult for others to provide necessary information or to orient the supervisor to the work of the employees in the unit. As a consequence, the unit devotes more energy to maintaining the facade of the new supervisor's so-called competence than to collaborating to build real competence and to meet real objectives.

Any individual moving into a new position needs to recognize that no one can hope to know everything about that position upon entering.

Part of career development occurs in learning the new position. You were not chosen because you were expected to perform at 100 percent capacity the first day. You were chosen for your proven skills, and also for your perceived potential to supervise effectively in time. So be a learner, not an authority. Get involved, ask questions—even though at first you may feel awkward. No one (except maybe you) expects you to be a super-competent supervisor in one day.

Truly competent individuals recognize their limitations and situational realities. They go slowly in their transitions, drawing upon the experience of their new subordinates, past supervisors in that position, and current supervisors in comparable positions.

The truly competent individual looks at the new position as a challenge and an opportunity, rather than as some threat to his or her image that requires covering up and "acting" competent. The stress some individuals put themselves under serves just to make them miserable, and the transition becomes abusive and taxing. Go easy on yourself. Recognize the realities of your situation.

In some of the units you supervise, your technical expertise will not be superior—or even equal—to your subordinates'. For example, you may supervise a CPA and a lawyer yet have no training in accounting or law yourself. However, you can still function effectively as supervisor for these employees. You are not expected to exceed the technical expertise of all your employees. Supervision draws on a different spectrum of knowledge and skills.

➤**Myth: "I feel like I'm out of place."**

You may feel unfamiliar being in a "higher," more responsible spot. You are now in a formal, recognized authority position. The former "them" is now an "us." Along with this strange feeling, you may also acquire a new perspective about authority and responsibility.

You may have to come to terms with being the responsible person, the one held accountable for results beyond one's own immediate work. Or you may find the position of getting the work done through others fraught with a feeling of greater helplessness than when you did it all yourself.

Anyone who assumes a supervisory position will sooner or later have to come to terms with his or her own feelings about power and authority. Sometimes the pain of having been oppressed or "sat on" by others will result in a new supervisor's passing on that resentment to subordinates, doing to them what was done to him by his former supervisors. Or a supervisor may personally identify so closely with subordinates that she finds it difficult to delegate and follow through on tasks. This supervisor will have to accept the authority of her position as well as the responsibility and tasks of being a supervisor—which involves delegating tasks to subordinates.

Taking on a supervisory position may be scary at first. You may feel vulnerable and out of place—like being on the big kids' swing or attending a meeting in the board room and expecting to be asked to leave at any moment. You may need to readjust your thinking before you are comfortable with the position and your rightful place in it. You will have to give yourself permission to advance and learn, to assume more responsibility and authority.

You will also have to learn to relate to employees on a new basis. You will have to consider them on the merits of their job performance and on the qualities that affect their job performance. That is the basis on which you are supervising them and by which you are all working together in the first place.

When you were younger, it was typical to model yourself after big people because they were older, more experienced, and more powerful. However, later on in life there comes a point when you have to accept what you have and work with other people on the basis of work to be done together. If you concentrate on tasks to be accomplished, you can get away from a hero-worshipping or awestruck-youth approach to others. Recognize that you are growing—that supervising is one of the accompanying strides of maturity, experience, and ability.

When you accept supervisory responsibility, you must make the role transition from employee to supervisor. The next chapter is about that transition.

3

Role Transition:
Moving Completely into Supervising

Even though you chose to become a supervisor, there may be some steps in the process of role transition from employee to supervisor that you have yet to take. Whether you are a new or a seasoned supervisor, you will benefit from determining your present stage in your own role transition. You may also begin to understand some of the steps that your colleagues, superiors, and employees have to traverse themselves.

On its surface this chapter may appear to be geared toward the newly promoted supervisor, but I believe any supervisor can incorporate this introduction to the loss/change process into many day-to-day interactions with employees. The loss/change process applies to people going through all sorts of changes that occur in organizations—especially changes in personnel. It is equally applicable to changes you and your acquaintances experience in your social and personal lives. Knowing these stages of loss will not only help you look at your own role transition into supervising, it can also make you more aware of the effect changes can have on a work unit when they are accompanied by some sense of loss.

YOU CHOOSE AND YOU LOSE

One of the more curious phenomena for most people who are promoted from employee to supervisor is a feeling of depression. It seems a little difficult to comprehend how one can feel depressed after being promoted. After all, you have just been awarded a new position with more power, higher pay, and greater career opportunity. How then is it that you feel depressed? And how can you tell your spouse and family, peers, and colleagues that you are depressed, when they are happy for you and want to celebrate? Perhaps they will not believe that you are really sad, and you will end up dealing with your feelings in silence.

As you read on, you will find that a feeling of depression is normal and natural at a time like this. Then perhaps you will not feel like such an odd duck, even though your depression will not go away.

At first, a feeling of depression just doesn't seem to match the reality of a promotion. Most supervisors don't discuss their experience with it, so you have no one to talk to about that feeling. On your own, you might consider the *loss* that accompanies accepting any new position or promotion. Even when you choose from among several desirable options, when you are limited to choosing only one, there is some sadness that accompanies your choice. For in choosing, you lose the other alternatives. You give up the other options. That is one of the realities of decision making—you live with what you choose.

For most of us, a change in job responsibilities, even within the same unit, means a readjustment or a loss of old relationships as well as the gain and challenge—some of it unsettling at first—of the new position.

When you know your position responsibilities, your supervisor, your peers, and other employees, there is a certain comfort in the continuity and security of your old job position. It is familiar. You are comfortable with the job, and your interactions with co-workers are somewhat predictable, even if they are not all pleasant. A new position involves breaking old ties, assuming a new role, and establishing different relationships. Certainly there is little familiarity or comfort in this new position, at least at first. Even if you are promoted to supervisor within your own work unit, your basic relationships will change. Former peers become employees. Things have changed.

THE PROCESS OF LOSS/CHANGE

The depression and some of the anger accompanying the move to supervision are explainable, for in most cases of loss or change—especially where it involves a major investment of energy or emotion—there is a grieving process that healthy people go through. As with heavier losses such as the death of a loved one, a divorce, or a crippling accident, people moving into a new position may experience a more or less sequential flow of feelings.

Numbness

When the loss or change comes suddenly and without warning, such as an accident or natural disaster, many people will just go numb. That seems to be one way the nervous system protects us from an overload of changed reality. Victims of a natural disaster, for example, are often found wandering in shock. Granted, such a loss is much more severe than what is involved in a job position change. Nevertheless, the process of loss/change still applies to role transition, though the feelings may be less intense.

The shock element (going "numb") in your promotion may stem from the suddenness of the announcement, some unexpected circumstances, or a sharp feeling that the position change will conflict with other plans you have made.

For most people, however, for whom change or loss is not sudden or shocking, the first stage in the process will be depression.

Depression

Most loss or change involves some sadness bordering on depression. There is a tearing, a breaking of former security, followed by a need to establish new bonds. Depression usually marks the first step in the loss/change process when the loss or change is *not* sudden or unexpected.

Some employees may feel self-pity, moving through a curious middle ground between the more clearly defined stages and emotions of depression and anger. As a swing mood self-pity falls more on the side of depression, and it often results from feeling trapped. Once an employee accepts a supervisory position, he may feel hemmed in by the decision, helpless. Ahead of him he sees a life of difficult work—a time of woe. Unable to turn back (what would he tell the wife? she, the husband?) he feels lost, overwhelmed, sorry for himself.

Usually, the new supervisor will soon begin to acquire new skills and feel more comfortable in the job. And he will also go through the other stages in the loss/change process, before settling into the new position. After depression, generally comes...

Anger

There is no sacred ordering of the feelings experienced in the loss process: However, the usual sequence is that depression is followed by anger. Often the two will be practically interchangeable. You are depressed one minute, mad as hell the next. The anger often stems directly from helplessness—not being able to continue in a familiar position, for example—and outrage, the seeming injustice of having to readjust relationships. Irritability will be one indicator of being in this stage—and feeling sorry for yourself.

These first stages—numbness, depression, anger—constitute an active refusal to accept the new reality, an overt emotional denial in dealing with the changed reality. The next stage shifts into a different way of dealing with the situation.

Limbo

After some of the more active experiences of depression and anger have worked their way through one's consciousness, the next phase is a settling-out stage. Limbo often feels like a neutral or withdrawn, do-nothing stage.

Nothing seems to be happening. You have quit resisting the change or loss, but you have not yet taken an active stance in dealing with the new situation. The person experiencing this stage in the loss/change process adopts a "just sitting" posture. The turbulence of acknowledging the loss is over. Tranquility and a new composure set in. There is a calmness to accept what is. After this do-nothing stage will come a time and a phase for acting on the acceptance of the new reality. The person promoted will begin to take some interest in the new situation.

Restructuring

If you are a new supervisor, there will come a day when you will no longer just tolerate what you have thrust upon yourself. You will dust off some of the policy manuals, take a look at the ledger, go to the file cabinet, open the door to your office, and start to demonstrate real interest in your new working situation. You are no longer just going through the motions. Now you are there to stay. You begin to involve yourself actively.

For someone whose home is destroyed in a tornado, the restructuring phase would involve beginning to discuss the costs of rebuilding and getting actively involved in securing a mortgage, recovering insurance claims, and the like. For the newly divorced person, this phase might involve getting spruced up for a night on the town with the hope of meeting someone new.

For the new supervisor, restructuring involves actively doing what is required to get the job done. Restructuring may involve holding conferences to clarify roles with subordinates. It may involve abandoning the duties once held as an employee. In the restructuring stage, you not only *accept* the fact that you are there to stay, you also begin to *act* on that acceptance.

The time it takes the overall loss/change process to run its course is different for each person. In most cases, when the individual is not repressing or denying the feelings that arise, the process will range from about six to nine weeks. More severe personal losses will take up to a year or longer.

When people avoid dealing with the feelings that accompany a major change or loss, they stand to carry over the results of that denial for some time. Some of the immediate consequences include psychosomatic complaints or illnesses such as sleeplessness, "nerves," irritability, headaches, or chronic stomach upset.

Knowing that the loss/change process exists in the first place can help individuals cope more readily and move through the phases more easily. Not knowing about this process leaves individuals to go through it feeling isolated, weird, wondering if they are going crazy. Actually this process is natural and healthy. The unhealthy thing to do is to ignore, suppress, or deny the process.

The healthy person will allow herself or himself to experience the natural ebb and flow of feelings in the loss/change process. Those undergoing loss or discontinuity of more major proportions may seek outside help and consolation. Recall the tradition of wearing black during a time of mourning, to put people on notice of an individual's loss of a loved one and possible need for understanding and compassion. Few people will be on notice about your need for support and understanding, especially when they are celebrating your promotion. So, during your mourning the loss of your prior position, you may well have to deal with your feelings alone. At least you are on notice that the process is normal, natural, and healthy to experience.

SEASONED SUPERVISORS MAY BE STALLED

I have worked with hundreds of seasoned supervisors and managers in training sessions. And even though it seems preposterous to confront seasoned supervisors with the issue of role transition and the loss/change process steps, once they self-assess where they are in their transitions to supervisor, some of these seasoned supervisors would report that they had stalled, usually at the "anger" stage.

Depression would be difficult to attribute to a simple stalling in the normal loss and grieving process. There are many competing syndromes and factors that could contribute to depressed feelings—including the environment, the work routine, some sense of status deprivation (see Module 17). If there were some supervisor activity traceable to being stalled at this step in the process, it would probably involve the onset of sadness and low morale in the supervisor at the time of promotion and a continuing sense of listlessness and depressed spirits toward the work situation due to the loss of specific relationships, interaction, or work activity.

Most seasoned supervisors who assess themselves as stalled pinpoint themselves at the "anger" stage. They may be short with employees and resent their having to take on particular responsibilities. They may try to get back into employee group discussions over coffee and be continually irritated if the group does not warm to their presence. Paperwork is a hassle, and they refuse to enforce certain procedures as their way of getting even with the organization, without losing their ties to their old employee position. They have yet to side with their own management responsibilities. Their refusal to accept the position responsibilities continues.

A few seasoned supervisors have stalled at the limbo or neutral stage of the process. They could well be stereotyped as "bureaucrats," putting in their time as a warm body. Their employees adjust by getting support elsewhere or by just being resourceful. However, employees receive little useful interaction from these supervisors.

Supervisors may have become stalled for a variety of reasons: there may not have been sufficient supervisory training available when they were finally ready to restructure and take on their own job responsibilities. The employees in their units may already have adapted, or been highly capable when they began, so that the supervisors had little to do and have never exercised even a moderate range of their responsibilities. A former supervisor who moved up one level in authority when an employee became supervisor may have continued to dominate the new supervisor's work unit and the new (now seasoned) supervisor has yet to assume and perform his job responsibilities. Finally, the new supervisor may have just been intimidated by the position and failed to come out to the restructuring phase.

Neither the shock or the restructuring stage are stall stages for most seasoned supervisors. First off, the numbness of the surprise promotion certainly wears off relatively soon, making way for at least the nonacceptance stages. And finally, the restructuring stage involves a movement toward full position performance. Of course, the supervisor could have limited training as supervisor, or limited exercise of responsibility, in which case there would be more for him to learn. However, set against the background of the role transition from employee to supervisor, the restructuring phase is a dynamic and healthy sign of having gone through the possible stall points, the prior stages.

The way in which most seasoned supervisors break out of their stall pattern is, first, to become aware that they are stalled. Next, they seek clarification of what they have to do to enter the restructuring stage and take on full position responsibility. And then they follow out their own action plan. Some form of role clarification is often essential to that action plan. Then, there are those seasoned supervisors who, upon reconsideration, decide that they did not and do not care to continue in a supervisory position. That is your choice also.

If you plan to break through your stalled stage in the loss/change process and assume your supervisory responsibility, the next section will assist you.

THE ACTUAL TRANSITION: WHAT IT INVOLVES...

In order to ease your transition to a supervisory position, it is useful to know what you gave up, what you take with you, and what you will be getting that is new.

A new supervisory position means new peers, a new supervisor for you, and new subordinates. As an employee, your sources of support might have been your peers and your old supervisor. Your sources of satisfaction might have been the actual work you did, your clients, or consumers with whom you dealt. Your new sources of support may come from your new supervisor and peers. Your new sources of satisfaction may be your work with your subordinates, though that satisfaction may take some time to develop while you first learn the job.

Figure 1 is a graphic illustration of your role transition. You may find it useful to think of the names of your previous and present superiors and subordinates to make the circles in the figure more tangible and real. These circles depict real relationships and show the readjustments you will be making.

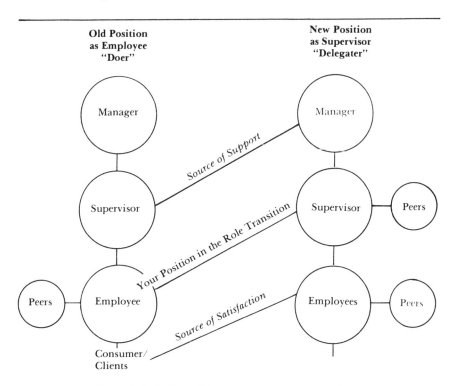

Figure 1. Role Transition: From "Doer" to "Delegator"

SMOOTHING YOUR TRANSITION TO SUPERVISOR

Beyond working through the stages of the loss/change process, and beyond acquiring new satisfactions and supports, several issues remain in making your role transition complete. Although not all of these issues will necessarily apply to your situation, some may—whether you are a new or a seasoned supervisor. You can continue to smooth your change-over by attending to them.

Perspective

Even in the absence of any formal orientation or training for your position within the organization, you can gain some perspective about your role and the role of your unit within the larger organization. From this perspective you can also at least partially determine what is expected of you.

One cornerstone of understanding central to your job and the organization is the *purpose* or *mission* of the organization, which then becomes stated in the form of fairly general *goals*. These goals, in turn, are then made more specific as *objectives* for the unit and for individuals. Individual employees meet objectives through *tasks* and *activities*, which they fulfill as part of their job responsibility.

At the very least you will benefit by gaining a perspective on how your unit fits into the overall organization, its purpose and the short-term production requirements. That begins to clarify your role and the work activities you are expected to accomplish.

Role Clarity

Precision in defining your new role—what is required of you—will smooth your job transition or complete your transition. Knowing your responsibilities, resources and rights can be a great help in exercising your supervisory position.

Role clarity means that you are clear about your major responsibilities—the tasks involved and the outcomes sought. It also means that you know specifically what is required of your employees and what is due your employees. Role clarity will also facilitate your dealing more effectively with colleagues, superiors, and staff. You know what you can expect (have the right to expect) from them—what activities their roles require—in terms of support, negotiation of action plans, allocation of resources, feedback, communication, authority, objective setting, and specific performance.

Each job role will have some basic complementary characteristics, some interdependence. Those complementary functions are set up or evolve in the interest of ultimately facilitating the production goals of the organization. Positions within the organization are set up to work in harmony, interdependently. So even though there may be some overlap in responsibility, there is a correspondence and collaboration between roles.

RESPONSIBILITIES, RESOURCES, AND RIGHTS

Each job and role position contains three major elements: responsibilities, resources, and rights. One job's responsibility may be another job's resource.

For example, when a supervisor sets an objective and reaches agreement with an employee within the unit to carry out tasks (the employee's *responsibility*), the employee is a *resource* to the supervisor. However, the employee may require some particular support to assist him in reaching the objective. It is the supervisor's *responsibility* to provide support, and support may come, for example, in the form of clearly stated objectives, a particular clearance for special hours, clarification of procedures, or access to word-processing equipment. The supervisor is then a *resource* to the employee in getting the task done.

This complemental factor demonstrates some of the interdependence that is the essence of true organizational interaction: each position relies on, turns on, interacts with, and/or supports some other position in the organism called an organization. There is a way job positions fit together—the choreography between supervisor and employee mentioned earlier.

Responsibilities and resources may vary substantially within one position, depending upon circumstances, time of year, press of activities within the unit, and personal activities on the job. If you have already been through a complete cycle of supervision, make note of the variations you have experienced.

Specific mention will be made of numerous supervisory responsibilities throughout this text. Take time right now, though, to spell out those responsibilities as you now know them. Divide a sheet of paper into two columns, and list responsibilities you had as an employee on one side and your supervisory responsibilities on the other. Update these lists as you continue your transition into the supervisory role.

You may have some difficulty spelling out all your resources in your position as supervisor, particularly if you are new to the job. And resources change. A new employee constitutes a new resource, for example. It may take longer than the probationary period to know fully to what extent that employee acts as a resource. You can, however, make a good start at identifying what you have available to you as a supervisor that you may not necessarily have had available to you directly as an employee. Begin that listing now, using the same format as you did before—resources you had as an employee on one side and supervisory resources on the other—and continue to develop your list of supervisory resources throughout your tenure in the position. Your job requires the ongoing assessment, planning, and direction of all the human and organizational resources you can draw upon.

Rights are a third factor in a supervisory job position—generally an overlooked or nonexplicit factor. Rights do not increase or decrease with job position. (Privileges and other resources may increase with position.) The rights one enjoys do depend, however, upon how one exercises those rights. Numerous supervisors I have worked with give the organization's personnel manual precedence over the Constitution and Bill of Rights. They see themselves as limited and vulnerable as personnel in the organization.

The failure to recognize, assert, and exercise job rights leaves many people—supervisors and employees alike—feeling constrained and limited in their job positions. Some employees will even suffer assault, slander, and specific nonperformance of contractual obligations toward them. Part of this comes from not being aware of their rights. Another part comes from their not really being aware of ways to exercise these rights.

Supervisors have the right to be endowed with all the authority required to perform their responsibilities. Yet many supervisors allow their own superiors or other staff to intervene with their employees, circumventing lines of authority, establishing unit objectives that exceed current resources and compensation, and the like. *The rights to know and to have authority to exercise your responsibilities are so fundamental they are often not discussed as being inherent in the position.* Often they are left implicit, almost bringing embarrassment from the supervisor who is moved to discuss "rights" with a superior—especially when the superior has not provided support or has intervened in the supervisor's authority.

Employees have the right to the most basic and simple creature comforts on the job. These are often backed up by regulations on employee health and safety. All employees have the right to know what is expected of them, the responsibilities they have, and what resources are available to meet those responsibilities. Without some clarity in the three R's—responsibilities, resources, and rights—one's role becomes increasingly ambiguous, and one cannot function fully within the unit or organization.

Many employees are wary of discussing their rights with their supervisor or a prospective employer. They think they will be perceived as uppity or contentious for doing so. However, this very discussion is necessary in order to help discern their role relationships with other positions and discover the full extent of their responsibility within that position to maintain its integrity. If one position collapses or is ill-defined and yielding with respect to resources and responsibilities, it then falls on another position to maintain the full brunt of responsibility.

A supervisor has the responsibility to maintain the integrity of his or her position (responsibilities, resources, and rights) to keep the role clear so that whimsical and errant responsibilities do not fall on the unit or particular employees, overwhelming and overstretching them or carrying them outside of their contractual job responsibilities.

If new sales quotas involve opening up a new sales territory or involve initiating sales calls in territories where salespeople formerly just responded to requests from prospective customers, there will have to be a commensurate increase in budget resources to provide increased per diem or mileage reimbursements, for example. The supervisor who accepts a higher sales quota (responsibility) without commensurate increases in reimbursements or time schedules (resources) places an unfair burden on employees in the unit. Additional resources need to accompany such changes in organizational objectives—unless, of course, a unit is presently underutilized or overbudgeted.

Of major importance here is the awareness of the interdependence of responsibilities, resources, and rights. Supervisors and other personnel will often accept excessive limitations or restrictions and still attempt to get results. This press on the accelerator with a corresponding depression of the brake leads to stagnation, frustration, and apathy in the unit.

In your job, you have the right to know what is expected of you and what resources you can draw upon to get results.

You can use a simpler format like Figure 2 to make a quick sketch of your responsibilities, resources, and rights—now and in the future. You may discover some imbalances among the three factors: extensive responsibilities without commensurate resources, for example. You may also use this form to clarify your role with your employees. Have each employee fill out one copy of the form for his or her job and another for your job. You do the same. Then get together to discuss any discrepancies and any items to be added or deleted.

THE CONDITIONS OF YOUR PROMOTION

In most cases more than one person is vying for a supervisory position at the time you are promoted and assume that position. Whether you come from outside the unit or from within, the politics of promotions and the conditions of your promotion may come into play to affect your fitting into the unit and smoothing your transition to supervisor. Someone will be displeased that you are occupying a position they wanted.

There is no sure-fire formula that says a new supervisor who comes from outside the unit may feel less animosity from employees than the one promoted from within. The tension of prolonged competition and comparisions after an in-unit promotion to supervisor can feel every bit as sharp as the general disappointment in a unit that the "local hometown favorite" did not win the job over an outsider. You will simply have to assess for yourself, through your own information-gathering methods, what the circumstances were.

List the responsibilities, resources, and rights in your position. This will allow a quick sketch of your role so it can be discussed in supervisory conferences to clarify roles, point up discrepancies, make additions, and so on.

Responsibilities	Resources	Rights

Figure 2. Role Clarification

If your transition is going smoothly, there is no need to dredge up potentially sore issues. However, you may receive an initial warm welcome to your new position only to find some unexplained resistance several weeks later. That is the time to investigate the conditions of your promotion, if you have not already done so during your interview or orientation.

If you came from outside the unit, find out who applied for your position from the unit. Also find out which people in the unit and the organization supported them. Compile other information such as the history of those who applied for the job, their past performance, cliques within the unit that might be sympathetic to this person's loss, and past promotions within the unit.

As a new supervisor, you might acknowledge the competition for your position, either to the individuals involved most directly or more generally in a unit meeting. You might say, for example: "I am aware that several qualified people applied for this position. I am sure that there is some disappointment at their not having been selected. However, there will be other positions available from time to time. For now, I am looking forward to working with you. I count on all of us working together to meet our objectives. Within the next _____ (time period), I will arrange to meet with each of you." You may select parts of this statement to fit your situation. In most cases employees will rise above their disappointment to help you with specific requests—for example, familiarizing yourself with the unit, information about the work and other individuals, and themselves.

If you were promoted from within the unit, the disappointment of your competitors may have a deeper base, manifesting itself in personal animosity or critical scrutiny of your performance. In addition, it may be more difficult to make the transition within the unit in which you have been an employee because other employees will tend to relate to you as a fellow employee until you distinguish yourself by taking charge in your supervisory role.

Clear the Air

One of your supervisory functions is to employ all the resources of the unit. The sooner you can move beyond any subordinate resentment about your new job assignment and position, the smoother the operation of the unit. Some individuals tend to surface their bad feelings some time later. By ignoring their resentment you may only delay the time when you will have to deal with it. It is best to deal with resentment now—while you are aware that it is there—so that you can clear the air and move on to more pressing matters.

Some of your employees may harbor a continuing resentment at not having been selected for promotion. Generally you can expect some work slowdown by those who are disappointed and experiencing their own process of loss at missing the expected promotion. However, if their work performance does not return to a near normal level within the first month, you will have to deal with them directly about meeting their job responsibilities.

In addition to clearing the air of some of the overt resentment and hostility toward your taking the job (and their own failure to obtain the position), you will still have to prove yourself. However, that will come with your applying yourself to the job. You can't talk your way into this kind of acceptance. You have to earn it by your action.

Sex, Ethnicity, Age, Degree, Tenure

Consider the composition of your unit from the standpoint of the employees' ages, gender, ethnic backgrounds, academic degrees, and tenure in the organization. You yourself may have encountered some of the adjustment difficulties subordinates experience. For example, a male employee now finds himself working for a female supervisor of about equal age. Some men may have difficulty working with women in the first place. Place a woman in an authority position over them and you have the makings of a conflict.

If you are a woman and a supervisor, find out whether your employees have ever been supervised by a woman, whether their experience was positive or negative, and whether they have any current concerns. You need to know if you are dealing with a helpful legacy or an obstructive one.

Consider some other typical employee biases about new supervisors.

Minority Supervisor: Believing that favoritism and tokenism is why ethnic minorities and women are promoted—to meet quotas.

Degreed Supervisor: Negating the ability of a person with a degree to deal with real-world situations.

Experienced Supervisor: Expecting that experience and tenure will automatically qualify one for a position.

Young Supervisor: Discounting a younger person on the basis of age alone.

Some of these factors may relate to your situation in such a way that your transition is never quite completed. Employee resistance based on one or more of these factors may linger and inhibit teamwork and productivity. After you have been on the job some time, you may tend to simply overlook some of these factors—even though they have been with you from the start. They do not automatically go away with the passage of time.

New employees coming into your work unit, even some time after your becoming supervisor, may greatly change the working dynamics of the work group. With each change, there are some in-unit transitions that have to be made. The new individual has to be included and has to deal with control issues before you can expect and receive full cooperation and teamwork. Issues of gender, age, ethnicity, tenure, degrees, and expectations may continue to restrict or retard your transition. Be aware of these factors within your unit and be prepared to deal with them.

The Supervisory Cycle: From Hiring to Firing

The following are the major supervisory responsibilities—spelled out briefly in a descriptive check list so that you can review the full cycle of activities that you will be conducting with the employees. (Several are described in more detail in the learning modules, which follow in Part II; the check list is provided for a preview of the supervisory activities you will encounter.)

SELECTION

The selection process involves the following items and activities:

Job Announcement: You are responsible for updating the job announcement, together with the personnel office, publishing it within the organization and outside, if required or desirable. The job announcement should accurately reflect the position available.

Interview: In most cases you will conduct part or most of the interviews for employees to be hired for job slots in your unit. It is important to accurately represent the organization and to fully inform the applicant about the job, the unit, and the organization. It is also your responsibility to assess each applicant's appropriateness for the position.

Selection: At the conclusion of the hiring interviews, you are to choose among the applicants to make the best match between your position opening and the applicant's experience, skill, and initiative.

Hiring: The applicant selected must be offered the job and informed of the requirements and benefits of the position. The applicant must then accept the terms of the position and the specific performance and benefits detailed or negotiate a more favorable contract. Some of this negotiation may fall under the jurisdiction of someone else.

ORIENTATION

The orientation process involves some unique activities, such as the probationary period, and also has some activity overlap with ongoing supervisory practices, such as supervisory conferences.

Orientation to the Organization: This generic orientation for new employees covers policies and procedures: leave, vacations, sick pay, insurance, family benefits, unemployment compensation, raises, promotions, and the like. In those cases in which the organization does not handle this part of the orientation (whether by video, film, program for all new employees, or personnel counselor) the supervisor is required to orient the new employee to the organization. One part of that orientation should include some perspective on the overall mission or purpose of the organization, as well as on the organizational goals.

> Handing a new employee a personnel manual and asking that employee to orient himself to the policies and procedures is a little like asking him to drink embalming fluid . . . a most unenjoyable activity for the living.

Orientation to the Unit: It is important for the individual employee to continue to track or follow the importance of his unit within the organization through his orientation. That perspective is crucial, together with the perspective on the overall work and interdependence of the unit team or members. Morale and motivation are stimulated when the employee can discern where he fits into the operation, whom he relies upon, and who relies upon him.

Orientation to the Job: This orientation completes the tracking of organizational purpose and mission as it is manifested in the duties and activities that are part of the employee's job description. It requires a complete review of the job as it was described in the hiring interview. And now the applicant-turned-employee has an immediate, real need to know all aspects of his job. A lot is forgotten after the hiring interview. This orientation should also include a basic and clear description of what the employee's job was created for—the purpose of the job. Out of this description should come a clear statement of the "difference" this job makes to the unit and the organization.

Employees need to know what difference they make. It is important to employee morale to be aware of the importance of their jobs, to know how their jobs fit into the larger operation, and to understand where they fit into the organization. It is essential to employee morale that their orientation include their interdependence within the unit and the organization and their particular contribution toward productivity or results.

> Employees from an Illinois manufacturing firm could take pride in the fact that most everyone in the U.S. was within a few inches of their products every day. They speculated that the screws joining the table they shared with me at a Chicago deep-dish pizza parlor had probably come from their factory. They had perspective on their contribution, and a pride in their organization.

Assessing Employee Capability: Even the best applicant may have shaded the truth a little about the dimensions or depth of experience brought to the job. Very early you have to assess your employee's capability and determine guidelines for bringing that employee up to full job capacity within the probationary period (or you will have to determine what will be an adequate indication of capability to warrant keeping the employee after that period). In essence you establish a bench mark against which to determine short- and long-term learning objectives (performance objectives).

Initial Supervisory Conferences: Generally you would meet with the new employee frequently, at least once every two weeks, depending upon the employee's needs for guidance and the availability of other guidance resources. Initial supervisory conferences establish a formal basis for an ongoing working relationship. They are generally used more to look at longer sequences of activities than do the on-the-spot coaching interventions of on-the-job training. Use these conferences to set and review objectives, provide information and support, update the common data base regarding the unit and the organization, and clarify roles to and with the employee. You would also begin to work the employee into unit objectives, as well as into his or her own job.

On-the-Job Training: Some new employees require direct and constant supervision when they begin a job, especially for technically oriented work. As managers of resources who must oversee the work of several employees, some supervisors designate one of their employees or an employee from a parallel operational level to provide direct hands-on training on the job. In effect, the employee doing the teaching accepts the supervisory, teaching responsibility that you have delegated.

> Herb, I want to introduce Jack Warden. Jack will be servicing our copiers in the third district in two weeks. Prior to that, I want him to go along with you and get firsthand experience with the variety of customers and situations that you confront daily. After a week or so, when Jack is ready, give him the opportunity to work with some of your customers. Give him some feedback on how he handles the situations. I'll meet with you Thursday of your last week together to catch up on your experiences in working together. By the way, Jack will be in orientation sessions for two days, but I will expect you two to work out your schedules when he finds out the dates for orientation.

Probation: Most organizations have a probationary period of six to twelve months, during which the new employee is to be supervised closely to determine whether he or she is to be kept on the payroll as a permanent employee. Specific criteria must be determined and established during this period so that the end-of-term decision provides the organization with a capable employee. Module 15 provides further details.

ONGOING SUPERVISION

The following are the major ongoing activities that mark the supervisor-employee relationship.

Supervisory Conferences: The primary use of the supervisory conference is to keep current on information (maintain the common data base), establish and follow an employee development plan, which may include job and career objectives; transmit, share, and negotiate objectives; and provide support and feedback. To fulfill a major responsibility of your position, you work your new employees into their jobs, getting them to develop skills and assume full job responsibility. For your more seasoned employees, your major responsibility is to continue productivity, sustain incentives, and focus on career development, with the employee's cooperation.

Coaching: Not all supervisor-employee interaction can wait for a formal conference. Coaching can take place right on the job site when the supervisor spots some shortcoming in employee performance. Coaching can also occur over the phone, in a tailgate conference, or at the water fountain. These short, spot interventions closely placed to the request for assistance or the mistaken activity constitute one major value of supervision to the employee. Coaching is a guidance procedure, which—like other types of feedback—is best done in a timely manner using specificity and detail to put the employee on track and show him how to stay there with developed skill.

Evaluation Conferences: Most organizations have at least an annual evaluation conference. Like the stockholders' report, this conference provides a summation of the employee's performance over the past evaluation period and may look forward to the coming evaluation period, in order to establish new goals and continue evolving goals. This conference is a time for overviews and feedback, based on a range or variety of activities observed over a period of time. The evaluation conference should hold no surprises if you have been meeting your responsibility of holding supervisory conferences during the year and keeping current on employee needs, progress, and developed capability. The evaluation conference depends heavily on the supervisor's ability to provide feedback, to be aware of the employees' activities, and to stay focused on job performance.

Personnel Action: One result of the evaluation conference may be a personnel action, including promotion, demotion, raise, transfer, or termination. These will all be discussed in Module 14.

You have just walked quickly through a check list of activities—in the supervisory cycle—of supervisory responsibilities to employees. The cycle begins with making the job announcement, follows on through selection and orientation, and is completed in ongoing supervision and a variety of personnel actions. Most of the items mentioned above are presented in detail in the modules in Part II.

PART II

SUPERVISING WHEN
IT'S ALL HAPPENING AT ONCE!

Introduction

If someone told you that supervision involves "doing what you have to do
to do it," you would probably think your leg was being pulled. If that
person then told you that "it takes as long as it takes" to get things done,
you might begin to feel irritation creep over you. But in many ways that
person would be "telling it like it is," rather than the way textbooks
usually tell it. The trouble is, in the world of textbooks things are as they
"should be," portrayed under somewhat limited or ideal circumstances.
In this world, where it has to happen, things do not wait their turn to
happen. There is not a line-by-line release of new information or a day-
by-day metering out of new complications to deal with.

It All Happens at Once! And there you are attempting to learn to
juggle a few balls in the air. And just as you are beginning to get the hang
of it, five or six balls come from nowhere, demanding to be included in
your supervisory act all at once. Can you handle it? Could anyone handle
it? How can it be done?

Like many people, you may enter your first supervisory job with an
empty feeling in the pit of your stomach. You may try to absorb as much
of your early orientation and on-the-job training as possible and then
attempt to make do with what you've got.

But there is learning after the first three months. You don't stop
there. You can learn from this book—and others. And you can continue to
learn on the job. First, let's look at learning from this book.

Many of us have been misled by textbooks to believe that there is a
formula, recipe, or correct answer at the end of the chapter. Even when
our schoolbooks had no answers, we knew the teacher's guide had them

all filled in—we knew the answers were there, that eventually we would see them. Now that we are big kids with adult responsibilities, we think that there should be a book containing all the answers to our job-related problems.

If that is your expectation, you may be disappointed. If there are any "answers," they will have to be somewhat customized or tailored to your work site. I attempt to make the following modules and topics generally applicable, but you ultimately have to make your learning from this book fit *your* situation. You finally supply your own "answers."

However, I hope you will find new insights here in Part II. It is made up of nineteen learning modules, covering topics from hiring to firing, from "Your Continued Learning on the Job" to "Dealing with the Violent Employee." You will be able to lift some of the practices covered in the modules straight from the book and use them. Others will require skill in applying, skill which you already have or will develop.

Part II is also intended to make you aware of some potentially new dimensions to supervising. Some of those considerations may not fit for you now. Remember, not every situation will lend itself to something you have read here. *You have to be discriminating. You* decide what fits and works for your supervisory performance. I simply provide you with a basis and a focus for your choices. Feel free to start with any learning module, irrespective of its number. Each module is designed to stand on its own. Turn first to the module that is most relevant to you now. Catch the rest later. Make this book work for you.

Learning Module 1

Your Continued Learning on the Job

You will have numerous ways of continuing to learn and to improve your work as supervisor beyond this book—and your first three months on the job. You will continue to learn, not only from working with your employees, but also from your peers and your own supervisor.

The supervisory position is set in the context of an organization chart. That means that each supervisory position will have some predictable relationships, both horizontally and vertically. And those relationships will to some degree influence the manner in which you carry out your supervisory role.

A supervisory position on the organization chart does not depend on a person for its existence. The position exists on the chart whether it has an occupant or not. The position also consists of specific responsibilities, resources, and rights within the organization—no matter who occupies the position. The major differences you will observe among supervisors have to do with the manner in which they exercise various combinations of the three R's. In addition to existing with or without someone in the slots, supervisory positions do not exist in a vacuum. There are numerous things that will influence supervisory activities. Some of these include the history of the unit, the mission of the organization, budgetary constraints, personnel allotments, personality quirks and variables, norms or practices existing in the organizational culture, system deficiencies, and the history and the development or evolution of your particular position. Consider these other factors in the organization—even external pressures on the organization—in assessing your impact and effectiveness from your supervisory position, and attend to the supports that are available to you.

BASIC SUPPORT—YOUR SUPERVISOR

Most of us will be simultaneously supervising and being supervised. The same kind of efforts we use to work our employees into their jobs will likely be used by our supervisors to work us into our job responsibilities fully and completely. So, whatever your initial reactions to learning a new position and taking on new job responsibilities, your own role as supervisee can serve as a continuing learning experience for your own supervisory role. Develop your ability to learn from experience.

In most organizations, people do not enter supervisory positions as their first job. Most of us began as employees, at the "doing" level of the organization, and then moved to the supervisory level. The fact that you have seen supervision in action—being supervised by your past supervisors—does not automatically imply that you can do it. Yet, some learning is likely to take place—certainly more than if you had had no supervision at all. Your learning is mainly dependent on you—on what you receive from your experience and what you transfer to your supervisory activities.

MAKING TRANSFERS OF LEARNING FROM SUPERVISORY EXPERIENCES

What readily transferable skills that produce desired results have you seen used by supervisors? From your stance of learning as a supervisee, what specific activities of your supervisor provided you with the clearest guidance in getting your work accomplished?

An Exercise

Put yourself in the role of a movie director for a moment. Recall scenes of experiences with your supervisor and with other supervisors.

Note specifically the activities that marked an effective supervisory exchange, whether delegation, clarification of task, or a simple communication (add your own applications). Once you have finished noting these activities, review them and select those activities you want to apply in your supervisory role. At times you may have to do a frame-by-frame (specific-activity-by-specific-activity) review to find some of the factors you will select for your supervisory role.

Figure 3 is a format for working through this exercise. Before reading further, make at least some sketchy responses to the items on it. You can always come back and fill in more detail, but you have a quick initial response that is worth noting *now!* You may require more time for an in-depth or detailed response later.

As a supervisor, you will continue to be accountable to your supervisor for the results of your unit as well as for the particular tasks of your job description. To assist you in doing your job, you may draw upon the direct support and encouragement of your own supervisor. You may also continue to learn from the interactions you have with your supervisor. Use your supervisor as a role model and as a consultant on specific situations you face with your employees.

ESSENTIAL FACTORS OF EFFECTIVE CONTACT WITH MY SUPERVISORS

INEFFECTIVE CONTACTS WITH MY SUPERVISORS | FACTORS TO CORRECT

WHICH WORK-RELATED CONTACTS WITH YOUR SUPERVISORS WERE MOST HELPFUL AND SUPPORTIVE FOR YOU IN THE PAST THREE MONTHS?

WHAT CONTACTS HAVE BEEN MOST SUCCESSFUL FOR YOU AS AN EMPLOYEE IN DEALING WITH YOUR SUPERVISOR?

Figure 3. Record of Learning from Supervisory Experiences

BASIC BUTTRESSING—LEARNING FROM YOUR PEERS

Now that you are a "member of the club" of supervisors, you will want to know how supervising is done in this organization. This does not necessarily mean that it is being performed correctly, but you can at least discover your colleagues' perceptions of the organization's expectations toward its supervisors. These expectations are what your performance will be measured against.

From them you can also learn a wide variety of practices for handling the situations you will confront. With them you can develop a network to exchange information, encouragement, policy interpretations, and the like. They will be a particularly valuable source of information and guidance when your immediate supervisor is not available.

Sometimes mandates that come down from above do not specify the activities and tasks required to implement the mandate. You and your peers may think that the folks upstairs are holding out on you. However, the lack of specific procedures often simply means that you are expected to work it out for yourself or with your unit. The top brass may not have it worked out either. In these cases—and for the sake of some diversity of viewpoint, some continuity and uniformity in the organization, and some security for your approach—consulting with your peers can be supportive and reassuring.

Some of your future planning may require interdependence with your peers, and some may need negotiations with your peer's employees for specific tasks. You can negotiate and accomplish these diagonal agreements more easily if communication with your peers is frequent and open.

Initially you may also want to determine what the norm is for supervisory behavior, so that you do not stray far from what is expected. Establish your credibility in the position before you decide to depart from the "acceptable" practices of your colleagues. You might also invite resistance from your peers if you deviate noticeably from their approaches. If you do stray from the norm, don't draw attention to yourself.

Peer supervisors can be a useful resource in dealing with your immediate supervisor and with the organization. This can be especially true when you need additional resources, cooperation on strategies, and the like. Even if a suggestion is all your idea, the support of your peers (explicitly or covertly) will increase idea acceptance from upper management.

Colleagues who have supervised in your organization for several years usually know personnel idiosyncrasies—the way the organization handles policies, rules, and goals. They have inside information about how the organization really functions, how higher-ups relate, what to expect from the grapevine, and other inner workings of the organization—which a bright supervisor will pick up on and use to his or her advantage.

Be aware of the balance of interdependence and autonomy allowed supervisors in your organization. Know the organizational range of tolerance for your position.

LEARNING FROM YOURSELF: PRACTICES AND PRESSURES

The overall daily operation of the organization may well have more influence on your work activity than any single contact with your employees, supervisor, or peers. External pressures, internal emphases, or just some particular nuance of the system you work in may require your spending much of your time justifying your budget, working on plans in fine detail (only to have them scrapped for new priorities), detailing your time expenditures, going to training sessions to prepare you for the job you are being drawn away from in order to attend the training session.

Sometimes you will work side by side with your employees during a rush job. At other times you will take work home over the weekend rather than delegate. You might hold on to the most important tasks because you do not want to entrust them to any one else—and you might be acting wisely. While these examples do not characterize textbook-perfect supervisory activity, that is what supervising may be in this imperfect world.

Supervising in an imperfect world means you will have to be resilient in many situations. If you are successful in doing most of what has been listed as supervisory activity, you may be far ahead of most people who carry the title of supervisor. The more you are able to follow correct supervisory procedures and practices, the more you will be developing conceptual, administrative skills that will aid your advancement in your organization. Even if not presently focused on career, this will serve you later.

LEARNING FROM YOUR EMPLOYEES

To some degree your employees' requirements will define your activities as a supervisor. Your main learning requirements for and from the position will come from the people you supervise. Without them you would not be a supervisor. You require the existence of the employee role to exercise your role as supervisor. The relationship is similar to the interdependence of performer and audience, pastor and congregation, parent and child. Your main activities will be interactions with your employees. So will your main effectiveness as a supervisor.

If you inherit a unit with experienced employees who clearly understand their job responsibilities, you may have little active supervisory responsibility other than comparing results with objectives or performance standards. Few of us will inherit such gems of units. However, such an inheritance would actually hinder the learning of supervisory functions. You will learn more from a unit in which employees are deficient in their job performance or discrepant in their tasks. Always begin your contacts with your employees with the knowledge that they have expectations of you in the role of supervisor. Their expectations may be based on their prior experience with supervisors or even on some attitude they have chosen to interpret in their best interests. Clarify those expectations very early. This is part of what I call establishing a common data base. Define your own role for your employees, and get your employees to specify to you what they understand to be their responsibilities to you and your responsibilities to them. If you don't, undefined role relationships can lead to disharmony.

Here's how it can happen.

Expectations Don't Often Match Reality

Employee D expects that you, as supervisor, will perform activities 1 through 8. You, meanwhile, perceive your responsibilities as supervisor to include activities 1, 2, 3, 6, and 8. These are legitimate activities of a supervisor in your understanding, and even though you may not know how to perform these activities expertly, you still recognize these employee expectations as legitimate.

You do not perceive activities 4, 5, and 7 as part of your supervisory responsibility. However, unless you clarify your position on the matter with your employee, the employee will continue to expect these activities of you. Your failure to perform according to employee expectations will be a continuing source of discontent in your unit. Since you did not count them among the responsibilities of the supervisory role, you will probably perceive these additional expectations as illegitimate pressures.

Employees determine some of the essence and unique activities of the supervisory role by their expectations, needs, requirements, abilities, skills, and individual idiosyncracies. The more complete your own understanding of your role responsibility, the less impact your employees will have in shaping your activities.

It will be useful for you to establish a common data base on the matter of role expectations and role clarity early in your work with each employee. Be explicit and precise about your own role responsibilities, and ask your employees what their expectations are of you as supervisor. Chances are you will find out more about their expectations as you discover more of your own assumptions about how they will function. You are also likely to discover expectations hidden behind such comments as "Oh, I thought you would take care of that" or "I'm not sure I have the authority to do that." Other approaches will attempt to put the "hot potato" squarely in your lap.

Often you can discover employee expectations in the course of goal or objective setting or when you get into detailed planning. However, expectations will continue to surface, even after you have thought you cleared up your role responsibilities "once and for all."

Employee expectations may come from individual employees or from the unit as a whole. And the expectations can be dealt with in individual or in group settings. In either setting the objective is to establish a common data base.

The importance of the common data base in a variety of supervisory situations was emphasized in Part I of this book. It continues as a theme through the rest of the modules and is underscored again and again. The prime concern of a supervisor ought to be establishing a common data base, and once in place, determining whether it is accurate, complete, and up to date—with your employees, your unit, your supervisor, indeed, with everyone with whom you communicate.

PUTTING INTO PRACTICE WHAT YOU ARE LEARNING

Very few supervisors have the capacity to change in a brief time their accustomed supervisory practices, their approach to working with employees. It is not for a lack of willingness that these changes are not completed, are not realized, or do not take effect. The problem is usually from a lack of one or more of the following requirements for implementing a new learning (even in situations beyond supervising): *understanding, conviction,* and *skill.* The lack of one or more of these requirements can account for the way a supervisor could attend and complete a course— with the clearest intention to make some changes in his activities with employees—and then promptly set aside those attempts or experience failure.

Understanding

After listening to a lecture and attending one three-day training session, a plant supervisor set out to change the way he got things done. He went back into the plant and held the type of meeting that had been held during training. However, the foremen had not participated in the training and did not participate in this meeting the way people had participated during the training meetings. Within three and one-half weeks, the plant supervisor was convinced that his new approach would not work in this plant. Furthermore, he was disenchanted with training, which he saw as seductive, simplistic, and misleading. What was so easy and natural in the training session just did not seem to work in this plant.

Unfortunately, the supervisor set out to implement some new activities without an adequate understanding of them or of what it would take to set them in place. You truly have to know what you are doing when you set out to implement new activities. You become almost a mini-organization yourself. You have to become aware of your purpose, your mission, or your goals and then begin to devise your objectives for setting the new learning in place.

The plant supervisor did not consider that the training session had introduced him to some new concepts and words. While that experience was "real," in some respects a person had to be there in order to fully grasp the meaning of the new terms. By bringing back words and practices that were unfamiliar to his employees, the supervisor not only threatened them a little, he also alienated them. The trusting, close-working environment of the training session was what the supervisor wanted to replicate in the plant. Instead, he got aloofness and suspicion. In short order he had in effect distanced the very people he wanted to communicate with and upon whom he depended in order to implement the system.

Conviction and Commitment

Conviction occurs when someone attaches value to an idea or activity. Beyond that valuing, you need a commitment to implement a change and to sustain it—"doing what you have to do to do it."

An assembly-line area had been studied for new efficiency techniques to increase production. Worker fatigue was found to be a factor, so the consultant recommended air conditioning for that particular southern climate. The management promptly installed a huge system to cool the entire assembly area. Upon re-inspection a year later, the consultant was surprised to find the air conditioner out of commission with a burned-out condenser and no immediate replacement plans.

On the surface, management appeared to understand the needs for increased comfort to induce assembly-worker production. They did all the "right" things by following the consultants' suggestion. However, they had not budgeted for maintenance of the unit, so for all their apparent conviction about the usefulness of the air conditioner, *they remained uncommitted.* It is *long-range commitment* that supports and maintains change beyond the early enthusiasm and short-lived conviction, through the pesky setbacks and unanticipated obstacles and costs.

Skill

The plant supervisor who tried to run the meeting with his unit "like it had been done in training" lacked the skill and understanding to make the changeover. People who have just been through training tend to mimic the activities they have observed in the learning process. What they fail to comprehend is the underlying rationale for the activity. Often the rationale for an activity is more important to know than the activity itself. Knowing the rationale, you can then make up your own situation-specific activity to accomplish the same purpose.

For example, one activity introduced in training is the publication of a meeting agenda. Since trainers are big on using flip charts, newsprint, and marker pens, the trainee tends to think that unless he has the same materials, he is denied adequate resources to do the job. In fact, the purpose of the flip chart is to make the agenda for the meeting visible to everyone. The agenda can be approached in perspective of other items and time available, and the meeting can be kept on track, if there is some visible map of activities. So a chalkboard, or 8½-by-11 inch copies of the agenda would accomplish the same purpose.

To implement your new learning in your unit, give the fullest possible rationale for the activities you introduce. This helps employees understand the new activities themselves, gives them greater flexibility to adapt activities to their circumstances, and increases the likelihood that they will go along with new activities—they will understand them rather than having to accept them on faith.

For any such implementation effort, it helps to develop a common data base, letting employees know where you are coming from (literally!). Taking part in an activity during a short training course may not qualify you to implement the activity any more than seeing a motion picture qualifies you to be a movie director.

Your own training in supervisory activities should be as explicit—step-by-step—as your directions are, in turn, to your employees. When you attend a training course, you will have to solicit sufficient information (and opportunities to practice) from those who direct the session to enable you to leave with an action plan for implementing your learning.

WHEN YOU HAVE ALL THREE

You will have to work for the understanding, the conviction/commitment, and the skill required to apply new learning to improve your supervisory practice. You can get additional understanding through courses, training, reading, self-paced textbooks, and training manuals. In this book, there are some practice components in the form of exercises. The conviction and commitment come only from you.

Enthusiasm without skill amounts to the same situation as Joe Citizen attempting to perform heart surgery just because he is convinced of its usefulness. Before you introduce a change in your supervisory activity, check yourself for your understanding, conviction/commitment, and skill in the activity you will attempt. Also, you may include your employees as allies in some of these changes if you have sufficient understanding of what it is that you want to do. They can make up for some of your shortcomings in skills needed for the change.

Learning Module 2

Supervisory Conferences

One of the formal focus points of supervision is conferences and meetings between a supervisor and one or more employees. Conferences may be regular and routine and have a relaxed tone to them. However, at times a conference will involve unresolved issues and generate a great deal of tension. This module covers both the "easy" and the "tense" conference.

All supervisory conferences should be held on a regular basis. Group conferences can be used to deal with topics such as unit planning, policy clarification, or work distribution. Otherwise, for employee development or correction and other individual concerns, the supervisor and the employee would meet privately.

PREPARATION

Bring yourself up to date prior to the conference. Take the routine out of the conference by building on the last conference. From your side as supervisor:

- review past and recent performance;
- note specific gains and improvement;
- develop tentative objectives prior to the conference;
- rehearse your role in the conference to keep the agenda moving from item to item; and
- prepare supports to assist the employee, line up resources, and review the budget.

Climate Setting—Holding the Conference

Whether the conference is expected to be pleasant or tense, there are certain "laundry-list" items to consider to ensure a smooth conference with a facilitative climate.

In most cases, running a conference follows rules of courtesy and good planning.

Conference Check List

Advance Planning

_____ Advance announcement of meeting or reminder of regularly scheduled meeting

_____ Preparation and distribution of advance (known) agenda

_____ Punctual start

_____ Time allotment for each agenda item

_____ Limitation on interruptions, e.g., holding phone calls

_____ Outside time limits

Logistics

_____ Place that affords privacy

_____ Sufficient space for comfortable distance

_____ Unobstructed meeting space (e.g., desk)

_____ Comfortable temperature

_____ Good lighting

_____ Ventilation, especially for smoke or stale air

_____ Refreshments

Tone

_____ Affirming feedback, positive strokes

_____ Data sharing

_____ Adult-adult, two-way communication

_____ Active listening

_____ Flexibility—conference paced within time limits

_____ Supportiveness—even when correcting, confronting

Focus

_____ Statement of purpose of conference

_____ Statement of agenda and allotment of time for each item

_____ Establishment of common data base—facts over assumptions—explanation of policy *and* rationale

_____ Objectives mutually set and rationale discussed

_____ Action-plan steps set prior to next conference

Learn to Say

_____ "I don't know

_____ "I'll look it up."

Here is more on what to do when there are difficult issues, conflicts, or tense feelings.

DEALING WITH A TENSE CONFERENCE:

When I tell you about the important considerations for beginning a tense interview or any other face-to-face conference in which either or both parties might be tense or nervous, you may question some of the procedures. However, give them a chance and see if they work. Some of the occasions to use these procedures are interviews, supervisory conferences, evaluation conferences, and the like.

Breathe!

Prior to the conference or interview, become aware of your breathing. You will have to continue breathing in order to take care of the excess adrenalin in your bloodstream during times of high excitement or stress. Many of us attempt to appear cool and unperturbed when we are excited or under stress, but our body chemistry does not change to suit our desire to look "cool."

Here is what happens:

Under mild threat or stress, extra adrenalin is secreted into the bloodstream. This promotes an increase in the heart rate, together with a body state of arousal, of readiness or alertness. While the adrenalin is coursing through the bloodstream, increasing your metabolic rate, your oxygen supply in the bloodstream is being consumed more rapidly. In your attempt to appear cool and in control as your blood flow quickens, you may also have some bulging veins as you subconsciously attempt to restrict the flow of blood, to hold back what you are feeling.

As the oxygen supply in your blood decreases, deep full breaths would break your facade of coolness, so you keep from breathing deeply (seemingly vulnerably). Because your brain uses about 30 percent of the oxygen supply in your blood, the now-reduced supply may cause you to feel somewhat dull or even a bit light-headed, almost dizzy. By working against your physical needs at the moment by not breathing deeply, you leave yourself at a disadvantage to deal with the mildly threatening or stressful situation, which by now has become increasingly stress filled just by the way you choose to cope.

There are other ways of coping:

The first is to admit that this increase in metabolism does occur for you. Furthermore, recognize that you have to draw in more air to provide your blood and brain with sufficient oxygen. So, rather than shut down your breathing, determinedly draw deep, full breaths down into your midriff, filling up your diaphragm or midsection, the area below your rib cage. If you can breathe deeply, you not only replenish the oxygen in your blood, you also begin to dissolve your tension or stress so that you feel less threatened. You should then be able to attend more directly to the person with whom you are conferring and to the agenda at hand.

You may practice inhaling with a slow one-to-seven count, then expel all of the air also to a one-to-seven count. If that is not sufficient, you might increase the count to ten or eleven or simply slow the count down. Breathe in deeply all the way down into your pelvis, if you can do so without straining. When you breathe out, let out all the air. Set your count so that you are not dying either to let the air out quickly, or to draw in another breath immediately. Breathe to suit yourself and your needs. You may also use this exercise daily at your desk to deal with stress or low energy.

Balance!

In attempting to appear cool and in control, many individuals displace the tension they feel by crossing their ankles, leaning heavily on an elbow, or in some other way contorting their bodies to drain off stress indirectly. This is a little like digging your fingernails into your palms to create pain so you do not feel a shot from a hypodermic needle. We tend to create stress to deal with other stresses or pain. Imbalance is created stress.

To the best of your ability, get yourself balanced. A quick check to see whether you are balanced and ready to deal with another person is to stand up directly from your position in your seat just before an interview. "Composed" postures (sitting back with legs crossed, for example) may be most immobilizing. To stand up directly from that posture you first have to uncross your legs. If you stood up with your legs crossed, you would fall forward on your head. If you find yourself under stress, pay attention to your balance—for if you feel threatened and then put yourself in a confining posture, you only compound your sense of threat. You subconsciously sense and signal yourself that you are immobile.

What to Do

Sit as straight as you can without appearing stiff. Find the support in the chair for your full weight on your buttocks, with support from the back of the chair for your back. Plant your feet (heel, arch, and ball of each foot) squarely on the floor, so that you can come to a standing position directly in one continuous, fluid movement from where you are sitting. That way, you are ready to move and you do not feel "cornered."

When you stand, be aware of distributing your weight evenly on both feet, bending your knees only slightly to maintain balance (do not lock your knees). Remember to keep breathing deeply at all times. The main thing is to be aware of your need to breathe and to maintain your balance.

Climate Setting for Tense Conferences

All of the courtesy accorded someone in the daily, easygoing conference situation applies here. It is most useful if you can make the person with whom you are conferring comfortable from the start. It is essential that you make some contact with that person when the person enters the conference area. While you may still be reading an application form for the hiring interview, for example, the minimum contact would be raising your eyes, welcoming the applicant, shaking hands if appropriate, and asking the applicant to be seated, saying that you will be ready to start in a moment. That makes the initial bond and averts the tension of non-contact, which would leave the applicant ill at ease.

Schedule potentially tense conferences at a time you will not be stacked up with other work and will be able to clear your desk in order to focus fully and completely on your discussion with the conferee. Attend to that person's comfort, both as a way of making that person at ease and facilitating the discussion, and also to get your attention off yourself and your own concerns. However, as we have emphasized, you need to attend to your own comfort first in order to be able to attend to the other person.

AGENDA—HOMEWORK

Some conferences, such as an interview, have ready-made agendas. However, for other conferences you will have an agenda determined by the situation or by the major concerns you want to cover.

Prior to meeting with the conferee, have the objective of the conference clearly in mind. Know where you are going with it. Know the business you are to accomplish. Remember that a primary activity in the conference will be to establish a common data base. One objective for a hiring interview could read:

> To establish a common data base by the end of each one-hour interview by describing the eight major job responsibilities and eliciting applicant skills, interest, initiative, and potential to meet those requirements.

YOU FIRST!

In most cases you will have called the conference, and so it will be your job to start it. Even when an employee asks to meet with you, protocol may dictate that you make the opening statement. That statement may be as innocuous as "I understand you want to talk some things over." Usually it is best to lighten up the atmosphere a bit to begin with or at least to deal directly with the facts. The simpler the statement you can make to kick things off, the better. Usually a simple statement of the reality of the situation will get the agenda rolling: "I have some things to talk over with you."

DEFINE THE BOUNDARIES OF CHOICE

One useful procedure in conferences is to specify the boundaries of the situation being dealt with. Some items are open for employee choice or discretion, for example, how the employee will proceed. Some items are open to mutual discussion and deliberation or negotiation by supervisor and employee, for example, deliberating dates for completion of immediate objectives and negotiating a work plan. That means that the outcomes are not fixed or sealed in concrete.

Finally, there are those items between supervisor and employee that are fixed and nonnegotiable. They are not "up for discussion." The job requires certain outcomes, or management has set them. It is important for the supervisor to realize and define the boundaries for the employee of what is—

- fixed, set, and nonnegotiable by employee (to be done as is);
- negotiable in part or entirely between supervisor and employee; and
- at the discretion or choice of the employee.

Once you have specified the boundaries for the conference, you can begin to lay down a common data base so that you both can begin the discussion with the same information.

As an example, a conference might involve a situation in which defective products are being reported by customers. There are several things that would make the supervisor's task with the employee clear. First, he should get specific and detailed information about the defects that are drawing the complaints. He should find out specific deficiencies, dates, shipments, and the circumstances surrounding the discovery of the deficiency. There may be some local conditions that contribute to the malfunction of the product, and this would come to light only by questioning the customer further, getting more detail. So the supervisor would first get additional information, rather than go off "half-cocked" or half-informed about the problem situation.

The supervisory conference in which the supervisor discusses the malfunctioning product could proceed this way: the supervisor begins by giving the background information he has received (building a common data base). Not accusing, only describing what he has been told factually, he asks the employee to comment and add anything to the facts the supervisor knows. The employee may want to get some more specific information before proceeding.

Once the employee has had an opportunity to add to the data base, the supervisor then comes to the point of exchange in which he sets forth his own needs or objectives. It is helpful if the supervisor can place his comments in context, describing the potential competition of foreign goods in the marketplace, for example. This adds to the common data base, provides the employee with an opportunity to stand in the boss' moccasins, and adds to general morale by highlighting the interdependence in the overall operation. Next, the supervisor moves on to state what he wants in that situation. In this case it could be increased quality control, guaranteeing the functioning of the product through a product inspection prior to packaging and delivery.

The employee's job description may not necessarily say anything about inspecting the goods. However, the job was created to handle the manufacturing phase of the operation, and even though there is no specific mention of product quality inspection, that task falls within the general duties of manufacturing. Often a lot will be assumed. The supervisor may have fully expected that "any fool" assembling the product would check to see that it met quality control standards before shipping it. Wrong again. He could not assume anything. Oh, it would be nice to be able to assume. But in this world such assumptions often result in foul-ups. *Specific discussion of expectations and mutual agreement is the only way to ensure specific performance.* The employee needs to know the full extent of his responsibility. So, if his products are defective, it is in his own best interest, as well as the interests of the organization, to explicitly add "inspection" to his duties.

It is entirely possible for the supervisor to manufacture all sorts of intentions, faults, personality flaws, or reasons "why" the employee let the flawed products leave the assembly line. He could attribute to the employee any number of far-flung motives his imagination could conjure up. However, when all the drama ends, even if a motive is nailed down, the supervisor still wants the inspection added to ensure that certain specifications for the product are checked prior to shipment. That activity is most likely to correct the deficiencies in the product's manufacture and delivery.

SUMMARY

The supervisory conference is a continuing mode of supervision. Certain procedures (using a check list, for example) can facilitate the conference, be it tense or routine and relaxed.

It is important to specify to the employee what realistically can be determined and acted upon in the conference—what is fixed, negotiable, or at the employee's discretion. Beyond that, it is important to establish a common data base for the context of the conference by providing information and eliciting information from the employee. Feelings can be an important part of that context. Finally, you have to reach agreement and document the accord you reached—the action steps that will follow.

Learning Module 3

Feedback:
Commenting on Employee Performance

The forward observer focuses his calibrated binoculars on the enemy position on hill number 462. About six hundred yards to his rear, a mortar is fired at an antiaircraft gun stationed on hill number 462. The mortar explodes some seventy yards to the right of the battery. The forward observer calls in that information to the mortar and suggests a degree correction of 1'15" NNW.

The forward observer has just provided the mortar with information that the mortar could not provide for itself because it is out of sight of the target. The information dealt with a "reading" on the position of the battery and then subsequent readings on the mortar hits with respect to the battery or target position. The subsequent readings all dealt with consequences of the mortar firing—whether it was true to the mark or off the mark. The subsequent readings were "feedback." Literally, the forward observer fed back information relative to the mortar firing—left, right, up, down, how far. This provides the initiator of the action, the mortar team, with guidelines for further action. Guidelines are gained from a reading of the consequences of earlier firings, which then provide a means of correcting further firing from prior misfires.

FEEDBACK DELIVERY MODES

In supervision, feedback is provided verbally and nonverbally. The nonverbal aspect could involve some prearranged series of signals or codes or some recognizable gestures. Sometimes nonverbal feedback consists of body language—a supposed signal sent out by way of body position. However, in many cases, body language has lost its innocence as a direct or readable method of gathering feedback information because of the popular and exploitative exposure of nonverbal communication as a tool for manipulating and analyzing people. In this module we will deal mostly with the use of verbal feedback.

THE WEAKEST LINK IN SUPERVISORY COMMUNICATION

Feedback is the weakest link in supervisory communication. Whether it consists of just a brief pat on the back or a more detailed dealing with point-by-point activities of the employee, feedback is either too seldom offered or ineptly given. Often, supervisors don't know what appropriate feedback is, let alone how to provide it. One result is that the supervisor dreads providing it, and the employee dreads the tension of receiving it.

More specific to the supervisory responsibility, feedback is essential to keeping the employee on track or reinforcing initial learning or skills. Feedback is also essential in daily performance evaluation, ongoing supervisory conferences, and in the evaluation conference. In most organizations, lack of feedback is a major deficiency in the supervisory relationship.

TYPES OF FEEDBACK

There are two types of feedback: *inappropriate* feedback—that is, feedback that is destructive or useless—and *appropriate* feedback—that is, affirming or corrective. In this module we will focus on the effective use of appropriate feedback, feedback intended in the spirit of affirmation or correction. But first an overview of the destructive and useless forms.

Destructive Feedback

Destructive feedback is feedback given with the intent of hurting, punishing, demeaning, or discounting the recipient. It involves more a denunciation for what was not done, than acknowledgement of what was accomplished. There is no particular corrective data involved to help the recipient improve performance. Sometimes destructive feedback even involves disapproval of some situation that cannot be changed—"I don't like your blue eyes" is an extreme example. Or it can just convey a dislike or disapproval without any indication of what is preferred—"I don't like the way you chaired the meeting."

Some additional characteristics of destructive feedback (or useless feedback) are that it is *general* rather than *specific* and *concrete*. It provides *no guidance* for a preferred state of being, situation, or activity. Usually the recipient is left feeling helpless in the face of destructive feedback, while the deliverer of the feedback remains aloof, dominant, and uninvolved, yet in control.

Useless Feedback

There are certain forms of inappropriate feedback that fall into a category all their own—"miscellaneous," if not useless. These include feedback that does not demean or demand or discount per se, but neither provides anything useful to the recipient. It adds nothing. There is no way to get a handle on this feedback, because it is general, and because it often seems to be given with the best of intentions. Examples include "I like you," or "You're a nice person." Most school children would respond "Yuk!" if this feedback were delivered in a syrupy tone of voice. There is something not quite genuine in it. It leaves you neutralized and certainly no more enlightened than before. Such general statements may be a result of ineptness. The provider knows exactly what he means by "like" or "nice." He just fails to communicate it, leaving the recipient to flounder or say, "Thank you (I think)."

In common parlance, feedback is most often categorized as "positive" or "negative." Under these terms, useless feedback would probably fit the "positive" category for most people since it can be pleasant and does not involve discomfort in the providing. Destructive feedback would be "negative" in anyone's book. It is unpleasant and uncomfortable to receive and even uncomfortable to give. Destructive and useless feedback are inappropriate in a supervisory-employee work relationship.

Part of the purpose of giving feedback is to provide people with information they might not be able to readily obtain for themselves. General statements such as "I like you" do not provide much information and may serve more as a teaser and disabler in a work relationship than provide a solid, concrete, specific, and available data base from which the recipient can draw his own course of action based on further knowledge of himself, his activities, or his job responsibility. Feedback from a supervisor should be, at the very least, job related.

Affirming Feedback

Affirming feedback involves information of a positive or rewarding nature. Affirming feedback tells you what you did right, what is on track, or what is working. Some supervisors have the facility to focus on affirming activities so energetically that the recipient is strongly influenced to make even more activity "right on track" and so receive more affirming feedback. The internal dialogue of the recipient is "I really like knowing and hearing about what I have done well. I wonder how I can get more rewards like this." Affirming feedback is supportive and disposes the employee to be open to further improvement in work performance.

Affirming feedback, like corrective feedback, includes all the essentials of appropriate feedback. From the recipient's point of view, these essentials are as follows:

Specificity. I was told what I did in detail sufficient to help me repeat (or not repeat) the activity, depending on what I want to do; I know what is required.

Timeliness. I have enough time to listen to what is being said, and I am disposed to listen. (For example, you would not give detailed information on running technique to someone who is still winded from a 10,000-meter run. Nor would you discuss detailed job plans or adjustments in a wedding-reception line.) Feedback should closely follow the activity affirmed.

Relevance. It has some importance to me, especially in terms of something I am trying to do or something important to the improvement or maintenance of my job.

When you provide affirming feedback, be sure the feedback is specific, timely, and relevant.

Corrective Feedback

Corrective feedback consists of specific information that provides an employee guidance and direction in focusing or refocusing energies on more appropriate job-related activity. Corrective feedback is an essential skill for the supervisor to use both in directing the new employee into effective task performance and in guiding the errant or derailed, yet capable, employee back to effective job performance.

When the forward observer calls back a reading in degrees to the mortar team, he is attempting to get them on target, to direct their firepower more precisely to their objective (target) on hill number 462. Each firing, hit, reading, and feedback constitutes some of the *process of approximation* similar to the tasks and activities, results, assessment, and feedback that goes on between the supervisor-counterpart of the forward observer, and the employee-mortar firer.

For the new employee the approximation involves being successively guided or coached toward an activity or result he has not yet achieved. The employee may need to be focused on many aspects of his job-related activity in order to proceed and develop his full job capability.

However, for the experienced employee who is currently off track for production, the supervisor attempts to reclarify that target area or range of performance possibilities to get the desired results.

These two essential tasks of supervising require the practice of corrective feedback. Even so, feedback is not always appropriate. As supervisor, you will have to decide what intervention is appropriate for corrective feedback. Here are a few considerations that will help you decide.

WHEN DO YOU USE CORRECTIVE FEEDBACK?

Personal Annoyances Versus Job-Related Activity

One of the first distinctions a supervisor must make in providing corrective feedback is to determine which employee activities are job related as opposed to which constitute personal annoyances to the supervisor. Annoyances may include garlic breath, dress, hair style, mannerisms, and the like—even a three-martini lunch. Where do you draw the line?

Three Bases for Job-Related Intervention

Unless these annoyances directly affect (1) job performance, (2) unit functioning, or (3) the organization's credibility or stability with consumers or suppliers, you do not have cause to intervene with corrective feedback. If you intervene on the basis of a personal annoyance, then your intervention is as a person, not as a supervisor. You need to make that distinction for yourself, as well as not letting it enter your work relationship.

Intervention on the basis of *job-related activities* may encompass such matters as dress (following the accepted standards of the community), hygiene (extraordinary body odor may repulse clients or customers), and drinking (when work falters after lunch).

The basis for intervention in terms of *unit production* may involve complaints from other employees. It would be best if the complaining employee dealt directly with the offending or irritating employee, but you may be left to do it. Your intervention may have to be based on very little direct "forward" observation, sometimes just on hearsay. For example, an employee may perform his own job-related activities to perfection and get all the results set forth in objectives. However, the employee may also finish tasks early and then distract other employees, visiting around. Or the employee may be "bad mouthing," spreading rumors, or otherwise disrupting overall unit harmony and morale.

A third basis for intervention is the determination that the employee is engaged in activities that currently or potentially could disrupt the *organization's interaction, credibility,* or *reputation* with the community. The social worker who works evenings as a go-go dancer in a conservative southern city is one example of a potential embarrassment for the organization. A doctor discovered to be a morphine addict, currently administering a drug abuse program, is another extreme example.

Intervention in the interest of unit or organizational functioning requires somewhat more precise information or analysis to establish the link between what is being done and how unit production or the organization are directly affected.

No matter what the basis for the intervention, there are drawbacks to giving corrective feedback. Here are some of them.

- You have to know what the correct activity—or the range of on-track, acceptable requisite activities—is in order to intervene.

- You want to intervene after the employee has exerted some initiative but prior to his becoming deeply frustrated or dangerous or destructive with his misdirection.

- You may not always be sure of the "right" time to intervene. For example, you may have sensed some early indications that the employee was swerving off course. However, only recently have you received sufficient indications that the employee is truly off course, you may hesitate and fear some recrimination from the employee ("Why didn't you tell me sooner?"), but you know you have to intervene anyway.

- Corrective interventions are sometimes difficult to accomplish without arousing defensiveness in the employee. You may want to jump right into getting the employee on track. It's obvious. However, you set the stage for corrective feedback with some lead-in, for example, "In order for us to work together effectively, I monitor your task performance. When you are on course, I let you know so that you may continue with some assurance. And when you seem to be off course, I hope I can tell you early enough so that you do not waste time and energy unproductively. I have been noting recently that you are doing _____ , which does not include some of the tasks required for getting output."

HOW TO DO IT

Affirming and corrective feedback is best provided in short, precise interventions daily at the work station, rather than just in periodic conferences. If you are able to be on site, this daily coaching activity serves to get the employee more effectively and efficiently applied toward his job responsibility.

When you provide feedback, keep your focus on specific job-related activity rather than on what you consider "personalities or character types" in your employees. Your feedback should be easy to deliver, factual and well received. However, that requires that you focus well on the job responsibility. Corrective feedback is not to be confused with feedback that is scathing, abusive or addressing a condition that cannot be changed.

Corrective feedback requires preparation and functions best when there is some specific activity, task performance, or results designated and sought.

Approaches to Giving Corrective Feedback

Corrective feedback may involve drawing attention to some deficiencies in employee activity or simply in getting some priorities that the employee can then use to guide further choices on the job. For example, a receptionist tended to write phone messages and answer the phone even while talking with a customer. She kept customers standing at the desk while taking care of phone business. Corrective feedback stated the priorities of the organization in this matter: "When clients enter the reception room, greet them as soon as they arrive at your desk, if not while they are approaching the desk. Put the phone on hold and let other activities wait, unless you are dealing with an emergency on the phone when the customer arrives."

Since most of us have some apprehension about how an employee is going to receive corrective feedback, there is a tendency to spend some time massaging the employee before delivering the message. The typical approach is to begin with a list of positives or affirming feedback. Depending upon your attitude and apprehension, this may come off more as a ritual litany than as a genuine affirming feedback offering. Your voice will be raised and tense as you squeak out the so-called virtues of your employee.

Meanwhile, a sensitive employee will be waiting for you to end your list of good points . . . , and . . . , and . . . , and get to the *but*. That is the same "but" we use to describe an unfortunate situation—and now for the bad news. You may tend to build up one side in order not to destroy the person.

Now let's review some basics. First of all, as a supervisor you are not dealing with an individual as a *person* when providing feedback. You are dealing with him as *personnel*—personnel with a contract to perform specific tasks and activities or to get specific results.

You as supervisor have a responsibility to provide employees with information that will allow them to perform their work more effectively.

One way in which you fulfill your responsibility is to provide them with specific, job-related feedback. That is your responsibility.

Once the employee understands this as a responsibility on your part and the specific focus on job-related activity, rather than as a generalized evaluation of the employee as a person or personality, the employee will begin to discover the advantage in receiving feedback. He will see it as a right and resource for his job and career development.

If you can approach your employee from this basis, that this is a useful bit of information you are providing, you may still want to precede the corrective feedback with some affirming feedback. Nevertheless, you can provide the corrective feedback whether you have some affirming feedback to offer or not.

The corrective feedback does not have to be offset by affirming feedback. It is part of your sharing of information, perhaps the most important contribution that you can provide in the supervisor-employee relationship. In any case it is your responsibility, and it may not wait on the generation of a one-for-one balance of affirming feedback. The more specifically you can deal with the activities that have to be done differently, the easier your entire task of providing the feedback. Come down to particulars.

INCREASING THE FREQUENCY OF FEEDBACK WITHIN THE UNIT

If you are like many supervisors, the extent of your feedback has been an occasional "boot in the rear" or "pat on the back." That may have been all that was required. Any increase in feedback now might arouse more curiosity than productivity.

Actually, increasing affirming feedback arouses more suspicion at first, than does corrective feedback. "What's going on around here?" "Why's he being so nice to me?" "What does she want?" Any activity out of the ordinary stirs employee interest. With affirming feedback there may be more hesitance to be open to it. One might feel vulnerable—almost set up—by being told what he performed well.

Affirming feedback is often met with embarrassment, shrugged shoulders, and a disclaimer of "greatness" by the employee ("t'warn't nothin"). You will see modesty and humility practiced at its best, and you may even regret inflicting such "punishment" on the employee.

But there are other useful outcomes for affirming feedback besides rewarding and impressing the employee to continue some tasks at his or her current performance level. It also reinforces the employee's sense of adequacy for doing some tasks.

Affirming feedback at its best will function to assist an employee in identifying job-related strengths, as well as strengths that require more work. Not only does it say to what degree the employee has "arrived" in *this* job, but also signals some acceptance by the supervisor. It is also important that the employee assess and acknowledge his job strengths for himself—as much for his own present peace of mind as for his future career development. The modesty with which employees confront an affirming supervisor is mostly culturally developed—in time, employees will get accustomed to affirming feedback, even revel in it.

Affirming feedback is best directed to a very specific point or activity so that the employee-recipient can learn from it—or at least know what you mean by what you say. When you give feedback, do so from your supervisory position, but acknowledge that you "own" the feedback.

Here are some examples of what I mean.

You say
"Jean, that was a good job."
You do not "own" the feedback.

Jean's unspoken response is
"Who says so? I disagree. What do you mean 'good'? I thought 'it' was superb."

A more specific comment—from your position as supervisor, but "owned" by you—would provoke less argument.
"As your supervisor, I appreciate your increase in customers last month. It helped our unit goals, and I will place a written commendation on your permanent record."

Now Jean knows what she did, who appreciates it and why, and what the consequences for her are.

You say
"Figby, your attitude and concern make you an ideal employee."

Figby's unspoken response could (rightly) be
"You are dealing in such nebulous items as attitudes, personality, character."

What would have told Figby more is
"Figby, when you worked late last Friday night to finish the new contract proposal, I appreciated your concern in helping me and the unit earn our livelihood for the coming year."

Now Figby knows the activity, the contribution he is being recognized for, as well as the basis for the recognition and how it fits into the overall operation.

ACCUSTOM EMPLOYEES TO RECEIVING AFFIRMING FEEDBACK

To accustom employees to receiving affirming feedback, you have to ask them to just listen to it without putting qualifications or conditions on what they hear. One exercise to make sure employees hear what you offer is to have them write down your feedback. That way they "put a bottom in their basket"—that is, even if they deny or forget hearing the feedback, they can remind themselves of it in writing, take it in, and eventually own or assume responsibility for that feedback from the supervisor.

Affirming feedback can also be a useful communication and support building device within the organization (see Module 9). Once you have begun to provide feedback more regularly and spontaneously, keep up the pattern you establish with employees. You can also allow them to provide you with affirming and corrective feedback. Responsibly provided, this is a major breakthrough in two-way communication within the supervisor-employee relationship.

SUMMARY

We have focused on some of the difficulties associated with providing employees with job-related affirming and corrective feedback. To make feedback most useful to the recipient, I would emphasize that you specify not only the activity that is "on track" or in error, but also any other activity that might be more effective and "on track" for the employee. A specific description of the activity is essential so that the employee knows what he is doing well or what requires improvement and how to improve that activity.

The more that feedback can be tied directly to job-related activities and results, the more appropriate it is in dealing with an employee. As a supervisor you cannot change employee characteristics or personality, but you can affirm or correct employee performance through feedback on specific activities. This focus keeps you within the range of both human and supervisory ability, rather than pursuing the magical "why" of the employee's activities, a thankless and useless pursuit that blocks communication with the employee and prevents the employee from having to take responsibility for his activities (see Module 9).

Through focusing on results, you can better utilize the leverage of the goal sought through employee activity. All feedback provided an employee ought to bear some relationship to activities affecting job performance, unit morale and productivity, or organizational functioning.

Learning Module 4

Hiring and the Selection Process

In Part I, you read a brief sketch of your responsibility through the supervisory cycle, from job announcement through termination. This module goes into some of the considerations, procedures, and mechanics of the selection process in more detail to help you with one of the most important decisions you make as a supervisor: the selection decision.

GENERAL CONSIDERATIONS

Some supervisors have the opportunity to hire the employees who will work under them. Others either inherit a unit to supervise, taking the personnel that comes with it, or their personnel are transferred in from other units, chosen by someone else in the organization. We will work from the assumption that you have the responsibility for hiring your own employees and discuss what that involves.

Anticipate Staffing Needs

It is helpful if you can anticipate the need for an addition or replacement in your unit. Anticipating allows you sufficient time to set up the selection process and to get all the necessary clearances. Often you have to have done it "yesterday," so you rush into the hiring process under some pressure to get someone on board. But sufficient front-end time (say, two to three months) allows for advertising the position and drawing in promising prospects.

If you are filling a vacated position, use the exit interview to get a clearer idea of the actual job tasks that employee has been fulfilling. Often job descriptions are brought out and dusted off for use on bulletin boards and in employment agencies and have little bearing on the position they purport to fill. Match that job description with the realities of the job. Make it specific and truly descriptive without overly limiting the activities you can negotiate or expect of the employee on the job.

The beginning of the selection process is an opportunity for you to make any revisions in the function and responsibilities of the slot you are filling. Assess what readjustments in job responsibility would best help your unit function, then negotiate those changes with other personnel in the unit and revise the job description accordingly, prior to publicly announcing the job.

Pitfalls

If possible, avoid situations in which the job position is "wired" from the inside—that is, someone is already designated to fill the position and the hiring interviews are just a courtesy or formality. In a wired position the job description is written so specifically that it practically matches the resume of the preselected person. Whether you are the one doing the wiring or someone else is, interviewing is then an empty exercise, frustrating for you and the applicants. Also, you could conceivably drive off some good prospects for future employment. Good applicants have some idea of their abilities and will be dissuaded from further attempts with your company, unless you also encourage those applicants to apply for future positions. Know what is possible, what real choices you have when you begin the hiring activity.

Advance Notice

Once you have updated the job description, allow enough time to draw in qualified prospects. Be prepared to extend the deadline if necessary rather than choose from among a group you would ordinarily cull out.

Develop Selection Criteria

In the best of all worlds you would know the exact criteria upon which you would make your decision of a new employee prior to holding the interviews. What often happens is that you will find yourself weighing some newly discovered competencies or characteristics—even experience—among the various applicants you interview. Although you will probably not develop all of your selection criteria as an afterthought, remember that some of the criteria that emerge during interviews are practical expressions of what is available to you—the labor supply.

Write out the criteria you use to make your selection. A written record is especially important in cases in which you can be "grieved"against, and the process of formulating and writing your criteria contributes to your own development as an interviewer, building up your sense of confidence in your decisions and judgments. Keeping careful notes and knowing the criteria for your choice will provide you with a basis for validating your skills over the long term as you see employees develop or wash out. You can learn from both experiences.

In some organizations, outside criteria may enter into the selection decision. Organizational quotas may come into play, as might administrative pressure in favor of a particular applicant, political considerations, or company experience with certain types of candidates. Some seasoned recruiting officers can make selection judgments based on certain educational or socio-economic variables that have correlated with performance in certain jobs over years of experience. Someone in your organization may have similar expertise. Talk with experienced personnel officers about these factors for your organization.

Know the kinds of people with whom you work best. Supervising does not include missionary activity, so consider your preferences, too, in establishing criteria. It is your job to produce, not wage a battle of wills with your subordinates or turn an ineffectual, though promising, individual into a star. Keep your perspective.

Building the Common Data Base

To build up the kind of information or data base required of an interview is the shared responsibility of the applicant and the interviewer. The applicant best knows his interests, experience, and capabilities. The interviewer needs to become aware of them. So, the applicant must contribute that information to the common data base.

Likewise the applicant needs to know more about the job. The interviewer has that information, at least the basics, so he must share that data with the applicant. The result of the exchange is that the available information is either shared fully by the applicant or elicited by the interviewer, or it does not enter into the interviewer's consideration. If there is information that is not shared, even though it is available, it does not become part of the common data base. When an employer says, "Oh, I was not aware of that about you," it is an acknowledgement that the information shared between them has been expanded with some new inputs.

BEFORE THE INTERVIEW

The applicant will get an initial impression of the organization through the interview. The setting, the climate you establish, and the interest you show can get your relationship off to a solid start. First you have to attend to some details: (1) arrange a clear and uninterrupted time for the interview, (2) read the applicant's application form prior to the interview and formulate questions to probe for more information, (3) arrange the physical setting so that comfortable contact can be established and maintained without crowding during the interview. Make sure the chairs are comfortable and that coffee or other refreshments are available, and (4) make yourself as comfortable and relaxed as possible so that you can focus on the applicant and put the applicant at ease.

Allow ample time for each interview. You may want some slack time between interviews in order to make notes and also time to extend some interviews.

INTERVIEWING

The face-to-face discussion with a job applicant is not the only opportunity you have to gather information in the selection process. However, it is probably the most important single part of that process. In it you begin to establish your relationship. The interview will also get you first-hand data you won't find elsewhere. But you may also draw upon the written application as well as the list of references of past and current employers.

Set the Tone Now for Shared Responsibility

Share responsibility with the applicant in the interview from the outset. If this applicant is to eventually work with your organization, he would profit by a preview of the autonomy, assertiveness, or initiative an individual needs to exercise as a member of your unit. Some opening lines might be the following.

"I would like to know, [*applicant's name*], how it is that you are applying for this job. Could you please tell me why you want this particular job?"

"Before you leave this interview I will tell you about the job, and then I would like you to tell me about any particular experience, ability, or interest you have in the job that would favor my choosing you."

"What interests you about the job?"

"How do you see your career with this organization if you begin in this position? What would you like it to be?"

"What would your past supervisors likely view as your strengths and weaknesses?"

Watch Out for Hidden Expectations!

This is a caution even for those who will not interview and hire their subordinates. Expectations applicants bring to an interview or to the job should be dealt with directly in the interview. Left obscure or unsaid, "expectations" can lead to nothing but trouble. They have to be uncovered at some point, and the interview is the best time to do it. Take this as advice, maybe even as a "red flag."

Oats in the Bucket

Often interviewers will attempt to put the job and the organization in a favorable light by promising the applicant almost anything. At best, this is misleading. At worst, another word for it is seduction—promising more than they can or will deliver. Furthermore, the person who makes the promise or assurance is seldom around when the employee comes to collect on the promise. This leads to disillusionment and low morale for the employee.

An applicant often will "hire on" to one job with the assurance or an imagined guarantee that he will be able to switch departments or shops when a job becomes available there. The important thing for him initially was to get his foot in the door. So there he is and once his dream job becomes available, the initial interviewer can't or won't do anything about it. Maybe the interviewer isn't even still with the organization. Maybe there never was an explicit promise that the employee could move over to another shop. The result will be the same—a disappointed employee, lowered morale, and probably lower production. And it all started with the interview.

That is why it is important to get at each employee's expectations of the job or of the organization. An employee who is chosen to be acting supervisor will probably expect to be next in line for a supervisory position. No one said so in so many words, but the fact that she was "acting" in that capacity is her assurance that she will or should be considered ahead of anyone else in the unit. Silent, unvoiced, and hidden expectations can be lethal.

Whether you interview, accept, or inherit employees, discuss their expectations with them during your initial contacts. They will not necessarily share them immediately. They may not even be totally aware of them. However, for those who have been promised or assured, find out what they expect. It makes no difference who made the promise. You, 'as the supervisor, are held responsible or are perceived as the agent of the organization in the matter, which is as good as "responsible."

So, get the applicant's expectations—and yours—into the common data base and make sure you qualify what you say. Be specific and to the point. Be explicit about what you individually can assure and what you cannot control.

FINISHING UP

Few supervisors are experienced interviewers, and you will probably not get all the information you want from each applicant. That is one good reason for putting some responsibility on the applicant. The applicant ought to have some idea why he is applying for this job rather than for a job as a cotton-candy concessionaire, stevedore, or flea trainer. Give the applicant part of the responsibility. Ask him what he especially would want you to take into account in making your selection.

And finally, at the end of the interview, ask him if he is still interested in this particular job. There is no reason to continue to consider someone who is not interested in the job you have open. Selection is sufficiently complicated, especially if you have good candidates. The more you can cut down the field to begin with, the easier your deliberation.

If the applicant says he is still interested in the job at the end of the interview, leave open the possibility of asking him back a second time before you make a decision. So many things happen during interviewing—you get tired and inadvertently careless about covering important areas, a crisis comes up and distracts you from your task even though you continue to keep appointments to interview. Also you tend to forget details about applicants you interviewed in the middle of the pack. So don't feel like you must rely on this single contact to get all the information you need. Also allow the applicant to provide further input to the data base for the selection decision. Invite the applicant to call or write you a note if he thinks of pertinent questions or information after the interview.

THE SELECTION DECISION AND FOLLOW-UP

Once the common data base is established from the interview, the application, the references, and any follow-up, you arrive at the point of selection.

By now you will have firmed up and added to your selection criteria. You will know what the talent supply is and who some of your top candidates are likely to be. You can look to match up job requirements with applicant skills, initiative, and potential. In the short and long run, you and the organization have to function based on choices such as this one. Much of your supervisory stress and effectiveness stems from this decision.

You may want to schedule a follow-up interview with one or several applicants in person or by phone. That way you do not make the interview session a critical incident in the selection process and you can elicit or confirm data to fit with any revisions to your selection criteria. Also, if you forgot an important question or item in the interview, you won't have to write off the applicant because of insufficient information.

When you have several qualified applicants for a job and you can choose only one of them, respectfully invite the others to come back for an interview when another job opens up. But under no circumstances assure them that they are next in line and need only show up to get the next job offered. You may have no control over the position that comes up next, and your generous offer would do more harm than good.

If an applicant is really unqualified for the position, you may do better to let him know as early as possible, rather than drag out the suspense. If possible, let him know what preparation he would need for such a job or what jobs within the organization would come closer to his areas of expertise or interest.

When you have decided whom you will hire, notify the other applicants promptly. Remember, your courteous treatment of all job applicants amounts to public relations for the organization and may provide you with willing and capable applicants for other positions in the future.

Learning Module 5

Playing the System the Way It Is

Most of us get a briefing on the organization chart early in our employment with an organization. The chart depicts clearly who is supposed to be accountable to whom, the line of authority, and functional relationships. Then, after a brief time on the job, you begin to find that the way the organization is supposed to be, or charted to be, is not the way it works. Now you have to work with that piece of reality. What do you do?

This module looks at an organization from the standpoint of the organizational culture, the way the organization is. It covers the phenomenon of turf building within an organization and how to work effectively in spite of turf building by other personnel. We begin with the assumption that there is an organizational culture and conclude that you can supervise more effectively by being aware of and working with it.

ORGANIZATIONAL CULTURE

Most groups of people over time tend to take on some distinct norms or ingroup practices. Even within a short time, a group that shares an experience evolves a bonding. Out of that bond grow certain understandings, practices, relationships, tolerances. People surviving a blizzard in the Midwest, living on a cruise ship, attending the same university, or waging war in Burma in World War II—all those groups take on some operating practices and norms that are peculiar to their group. They begin to have their own culture within the group, and that culture affects the way they operate together.

We have all experienced "group culture" in some context. Families have their own cultures, manifested in their practices at Christmas, family reunions, marriages, deaths, and so on. There are "certain ways" things are done. Everyone expects them to be done that way, and there is a noticeable disruption if these practices are changed.

Similar collections of practices and norms for activity and interaction grow up around an organization. These practices evolve as a result of current fashion, individual efforts, administrative influence, regional differences, and experience within the organization. Part of most employees' informal initiation into the organization occurs when one is taken aside and told about the "house rules." The message is "Now you may not know this, but around here we . . . "

A unit may have a fund to celebrate personal events such as birthdays, promotions, and transfers. Such events are marked by a cake, punch, and an afternoon break complete with a gift. There may be one person who is always counted on to get a card for an employee who is in the hospital, gathering all of the signatures of the staff before taking it to the hospital. These practices are not on anyone's job description, nor are they listed in any personnel manual or policy. They are just "done."

Organizations have their own way of dealing with time (coming late, long lunches, working late, leaving early on Friday) and space (who has a desk near a door or window, a private space, access to a conference room, a view from a higher floor, an office near top management or the copy machine), materials (rug on the floor, wood desk, car, floor-to-ceiling partitions, coffee pot, or dictaphone), and other support (access to secretarial pool, response from maintenance, or administrative contacts).

An organization has its own list of sanctions, punishments, and rewards. Actions that would result in losing annual leave in one organization—leaving early on Friday, for example—might be common practice in another organization. In fact, in some organizations you might be considered odd if you stayed around till five o'clock on Friday. At the same time, the organization that permits early departures on Fridays might have different norms for crunch or crisis periods—maybe *everyone* is expected to work overtime to meet deadlines.

The organizational culture is the way things are, not the way things are supposed to be. Organizational culture contains such important elements as the "grapevine" and recognition of who has the potency or gets things done in the organization rather than who has the position power. The boss's assistant may be the most potent person in the organization because she can arrange the boss's schedule, control information flow, set priorities, and grant or deny access to the boss.

The organizational culture includes who has the clout and how things get done most expeditiously (though not necessarily according to formal procedure). *These are the ways known by those who work effectively in the organization.* You can discover these peculiarities of your organization through careful observation and from your colleagues. What gets results?

Organizational culture is often recognized when someone comments, "It's not *what* you know, it's *who* you know." Anyone who chooses to ignore the politics inherent in any organization with human participants is grossly naive. When you realize this political element, you have to work your own compromise between the way things are *supposed* to work according to the book and the way things *are.* You can continue to follow "correct" procedures as you see them, but you may do so at the risk of being ineffective, even alienated within the organization.

In most organizations, you can effect your own mode of operation only within your own mantle of authority. As a supervisor, this mantle includes those tasks for which you have direct responsibility and the interactions with your employees and those under them. You may influence the way in which all other personnel interact with you in your position to some degree. But when you enter into organization interactions beyond your immediate employees, those over whom you have position power and authority, you can only follow the most effective activity you know, cognizant that you are also dealing with the organizational culture.

Once you recognize the organizational culture, you will also recognize the manner in which individual personnel take on roles to reinforce and maintain the practices of the organization.

The following is an example of one theme being played out:

A secretary brings a gruff message to you, a subordinate, "The VP wants to see you right now!" in such a way that it portends dread and threat. You accept the manner and tone of the secretary as an extension of the vice president and do not confront or contend with the secretary about her manner. In fact, the secretary sets the tone for confronting the "fire-breathing dragon" on the other side of the door.

You wonder if the secretary is only creating an image of the VP, making the image more blustery than the person really is. However, it is part of the organizational culture to stand in awe and terror of authority, so the secretary's activity fits the script. The VP, of course, can act like a real bear at times.

You enter the office all tensed up, only to find the VP on the phone laughing heartily. When the phone call is over, there is a relaxed, happy human being before you—hardly a fire-breathing dragon. And guess what— the VP wants to talk with you about changing to an office with a window! Meanwhile, the secretary continues to be abrasive and abusive, using her closeness to the vice president as a backstop. Sitting nearer to authority, others are less likely to confront her. Given her meager salary and constant work, the ability to intimidate the staff while seemingly representing the VP is an additional fringe benefit.

In some organizations, abusive or abrasive activity is not allowed. The example above, however, suggests an organization fraught with intimidation, poor role definition, whimsical supervision, and sketchy lines of authority for all but the upper echelon, where there is plenty of latitude for and tolerance of personal individual styles and agendas, even over organization objectives.

Know your organizational culture, especially the distinctions between position power and personal potency within the organization, communication lines, informal practices and procedures, unofficial priorities, internal accountability, those with major access to the decision makers, and the decision-making process.

Here's one way to start.

Take two blank sheets of paper. On the first one, draw an organization chart showing the way the organization is *supposed to be*—according to the personnel rolls, the policy and procedure manuals, and the official organization chart. Label the first chart "Formal Organization: The Way It's Supposed To Be." On the second sheet, draw a chart of the organization as you see it operate. Draw this chart at least two position levels out, up, and down from your position. Label this one "Informal Organization: The Way It Is" and put down the date you drew it. Update the second chart whenever you discover anything new about your organizational culture—lines of communication you never saw before, a new way to carry out a certain procedure, a shift in decision making.

None of this is to say that the norms, practices, and procedures that make up an organization's "culture" are somehow "wrong." They most often may be taken simply as what is. It is important to know, however, that there are numerous practices in any organization that either contribute to overall operation and productivity or seriously hamper operations. Since organizations rely on a division and sharing of functions in order to operate properly, practices that inhibit interdependence between departments also restrict the life flow of the organization. "Turf building" by employees is one such practice that can seriously obstruct an organization's health.

TURF BUILDING VERSUS ORGANIZATIONAL INTERDEPENDENCE

Turf building occurs in most organizations. One employee or more begin to carve out a larger, disproportional piece of the budget—accumulating resources, staff, power—at the expense of the others in the organization. Even in organizations where the more capable employees generate and command more effective results, this is done at the expense of some other part of the organization. Payoff for the capable employee is the greater responsibility and resources channeled through his unit. But the organization loses some of its effectiveness and balance of functions. The turf builder grows strong at the eventual expense of the organization.

For some people, turf building is an end in itself. The employee gets and holds on to resources whether they are used or not. For example, the bureaucrat who does little during the fiscal year in managing existing programs celebrates the last week of the fiscal year because he has just committed the remainder of his budget—and can now count on having the same amount allocated to his control for the coming year.

Organizations function by providing an appropriate allocation of resources—people, materials, space, and other support—to the accomplishment of the organizational mission. The employee who builds turf or creates a kingdom is losing sight of the purpose of having an organization in the first place—the interdependence required for the accomplishment of goals and objectives. The turf builder is more involved in aggrandizing the particular slot he occupies. His least concern is the connecting lines on the organization chart—unless they designate his subordinates, symbols of his status and free exercise of power.

Action planning comes hard for a turf builder, except maybe when he plans within his own unit. Action planning involves lining up all the organizational resources and sharing responsibility across units for the accomplishment of the plan. An action plan involves interdependence in action, an acknowledgement of the interreliance of the units to perform various functions. The turf builder is threatened by this concept—unless somehow he holds the key factors in the plan and so can use them as the leverage for even more power.

It would be nice if one could just help the turf builder realize that his major energy is focused on himself and not on the work of the organization. One would hope that would deter him from further hoarding, but it does not always work that way. What may help you in continuing your work within an organization where turf building occurs is to use some of the practices summarized in the next section and discussed in more detail throughout this book.

WORKING THE SYSTEM

Here are some of the highlights to remember when you're "working the system."

Continue Two-Way Communication

Generally, good supervision and management of a unit will provide a continuing flow of communication between supervisor and employee. That two-way communication will provide the supervisor with a clear picture of the reality of the employee and keep the supervisor current on unit operation and knowledgeable on unit resources and requirements. As long as there is individual role clarity and continuing update on responsibilities, resources, and rights, it is difficult to covet and possess those responsibilities and the accompanying authority, rights, or resources.

Maintain Your Job Responsibility

When one builds turf, it is generally at the expense of some other position. It is admirable when someone can take on and fulfill the responsibilities of an unfilled position. But when one employee's activity detracts from another employee's having access to resources or blocks that employee's access to his own job responsibility, there is a clear infringement on the rights of that denied employee.

Provide Incentives

Turf building can occur most easily in organizations where there is little incentive in the form of advancement or in-house promotions. The organization will tend to indulge employees whom they acknowledge to be underemployed or for whom there are inadequate incentives. That indulgence is expected to obligate the employee to continue with the organization without further demands for career advancement. Career incentives should be available and clear.

Role Clarity Makes Good Boundaries

Turf building can also occur when there is inadequate role clarity or task structure in an organization. When supervision fails to establish and maintain some role clarity, the organizational culture may develop a lackadaisical attitude about firming up job descriptions and just accept things as they are. In that situation, when higher-ups have given up by accepting blurred roles and responsibilities, the employee who is victim to the turf builder's infringing on his job or resources is likely to become complacent and lose incentive for his job. What is required in these circumstances is an explicit structure of roles and responsibilities.

Coordinate

Wise supervisors will encourage coordination throughout the organization in addition to stimulating interaction within their own unit. At times a project will require clearances through other supervisors to set up a schedule of activities. The marketing department, for example, may have to coordinate with production prior to setting up a schedule with sales personnel. Wise supervisors will check out and open up interconnections within the organization. The turf builder will, of course, claim that no one else is doing it (adequately), or that whatever they are doing, it is none of his concern. The turf builder has to deny the essence of the organization—personnel working together to blend and reinforce their separate and specific activities toward the organization objectives, goals, purpose, or mission.

Organizational Good Precedes "Lines of Authority"

At times the "line of authority" can become a real kink in the chain of command for an organization. It can also become an immense block for the employees who wish to initiate two-way communication, yet know that it is not going beyond the first level above them. In dealing with such situations, it is wise to counsel that in the first place, one can do anything he wishes—he only need deal with the consequences. The organizational culture—besides individual personnel—may be against you. So, if you are reading this book with the idea that there is a succinct plan or answer to your dilemma back in the office, you are reading the wrong book, or you are reading this book in the wrong way. In order for you to decide to take action—for example, to circumvent the line of authority above you—you will have to weigh many factors which only you know by virtue of your experience in your organization. What is your organizational culture? How high an emphasis is placed on the chain of command? What has been tried in the past in similar situations? What are the likely consequences for yourself? Long-term? Short-term? Career consequences? Organizational consequences? You can do what you want. You only need deal with the consequences. Check them out.

Keep Superiors Informed

In most cases, by doing your homework and preparing a clear factual presentation to your immediate supervisor, you will gain some hearing and maybe even action.

You can, of course, question the entire idea of having to prepare a factual presentation of something that may be obvious to you. However, it might not be obvious to anyone else, least of all to those who will have to take this action. Or you can complain that those above you are getting paid to seek out the very situation which you have uncovered. Why should you step out and take a chance? With that kind of rationale, you will choose as you wish, to act or not. However, you are required by your job responsibility to keep your superiors informed.

If your perceptions of some needed activity are correct, you may be doing the organization a service, and you might benefit from your action.

Your particular position on the organization chart does not need to limit your contribution to the organization. You can detect and develop additional products or delivery systems for your organization from the bottom up. Those new products have to start somewhere. If you wait for research and development to come up with all the bright ideas, you just stifle your own creativity.

Once again, no matter what action you wish to take in your organization, you have to explore the situation, your own objectives, and the likely consequences. You may have to set the value of maintaining the chain of command up against the value of some potential benefit to the organization. What you will have to do in that situation is to explore your alternatives and detect if you have a way of merging both values. You will also have to examine what precisely you want—to be effective or dramatic.

One of the favorite games played in some organizations involves an immense amount of "trying." Great flurries of energy and activity are directed toward an objective. However, for some immediately hidden reasons, the objective is not reached. Much of the superfluous, dramatic activity in an organization has as the hidden objective demonstrated proof that the individual employee involved in the activity is truly "helpless" in light of organizational constraints.

The turf-builder—in contrast to totally ineffectual employees who try hard—obliterates or preempts organizational priorities by controlling the means to production or service delivery. Neither the "trying" nor the turf-building employee is functioning in an organizationally appropriate manner. The turf builder overcontrols and infringes on others' rights, resources, and responsibilities; the "tryer" who fails to assert his own rights, manage his resources, or take on his responsibilities detracts from the organization.

HOW THE EMPLOYEE CAN CONTRIBUTE
TO THE ORGANIZATION

To function properly, the organization requires individuals acting as personnel who are resilient enough to step beyond the written word and closely defined tasks to interact effectively with each other and with other units. No job description will ever be able to capture each and every activity required of an employee. What is required is a good-faith attempt to delineate the job duties of the employee in light of the rationale for which the position was created in the first place.

What is required of the employee is a willingness to carry out job responsibilities that will emerge because of the *specific job description he holds, the evolution of the job, the interdependence within the team or unit,* and *the interdependence within the organization.* An employee relates to the organization at several levels of interaction. It is absurd to expect to have every aspect of that dynamic interaction anticipated and stipulated on a job description.

Nevertheless, it still behooves each supervisor and employee to be current and specific on those aspects of the job that are known and describable. It behooves them to come to an early understanding that goes beyond the "letter" of the job to the function and purpose of the job.

SUMMARY

Each supervisor-employee team and each supervisor-unit group need to be clear on their responsibilities to one another and to the organization. Those responsibilities have to allow a creative *balance* between *organizational requirements and payoffs* and *employee initiative and incentive.* A fully functioning organization cannot afford turf building, since it inhibits organizational operations. As a supervisor, you can best cope with turf building by maintaining your own role boundaries and responsibilities with your employees and with other personnel outside your unit.

Learning Module 6

Meetings

Few supervisors can fulfill their supervisory responsibilities without ever having a meeting. This module is about running unit meetings more effectively: preparing for the meeting, planning the agenda, running the meeting, and getting results. Learning to plan and run meetings effectively can result in more productive use of your and your employees' time and improve morale and teamwork in your unit.

HOW MEETINGS GO BAD

How many times have you heard someone you work with grumbling about having to attend another meeting? How many times have you grumbled about meetings you are required to attend? A meeting can be a useful or an ineffective tool in communication: so many meetings end up being boring, unproductive, or a waste of time because the person responsible for the meeting had not planned and run the meeting well.

The two purposes for holding a meeting are (1) to establish a common and current data base, to gain a common understanding, or (2) to engage in some common enterprise such as goal setting or action planning. Meetings are often mistakenly held to make individual assignments to deal with issues that do not concern all the participants. Meetings are also misused when they are held for "window dressing" or other inappropriate purposes: opinions and information are elicited with no intent to apply them in decision making. Even when meetings are held for an appropriate purpose, they go bad when no one maintains the agenda, participants wander off on tangents, and no practical action steps are outlined to follow up the decisions made during the meeting.

When participants see no purpose in participating in meetings and no prospect of having their contribution count in the operation of the unit, they will have little incentive to involve themselves actively in future meetings. They will be there in body only—and then hardly awake.

KEY ELEMENTS TO IMPROVE

Here are some key considerations for making your meetings more purposeful and productive.

Involve the right people in the meeting. What is the reason for bringing these people together at the same time? Invite only those people who are directly concerned with the purpose of the meeting. *Establish a common data base,* to give structure to the meeting and to encourage mutual involvement and shared responsibility throughout the meeting and during any implementation phase that follows.

Have a printed or public agenda for the meeting, to help keep the meeting structured and on point. A public agenda constitutes some agreement by participants to deal with the issues listed, and it allows better control, keeping the discussion centered on the agenda rather than going off on tangents. A chalkboard, overhead transparency, or newsprint on a flip chart can be used to make the agenda public. They can also be used to record notes on the proceedings and issues that arise during the meeting. That way, everyone can visually follow the proceedings and have equal access to the evolving agenda. A secretary taking notes is not enough: data is not common during the meeting when it is hidden on someone's note pad.

Other ways to give structure to the meeting: set a start time and an end time for the meeting and assign a block of time on the meeting schedule for each agenda item. If additional time is required for a particular agenda item, you may negotiate with participants to take time from other parts of the schedule. Usually, once everyone starts to focus and stay with one item at a time, time is saved and additional time is available at the end of the meeting for other issues.

THE UNIT MEETING

To repeat, the two purposes for holding a meeting are to establish a common data base—to gain a common understanding of some event, issue, problem, requirement, and so on—or to engage in some common enterprise such as goal setting or action planning.

A unit meeting can provide a special forum for dealing with issues of role clarity and interdependence in the unit, for example. It can elicit expectations employees have of each other and allow the supervisor to clarify his or her relationship with the unit as a whole. Above all, such a unit meeting can serve to replace assumptions or rumors with explicit discussion of issues. In meetings for these purposes, each member of the unit can learn early to be a gatekeeper, drawing out silent members for their opinions and ideas, so that everyone participates in matters affecting the unit.

A unit meeting is also a correct forum for creating action plans. When most of the major players in an action plan are gathered together this way, the matter of who is responsible for what within the plan can be resolved or clarified as the plan is being developed. This immediate assignment and clarification of responsibilities is especially important when the plan requires a complex sequencing of activities, a tight time schedule, or some distinct specialties to be brought together to accomplish the entire objective.

When you bring the key people responsible for carrying out a plan together in a meeting to discuss, delineate, and delegate duties, you remove some of the cause for employee claims of favoritism or being denied opportunity for input. You also establish a framework that encourages them to work together harmoniously and effectively. However, employees involved in planning meetings need to have a clear statement of what they can consider and effect, what is already fixed and nonnegotiable. That eliminates an element of seduction about meetings—that we can do anything. Not so. You can do only so much.

The incentive and spirit with which unit members participate will reflect the effectiveness of a meeting to involve them and to get results. Involving them may require some change in meeting activity, so that everyone has access to the floor, to be heard and to listen.

TIPS FOR IMPROVING THE PROCESS

There are a number of things you can try in your overall meeting process. You can invite members of the unit to add to the agenda before a meeting and then to take responsibility for the part of the agenda they originated. You can hold separate meetings on the same topic so you can work a smaller group of people each time. You can introduce a topic or issue at a large-group meeting, then hold a series of small-group meetings as a continuation.

You can also introduce, implement, and maintain such practices as establishing a common data base, keeping a public agenda and record, in most meetings you attend. Your use of these practices need not be limited only to meetings with your subordinates.

Here are some more specific tips for improving your meetings, no matter whether you are "in charge" or someone else is.

Slow Down Discussion

In most groups the tendency is to speed up and escalate discussion, both in tempo and loudness. This happens especially when people sense they are not being understood. So they just yell a little louder and talk faster. What results is defensiveness, frustration, and exasperation—rather than an effective attempt at understanding.

Rapid speech does not make for clear discussion or fuller considera-tion. Nevertheless, through most of our early upbringing we learn to equate rapid, articulate speech with intelligence and ability to succeed. Teachers responded to us more favorably; we got more attention. So it is not surprising that we continue that early group behavior in meetings now. We are programmed to speed up when we get together, to come off as competent even if we don't communicate.

To purposely slow down group discussion initially carries the risk of being judged incompetent, perhaps raising feelings of awkwardness or ineptness. But in the interest of communicating, to maintain the common data base for the meeting, you will frequently have to slow things down—maybe even slow yourself down—to make sure everyone is getting the information available in the meeting.

Speak in Declarative Sentences

Individual opinions and agendas so often remain hidden behind ques-tions: There are very few questions that do not contain a "statement." In establishing a common data base among meeting participants, it helps to get everyone's interests, purposes, and agendas out in the open. That means establishing a ground rule that everyone must speak the statement-behind-the-question, rather than set other people up to take responsibility for getting that information out. Let other people know what you want to know. The more direct and explicit, the less gamey and manipulative your own statements in a meeting—and the more likely you will get shared information and establish a common data base.

Only One Person Speaks at a Time

A common data base is most likely to evolve when only one person speaks at a time. Although the one-at-a-time ground rule may allow less "air time" per person, at least everyone has the opportunity to share informa-tion openly, without having to compete with other discussion. And everyone has the opportunity to hear all of what is said. As obvious as this is, it is violated in most meetings.

Speak for Yourself!

You often hear the royal "we" from people speaking within a group, whereby they loosely include in their statements all the people in the group or some other vague collection of people. The only appropriate time to speak for others is when you are a fully authorized representative or spokesperson.

Keep It Relevant and Specific

A simple ground rule: get on the topic and stay there. When someone starts to ramble all over the map, it is then easy to intervene by inquiring, "How does this relate to the agenda? . . . the last point? . . . the topic under discussion?"

Whatever rules you would like to function with in a meeting, it is important to get the agreement of all participants to abide by these rules. Agreement allows you to escape the constricting stance of being the enforcer, the muscle, the one who "makes" other people perform in a certain way.

Initially it may take time and energy to get some agreement on ground rules in meetings until participants see their usefulness. Breaking through past patterns of ineffectiveness and frustration will also take some time and energy, but it should be worth it to establish a more effective, productive way of working together.

SOME THINGS YOU CAN SAY

Whenever you are in a meeting—whether you are running it or somebody else is—you can intervene at any time by making statements or posing questions like the ones below to bring people back on track. Remember, the simpler the question or statement, the more powerful your intervention is.

"I would like to know whether we have gotten out all the facts about this situation before we proceed further. I want to just check with you, _____ and _____ , because I didn't hear your opinions and we are already talking about options."

"I'm not sure how what you are saying relates to our agenda of _____ ."

"I'm having trouble hearing what you are saying to _____ and what _____ is saying to the group at the same time. I would like to benefit from what both of you are saying. If you don't mind, please wait until _____ is finished and then let me hear what you are saying."

"I'm not sure to whom you are referring when you say 'we.' I know that I have some different thoughts on the topic that I'd like to bring up."

"I hear your question. And I want to answer it. However, I would like to be a little clearer on what you are specifically looking for."

Notice there are "I's" at the beginning of those sentences. If you had already reached some agreement in the meeting to collaborate in establishing a common data base, then you could begin your statements with some phrase like "We agreed to . . . " which would let you off the hook as the one seen as continually requesting, focusing, and qualifying, even though you are actually constructing the common data base and maintaining a healthy, explicit, non-defense-arousing climate for discussion.

SUMMARY

A common data base is essential at all phases of supervisory activity as well as for communication in general. Strive for a common data base in meetings you chair as well as in meetings you attend.

To establish and maintain a common data base in meetings, remember:

- Get initial agreement from others to work toward a common data base
- Slow down discussions to be understood
- Speak in straightforward, declarative sentences
- Allow only one person to speak at a time
- Speak for yourself
- Be relevant and specific

Learning Module 7

A Model and Procedure
for Problem Solving, Decision Making,
and Planning

This is a general overview of the model and procedure for planning, problem solving, and decision making. More detail on the model and procedure follows in Module 8, which deals specifically with how you can train your employees in problem solving and decision making.

There are numerous problem-solving processes, though most of them merely provide a slightly different emphasis among the five steps spelled out below. These are the steps in the process we will use:

- DATA GATHERING: COMMON DATA BASE
- PROBLEM IDENTIFICATION
- GENERATING ALTERNATIVES
- DECISION MAKING: CHOICE
- EVALUATION

ADVANTAGES OF THE PROCESS

A process is a little like an organizational chart—you can have a problem-solving process without having a problem to work on. The process exists apart from the content. Just as a comb can provide a means of arranging numerous hairs that are in disarray into a rough approximation of the order you desire, a problem-solving process can provide a means of sorting out the chaos of complex situations in disarray. Once you can get a handle on what is going on, you can begin to deal with it more effectively.

During your work day you can use this process to provide some order and structure to your problem solving and decision making. With the process you can exercise some control of the situation, even if it means acknowledging that you have to gather more data before proceeding. Getting some handle on your situation can help alleviate stress, both for present circumstances and for the future. And you can cover your rear end in chaotic situations by knowing you have brought some order out of the chaos.

The further usefulness of having a problem-solving process lies in being able to deal more effectively and explicitly with issues you face daily. Beyond that, you can also provide your employees with the process on a step-by-step basis, and so teach them a usable skill which will benefit your unit and your employee as well (see Module 8).

Most of us have a developed problem-solving process. To some extent, becoming supervisors, getting to this stage of career recognition, implies we have some developed sense of problem solving. The difficulty with most individuals' problem-solving process is that it is not explicit. You don't know you have a process. That means, for example, that at 10 A.M. this morning you coped with a situation for which you were able to derive several useful alternatives and then send out an employee to check out the feasibility of each alternative. However, at 11:15 A.M., you might be confronted with another problematic situation and not know which way to turn. That is the time when you will benefit from an explicit, step-by-step process to structure your approach to problem solving. You need not always employ the problem-solving process offered here. However, you can use it when the methods you are used to using come up short. Before you find yourself confused about where to start in using the following five-step process, we need a word about processes.

A process, like a comb or some other tool, does not become useful until you begin to use it. With a comb, you would pick it up, direct the teeth toward your disordered hair, and begin to rake through the tangles. With a process, you may not have the same visible, tangible starting point, for example, the back of your head or the front.

A process is a little like the Chinese puzzle ball—a carved ivory piece with one ball contained within another ball within another ball. With a process, when you have a question about where to begin, simply know that you have to start somewhere. The five-step process spelled out here is not sacred in the order in which it is presented. Generally though, it is best to start with facts and data.

THE FIVE STEPS: ONE BY ONE

The problem-solving steps spelled out below are common to a number of problem-solving methodologies: They represent a certain way of categorizing the required activities for sorting out the facts, the alternatives, and the feasibility of various choices. Of immediate importance to you is the awareness that there are processes such as these available . . . that one is not necessarily born with problem-solving ability. You can develop it. You can learn it and practice it. This is one approach.

1. DATA GATHERING

When Sergeant Friday of the Los Angeles Police Department went to investigate a crime or complaint, the first request he would usually make (often to a hysterical victim) was, "The facts, Ma'am, just the facts."

An initial concern for good problem-solving technique is to establish a common data base by gathering all available facts and information. Available facts in an organizational setting might include:

> Background information, history of the organization for this kind of situation, history of the unit, prior personnel involved in this kind of situation, current information, information sources available, external pressures, organizational culture, all personnel involved, known policy and procedures, legislation, administrative preferences, time available, and the like.

One of the most effective applications of problem-solving or decision-making procedure is in *slowing down the rush to solution or decision by first gathering data on the problematic situation or the situation of choice so that involved personnel know what they are talking about.* Excessive speculation and unfounded interpretation are forestalled when involved personnel take on the explicit responsibility of gathering and sharing all available information.

As you work through the problem-solving steps, one of the more useful approaches is to continue to build up the common data base as relevant and important information surfaces. Often what is initially presented as relevant, represents only one person's immediate judgment. Often that person (who may be the problem presenter) is so narrowly focused that not only does he miss in representing the central problem, but he also does not adequately present valuable information to begin with. Fact gathering is an ongoing activity in problem solving.

2. PROBLEM IDENTIFICATION

One aspect of daily living as well as organizational life is that we all have to deal with problems. While the word *problem* is itself very nonspecific and overused, it covers a multitude of circumstances, not all of which are problematic. Here is some background on the matter of problem identification.

Having problems is part of being alive. That is not to suggest that you wallow in them, but that you do acknowledge the problems you have and then begin to work through them.

Problems stem from the central tendencies of human beings to have energy toward, to approach, to want, to desire, to need, to incline toward, or to take on responsibilities to accomplish certain activities, tasks, objectives, goals, or purposes. Each of us has certain fundamental, and sometimes whimsical, "I want . . . " statements in what we do and in our problematic situations. *We would not have problems if we did not want something,* either for ourselves personally or as personnel within the organization. In dealing with problems, we are dealing with some of the basic and essential energy of living, our fundamental concerns and drives. We have goals.

You see, a problem is essentially a conflict. The two types of conflict embodied in problems are a goal in conflict with another competing goal and a goal in conflict with an obstacle. Notice that in each case the conflict involves at least one goal, one "I want" or an "I want on behalf of the organization."

If one looks simply to identify a problem, one begins a vague exercise with little structure. However, if you begin to look for the basic "I want . . . ," the major goal of the problem presenter, then you can begin to discover the underlying conflict, determining whether it is a goal-goal or a goal-obstacle conflict. Simply knowing how to make the distinction between these two types of conflicts should assist you in diagnosing or identifying problems you encounter.

Be aware that the problem presenter—whether it's you or somebody else—needs to define the problem in the terms which most closely demonstrate ownership of the problem by the problem presenter. So, rather than describing the situation in abstract terms, you can focus the problem by asking the question, "What's your problem (goal)?" Now, let us consider the first of the two major conflicts which typify a problem.

Goal Versus Goal

There are times we want two or more things at the same time; we find we have a conflict between our goals. Jo wants to watch a TV special at 11 P.M. tonight and Jo also wants to get 8 hours of sleep tonight (and it is now 9:30 P.M.). In this case the conflict involves a real shortage of time (the precipitating element). The conflict is essentially a clashing of one person's goals: viewing versus sleeping. Disregarding the possibility that the special will be replayed at a later date, Jo has to determine her priorities in this case. Which does she value more, the special or the sleep? In many cases, when the basic conflict is between two or more goals, the resolution involves assigning priorities.

In organizations there are often goal-versus-goal conflicts between quantity of production and quality. In human services organizations this conflict also comes down to quotas on number of patients or clients served versus the quality of service. Once you have attempted to find a resolution to this kind of conflict and find no clear first-priority goal, someone else has to determine the priority goal. When conflicting requests come from higher up, the decision of a priority needs to be made by the person(s) making the request(s). Choose one.

Responsible personnel will, time permitting, conduct a fact-gathering study on their own to determine what—given the resources available to them, the quotas, and the quality standards—they will be able to deliver. In a manner similar to that used in zero-based budgeting, the employees would provide a capability statement to the effect that given present resources, they will be able to deliver X number of a given product service at Y standard of performance or grade (for which standards are specified). The capability statement can also include what additional resources would be required in order to attain the quotas requested or established by management. This type of capability statement helps to establish a common data base with decision makers and provides useful information for future planning and objective setting for both the employees and the supervisory levels above.

Goal Versus Obstacle

Conflicts also occur when a goal is being pursued but is blocked by an obstacle. Rather than making a choice between two competing goals, the goal-obstacle conflict requires a gimmick or novel response to facilitate the underlying goal. Often the obstacle is a shortage of resources—time, space, materials, or skill. In these cases, one does well to factor out the essential variables in the situation: who, what, when, where, and how much. From these factors, you then begin to determine what is "fixed" and what is "negotiable," what you alone can change and what requires the cooperation and support of others. You would then begin to work on the negotiable aspects of the situation during the next step, the option- or alternative-generating step. But a few quick comments prior to moving on to that step.

Goals: Real, Ideal, Illusory

There is an important nuance in my emphasis on identifying the major goal in the problematic situation. Just because you can recognize and identify a major goal in a problematic situation does not mean that achieving the goal is possible. By stopping short of manufacturing miracles, the problem-solving process requires working on *possible* situations and goals. That is a test you will have to subject your goals to—are they possible?

Possible does not mean that they have been done yet. It simply means that they are within the realm of human possibility, achievable within the time allowed and other constraints that contain that situation. For example, the four-minute mile was not run (or recorded) on the earth's level surface until Dr. Roger Banister broke it in 1956. As a goal, the four-minute mile was thought to be possible. But until it was broken, it remained an ideal—within reach, but a little outside our grasp. Many goals set within organizations will initially be a little outside the grasp of employees. That is why they are the ideal. But the ideal does not have the starry-eyed, floating-in-air connotation that most people attach to "idealists." It simply means that the goal, your "I want..." is possible, but it carries no guarantees that it can be attained right now.

The "real" goal is one that is readily within reach of those who are attempting it. The day-to-day work of an organization involves the repetitive or maintenance goals. However, even these real goals can run into obstacles or other competing goals.

It is important to recognize that there are illusions that may pass for goals. They are simply not possible. Yet they are allowed to exist on paper and within the intentions of employees. At times, "impossible goals" are set so that personnel will keep on stretching and striving. However, working toward impossible goals injects an element of unreality into the situation. Anyone becomes exhausted at pursuing the unattainable. To deny the impossibility of the goal leads easily to the demand to keep on, even when it may not benefit anyone. Look at the goals your employees set. See if there are some that are definitely illusions. If so, attempt to set more attainable, ideal, if not real, goals with your employees. Be aware that allowing illusions to pass for goals will lead to a high burnout rate in your unit or for yourself.

When you find, in working with yourself or with an employee, that a major goal set is an illusion, you benefit most from (1) pointing out the impossibility of the goal and the likely consequences (you need not play into fantasy goals) and (2) getting the employee structured into realistic or possible goals.

Refocus on Problem Identification

To identify the problem beyond the gathering of facts, look also for the precipitating issues. Then determine from the employee working on the problem what his major job requirement or goal is. Examine it for its feasibility, and identify whether that goal is competing with another goal (goal versus goal) or whether that goal is presented with an obstacle (goal versus obstacle) in the guise of deficiencies. Sometimes it can be very important how you define the conflict. You may already be entertaining a goal that, as stated, is an illusion. For example, a unit production quota is set at the same number every month even though half your staff is out on vacation in August. Look carefully.

A certain production quota, given current technology and resources, may well be impossible. Initially you might perceive the basic conflict as goal versus obstacle: you want to produce "x" number of gastors and you only have so much time, machinery, and personnel. You might take each factor, including the techniques you use, and make improvements. However, you discover shortly that even with all known gimmicks and improvements, the major goal is impossible. You would then do the possible by relieving yourself of the stress of a task you cannot accomplish. When you define the conflict as *goal* versus *obstacle*—that is, a certain quota versus lack of resources to produce—you could continue to frustrate yourself by failing to acknowledge the realities of the situation. However, if you were to define the problem as *goal* versus *goal*—that is, quota versus quality—then you could chart each goal and determine what you can do to satisfy each goal. Such a capability statement could be sketched out as a graph (Figure 4). The graph shows what is possible, and what the trade-offs are between quality and quantity so that whoever makes that choice, does so on the basis of accurate information clearly presented.

Another way to factor out the major variables in a problematic situation is to draw a visual representation of the circumstances—for example, sketch an organizational chart to portray the personnel involved. The problem may involve communication links, for example, someone going around the chain of command. So you would draw the chart to illustrate how the line of authority is being circumvented.

Another helpful approach is to determine the extent to which the situation is cleary credited to the problem presenter, to others, or to the

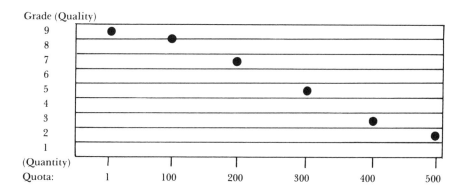

Figure 4. Quality/Quantity Capability Graph

context—the department or unit—in which it occurs. When discussing a problem with the person who first raises it, it is useful to ask, "What specifically is the problem in this situation you are describing?" After a clear description of the problem with that situation, you want to get at the *source* of the problem. Find out whether the "source" is seen as oneself, others, or the organization (unit, another department). You see, if the problem focus is "out there"—on others or the organization—then there is probably little you individually can do to solve it without going through channels. However, if part of the problem is yours, then you can exert some control on the situation toward solution. A problem is easiest to resolve when you own it as your problem. But in most organizations there is a tendency to view problems as free standing entities, disassociated from anyone in particular.

Another useful way to classify problems raised by employees in the organization is to look at them from the standpoint of the three R's— responsibilities, resources, and rights. Is the problematic situation a result of insufficient or excessive responsibilities, resources, or rights? This then helps to pinpoint some of the factors to be examined in-depth and suggests what might be changed or negotiated in the alternative-generating step.

3. GENERATING ALTERNATIVES

Most individuals working on a problem—with another person or in a group—will jump almost impulsively from hearing a few of the facts to presenting their suggestions, advice, and other solution options. Those suggestions often will come in the form of long statements that begin as questions: "Have you ever thought that by cutting down on paper processing time you would have more time for meeting with employees at the work site?" The inquisitor is making a suggestion. And the general tendency seems to be to leap immediately from facts to options before adequately identifying the problem. What then results is that more effort is placed on addressing the problem presented, rather than the facts.

In many cases, the initial problem presented is not the central problem. Often the discussion of the perceived problem will lead to an uncovering and exploration of the more central problem. Be aware that the problem you first hear is probably not the problem you will have to work on. Make sure you get all the facts and employ methods to refocus the problem identification, then move to generating alternatives or finding options.

In one approach to option finding, you look for the variable factors you can change or influence in the problematic situation. For example, suppose you arrive home alone one night without your front-door key. If the key were the only way to gain entry, then that key is specifically what you would have to obtain. But if you look at various ways to gain entry, the key/door-open sequence may not be the only resource available to you. There could be unlocked windows, other accessible entry points, a locksmith, or taking the door off its hinges. If you define the obstacles as *one specific key for that door,* then you either have it or you don't. If you emphasize that the goal is *gaining entry,* however, you can generate numerous alternatives—and "entry points" would be one variable factor.

So often we fix on only one possible solution, when there are numerous options—how many times have you heard "she's the only one for me"? If you are willing to consider reality, there are plenty of possibilities. Some of your options or possibilities depend upon whether you limit or open up your reality. One way to expand your reality is to use brainstorming techniques, whether working with a group or just one other individual.

Brainstorming

Brainstorming is a technique used to elicit the optimum number and widest range of options from a group searching for alternatives. An essential part of finding the novel response required for problem solution involves testing and extending the reality that you have initially accepted as fixed and final.

Brainstorming employs a rule of reserving judgment during the course of the exercise so that participants can feel free to generate ideas. All energy is to be directed toward coming up with creative ideas, free flowing, unconstrained, so brainstorming allows the range of possibilities open for problem solution to be expanded. Here is how it works.

The brainstorming technique is explained to the participants. It is useful to have someone act as a recorder and to have newsprint and an easel, or a chalkboard available to record the ideas so everyone has a common data base on which to check their contribution and to bounce off new free associations.

A specific time period is set aside with one participant watching and calling time . . . often 3-5 minutes. A focus is selected for the brainstorming session, "ideas for improving service without increasing the budget," for example. Participants are advised to concentrate on producing and sharing their ideas. Instructions to participants emphasize that any idea is acceptable—"pink elephants," or whatever. And that while ideas are being generated, there is to be no request for an explanation and no judgments expressed about the ideas—even in the form of laughing, frowning, or looking around. It is important to emphasize that judgment of ideas—even unvoiced judgments—during the brainstorming process can stifle creativity and idea generation, which is the purpose of the exercise. Then you set the focus, begin to keep time, and write down the ideas. Keep the ideas flowing by coaxing when necessary, reminding the participants how much time is left.

Once the time period is up, you can then get clarification on various ideas listed. Participants may also come up with additional suggestions after reviewing the list. This is not like school—the list does not close at the end of five minutes. Continue to add ideas as you go. There will come a time when ideas quit coming and then you can move to assessing the feasibility of some of the ideas. Attempt to remain open-minded to the suggestions. Remember that often the problem remains stressful because some obvious, simple use of available resources is being overlooked. Once we get the novel response, most of us say, "But, that is so simple." And indeed it is. But you have to remain open to the simple response.

You can begin to hone down the list by moving from those suggestions which are merely possible, and beginning to note those with more immediate probability . . . what is more likely. One technique which is helpful to demonstrate the usefulness of brainstorming is to ask the problem presenter to pick out one of the least probable options. Then make that least probable option the focus for a separate brainstorm. This amounts to showing the power of group contribution. But it also points out that the problem presenter may be overlooking some potentially valuable options. Try it!

Once you have elaborated on the options generated, you can begin to rehearse the manner in which you would implement that option and anticipate the likely consequences. The *major consequences* you will consider at this stage are long term, short term, career, and organizational. Part of the rehearsal process prior to choosing an alternative, or combining alternatives, is to check likely consequences against this list. Once you have visualized and anticipated them, you are ready to make a choice.

4. CHOICE OR DECISION MAKING

This step combines the actual decision made toward problem resolution with the implementation steps taken to activate the option. This step in the process involves a commitment to action. Up to now, one could pretty much "ivory tower" or observe the problem-solving process and play around with it. But this is the pivotal bite-the-bullet phase. You make a decision, a choice, which you then have to act upon. Once you have made that choice you may want to run a force-field analysis to determine the action steps you will take to implement your plan.

Force-Field Analysis

Force-field analysis was first introduced by Kurt Lewin. It is a model for demonstrating and working with certain perceived forces in the environment to effect change. If a certain situation now exists, then it is said to be in balance: The driving forces equal the resisting forces. So that if you wish to effect change you will have to establish some disequilibrium in the situation. The force-field analysis provides a format for dissecting the situation and determining where to create the imbalance to lead toward the new situation.

Figure 5 is a force-field analysis format. To use it, write in the situation, then state the choice, decision, or objective in the spaces at the top. Then in the columns labeled "Driving Forces" and "Restraining Forces," list all the distinct forces that support or oppose your endeavor. Once you have completed this listing of forces, you will engage in some speculative weighting of each force (from 1 for the lowest possible weighting to 3 for the highest weighting) for its relative strength or impact in the situation. If you have listed all forces operating on the status quo, the weightings of both sides should balance out.

Here is how you provide the weighting:

Suppose that you are one of the main driving forces for a desired change. Then you would place your name under driving forces and place a "3" next to your name in the left-hand column. Next to each of the other forces on the driving and resisting sides you would also assign a relative weighting from 1 to 3 depending upon how you view the relative influence of that factor in the situation. You might also list some factors

Situation:			
+			**—**
Add to and/ or increase strength	Goal:		Decrease number or strength
	Driving Forces	Restraining Forces	

Figure 5. Force-Field Analysis Format

on both sides if they have both driving and restraining effects. But you would only assign a combined weighting of 3 for each of the single factors you list in both columns this way.

Once you have listed all the driving and restraining factors and assigned weightings, your totals in the + column should roughly equal the totals in your — column. That depicts the status quo at present. If there is a great discrepancy between the numbers in the two columns, then you are probably overweighting one side, or have left out some factors on the other side. This balancing of the assigned weightings is not so important as the complete listing of forces. However, it can serve to stimulate a more complete listing and analysis of driving and resisting forces.

Next you have to decide where to focus your energy to change the forces in the direction of the change you desire. Generally, you would do better to diminish the resisting forces, for example, talking with resistant personnel to attempt to win them over. You might gain their support, in which case they would swing over from the column of resisting forces and enter the column of driving forces. With that disequilibrium started, you have begun some change. At least, you can diminish their resistance, possibly only swinging them into a neutral position and out of the force field entirely—no longer an active factor.

According to Lewin's theory, if you increase the driving forces, you set off a chain reaction in the resisting forces to resist even more. So, an increase in weighting on the driving side simply increases a weighting on the resisting side. The smarter move is to pick out some of the resisting-forces factors and set out a plan of action to diminish them or to win them over completely. That is where your action planning begins.

Choose one of the resisting forces as a place to start. Then begin to map out your strategy for dealing effectively with that factor—be it space, time, or an individual. In most cases you will be dealing with individuals or personal groups no matter what factor you ultimately expect to diminish or win over. So you will have to rely upon your ability to persuade and communicate without arousing defenses in implementing your action plan.

Do your home work before embarking on the actual implementation. Gather facts on the individuals you will deal with, set your objectives clearly for each contact, and then establish a common data base on the important information involved in the change desired.

5. EVALUATION

Is the conflict resolved? What are the criteria by which we can check the resolution of the conflict and any other consequences of our problem-solving and decision-making procedure?

When you function in an organization as personnel, the major consequences against which you weigh the success of problem solution are:

- Short-Term Consequences
- Long-Term Consequences
- Career Consequences
- Organizational Consequences

If you were making decisions just for yourself as an individual, then you would change the "career" and "organizational" consequences criteria to "personal" and "social" consequences as criteria for yourself. Our concern here is with the organizational consequences.

Some of the consequences normally considered in evaluating one's problem-solving ability include a reduction of stress in the situation, a lessening of tension surrounding those circumstances, and some resolution of the very conflict which constituted the problem. More than that, though, you have to look at the wider picture. Sometimes short-term results provide a ready resolution to the conflict, but in the long term things are worse.

In one organization, the board of directors responded to employee and community complaints by getting rid of the chief administrator. To all intents and purposes this solved the problem in the short term. However, the board then fired half the staff, and the organization lost much of its public funding, because fund raising was the one thing that the fired administrator did well. The long-range consequences for the organization were disastrous. Individual careers were cut short. Funding was lost with a resultant loss of clients and more staff. Soon the organization was only providing a minimum of service to clients, since it no longer had the client load to justify its budget. As an illustration, you can perhaps see the range of consequences which have to be considered in a thorough evaluation of a problem-solving situation.

Evaluation according to the consequences is borne out in practice and experience. If the problematic conflict that originally surfaced does not prove to be resolved, then you would revert to one of the appropriate process steps and work on the conflict further.

SUMMARY

The order of progression in problem solving and decision making has been laid out in a five-step process. However, practicality has to govern the order in which you consider those five steps in the process. What works? Sometime when you feel stifled in defining the problem, move right into generating alternatives or options. In a short time you will find out why the options you are generating have little to do with the actual situation. Then you can begin to refocus the conflict.

Whatever the particular circumstances of problematic situations, you have this five-step process with which to structure and cope with the chaos of those circumstances. Figure 6 offers another format for working through the entire process. But the important thing is for you to determine how the process serves you best. The process itself is never to be the central focus. It is merely there to facilitate and structure problem solving, decision making, and planning. If the process provides an impediment, then it no longer serves you as a tool. The process then runs you. Stay in charge. And direct your employees in learning this process in the next module.

FORMAT FOR PROBLEM SOLVING AND DECISION MAKING

DATA GATHERING   *The Situation:*

PROBLEM IDENTIFICATION   Explore the situation and develop your own solution. The effectiveness of a response depends on the consequences of one's actions. To be maximally effective, your response should reduce or eliminate the conflicts and uncertainties in question, plus minimize negative consequences that might ensue. With luck and foresight you can devise a means of preventing a similar situation from occurring again.

What precipitated the present conflict?

What is the conflict (problem)?

Goal: _____ versus Goal: _____

-or-

Goal: _____ versus Obstacle: _____

GENERATING ALTERNATIVES   Goal: What do you want to do? Be specific.

What are the possibilities?

What are the probabilities, more likely choices?

DECISION MAKING   What is your choice?
Write your choice in the form of an objective if appropriate:

By_____ , 19_____ , _____

**Figure 6. Problem Solving, Decision Making,
and Force-Field Analysis**

FORCE-FIELD ANALYSIS
Implementation Situation (Additional Considerations)

Driving/Supportive Forces	Restraining Forces
•	•
•	•
•	•
•	•
•	•
•	•

Action Steps

1.

2.

3.

4.

5.

6.

7.

8.

EVALUATION   An effective response is one that best resolves the problematic situation, tends to maximize other positive consequences, and minimizes negative consequences. Response effectiveness is evaluated ' through these *consequences:*

Short-Term

Long-Term

Career (Personal)

Organizational (Social)

There is no "right" response. Much depends on your personal style, your desires, relationships, expectations, and goals. The most effective response for one person will not necessarily be the most effective response for another.

Figure 6 (continued).

Learning Module 8

Helping Your Employees To Become Effective Problem Solvers and Decision Makers

In the preceding module we considered the problem-solving process and the decision-making and planning aspects of that process from the standpoint of someone who is working on a problem or guiding a group or unit through that process. Now we will make some specific applications of that process in supervising individual employees by teaching the employee the process for him to use on the job.

WHAT'S THE USE?

Teaching employees the process provides them with a basis for participating with you in decisions affecting the unit, as well as decisions that affect them directly. If they know the process you use, you can employ them as resources, and you can all approach a situation to work on it as a team.

More than that, unless someone has a totally lock-step, prescribed job, most employees have some opportunity to work on their own job-related problems, to make job-related decisions. Teaching the employee this process helps him to work more completely into his job. He can assume responsibility for his own tasks more completely if he is capable of making decisions rather than bringing them all to you. You can be more assured of his capacity if you know he has the problem-solving process as a point of reference.

This is not a simple case of teaching your employee in order to avoid responsibility. It is a case of working the employee more fully into his job responsibility, consequently working you out of his job responsibility. Beyond that, your employee will acquire a skill he can use effectively the rest of his life, on the job as well as at home.

The fact is employees are solving problems and making decisions daily. Teaching them this skill provides them with some support and assurance in the process.

A main concern in your initial work with a new employee involves assessing what job tasks the employee can perform capably and which of the employee's responsibilities will have to be taken on temporarily by other employees. Most often this initial learning involves technical aspects of the specific job.

Once the employee has attained full job capability in the technical aspects, the fixed or set part of the job is established. Then it is important to set in place some of the generic capabilities that can ease your supervisory tasks and prepare the employee for greater job performance and security, as well as career advancement. The farther up the career path an employee moves beyond direct production, the more decisions and choices he will have to make. This process prepares him for that career change.

Problem-solving and decision-making skill is generic. With it, the employee can make solid decisions, set attainable goals, and solve problems. The five-step process provides the basic guidelines to accomplish these tasks.

HOW YOU DO IT

Described below is a methodical approach through which you as supervisor can work your employee into full capability as a problem solver or decision maker. You will be able to assess the employee's current capability and also provide employee development in this skill, which is paced to the individual employee.

The format used to illustrate this approach is a rectangle with a diagonal line from the lower left corner to the upper right corner (see Figure 7). At the upper right corner the diagonal line represents the employee's full capability in the activity, while at the lower left corner it represents no capability—the employee knows practically nothing of the tasks. The vertical line from the upper left corner to the lower left corner demonstrates that the unit, the supervisor, or someone other than the designated employee will have to provide the activity represented in the rectangle, if it is to get done. As the employee moves from no demonstrated capability (and total dependence on others) to full capability, his progress is recorded along the diagonal line. For every new activity the employee masters and demonstrates capability in, the activity required of the unit is reduced or diminished. The diagonal line shows the proportions of the task being performed by the employee and by others.

The base of the rectangle is a time line. It will vary with each employee and is flexible and negotiable. It is used to trace the time it takes the employee to acquire capability in each activity, allowing the supervisor to track and assess the pace of employee learning. The horizontal

lines on the right-hand side indicate the particular activities that constitute an incremental build-up to full capacity in the process skill.

An Example

Here's an example of how this approach can be used to track employee
progress and development.

Say you start working with an employee on the fact-gathering stage
of the five-step problem-solving/decision-making process. It is important
that you and your employee reach some agreement on the usefulness of
learning a decision-making and problem-solving process to begin with.
Explain that the *short-term objective* will be to familiarize the employee
with all the data sources in the organization, while the long-term
objective will include the employee's learning better skills for decision-
making and problem-solving activities that arise on the job.

Initially, you may want to lay out a simple rectangle that includes
just the incremental activity steps involved in fact gathering.

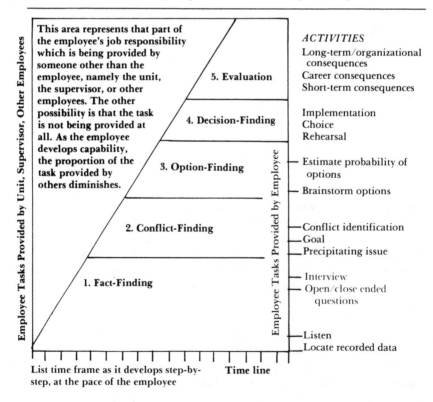

Figure 7. Capability Building: Decision Making/Problem Solving

Fact gathering involves numerous activities, depending on the particular job. What we mean by fact gathering is the ability to retrieve, gather, or generate information or data about a situation. For purposes of the example here, we will present a sufficiently broad spectrum of activities to touch on the full range of fact gathering.

In some jobs, the fact-gathering step in problem solving may just involve the *location* and *retrieval* of already published or available information. The process of retrieval consists mainly of locating the source (file cabinet, person, computer terminal, water level indicator, graph, or chart) and then getting the information from it. For some employees involved in data retrieval, this may be the major activity of their job. For others it represents only a part of their work.

Gathering information for problem solving may involve more complex activities than simply retrieving hard data: It may entail coordinating sources in order to provide a fuller complement of information. It may also involve interviewing—and all that interviewing requires. Without getting into a primer on interviewing, let us just mention a few points.

Interviewing involves getting information from the interviewee. It may require that the interviewer have some technical knowledge to understand or interpret responses to interview questions in addition to an ability to probe for more information with open-ended questions. Preparation for an interview may require familiarizing yourself with the content of the interview—the general area of interest. It also requires some of the climate setting (see Module 2) and non-defense-arousing communication techniques important to good communication. The interviewer will usually at least state the objective and the rationale for the interview at the beginning.

Interviews may be conducted with open-ended questions alone if your employee has a willing interviewee, one who is able and willing to provide your employee with the information he seeks. However, if 'he needs specific information which is not elicited with open-ended questions, then he will have to become more focused in his questioning. And that requires some technical expertise in the areas he is exploring.

A journalist pursues an interview with the more general questions "who, what, when," and the like. However, for an in-depth interview, one needs to know more specifics to begin with. "John, what were you doing away from your work site on June 15th, at 3:45 P.M. in the middle of your shift?" Close-ended questions focus in more finely for specific information. But if they are not posed with skill, close-ended questions may elicit nothing more than a "yup" or "nope." Someone looking for impressions might use general open-ended questions. An attorney cross-examining a witness would use more pointed close-ended questions.

So, the facility to gather information gets closer to the source and the availability of the information in terms of time. Expert gathering of information will sometimes uncover additional information or gain access to information that was formerly not shared. Then once an interviewer becomes more adept with probing questions, that interviewer might even elicit information the interviewee was not aware he possessed or was not prepared to share. The point is that increasing skill in data gathering provides information which formerly might not have been available or accessible.

Figure 8 shows the way the incremental build-up of activities for Step 1, fact gathering, would be portrayed.

Your employee may not require the full gamut of fact-gathering activity portrayed here to become fully capable in his job. So the format you would use to track your employee's development and progress in fact gathering might only include, for example, awareness of data, request for sources, locating sources, request from sources, retrieval of information, and presenting information. You will have to look at the extent of fact gathering involved in his job, whether for normal, required performance or for the discretionary or negotiable aspects of his job.

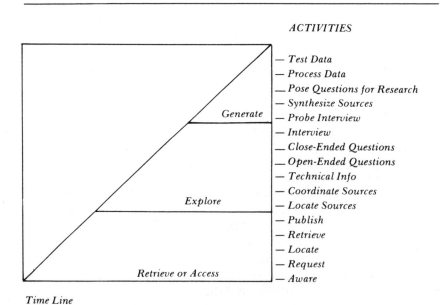

Figure 8. Capability Building: Data Gathering

As you progress through the rest of the problem-solving model, you will have to make similar judgments about what specific activities are required for your employee to become more fully functional at each step—in problem identification, goal setting, generating alternatives, and so on. Table 2 presents the full problem-solving process—all five steps—with some of the activities to learn in each step.

Table 2. Problem-Solving Process and Activities for Capability Building

Step	Activities
5. Evaluation	Compare consequences with initial stress or conflict Assess organization outcome Assess long-term outcome Assess career consequences Assess short-term outcome
4. Decision Making	Implement plan Develop action plan to diminish resistance Choose second resistance force to diminish Develop step-by-step approach to highest resistance Choose resistance force to diminish Assign relative value to + and - forces Specify + and - forces for force-field analysis State option choice objective Choose best option or combination of options
3. Generating Alternatives	Anticipate probable consequences of options Rehearse each option Priority rank probable options Develop probable options list Test each factor for option Refine negotiable factors List possibilities Brainstorm
2. Problem Identification	Identify conflict Assess goal feasibility Identify major goal Identify precipitating issues
1. Data Gathering	Test data Process data Probe interview Interview Pose closed-ended questions Pose open-ended questions Coordinate sources Retrieve Locate

HOW TO USE THE MODEL IN SUPERVISORY CONFERENCES

Here is a brief glimpse of one approach which you can use with your employee to work the employee into this process. It uses an incremental, step-by-step approach geared to the employee's own pace. The first time the employee comes in, you might simply ask him to get more information. Perhaps he just brings you a file on the situation. Or he may have to do some more complex information gathering.

Here is a mini-case to illustrate.

George, a salesman with a large manufacturing firm, recently lost one of his biggest accounts. His supervisor asked him to find out the reason why the customer switched to a competitor.

In the first conference George came back with some information he had heard from one of the other salespersons who had a friend who played golf with the customer's purchasing agent. George's "source" said that the company had changed suppliers because the chairman of the board had recently purchased controlling interest in the other supplier.

The supervisor told George to get more information next time rather than accepting a rumor—to get some specifics and check out the sources.

In the next week, George loses another large account. The supervisor calls George in for another conference. They both agree that there is probably a serious problem here and that George should identify the problem and decide how he wants to solve it and perhaps what results he would like to achieve.

At this point the supervisor might also request that George generate several possible courses of action to deal with the situation and present those to the supervisor, along with laying out the background information and attempting to specify the central problem (why are we losing customers?).

In the next conference George reports that after talking to the two customers he lost, he discovered that both companies had been experiencing significant delays in deliveries and that this was the reason why they had changed suppliers. George tells the supervisor that he had checked with the other sales staff and none of them had received reports that their shipments were not being delivered on time but that two other salesmen, working under another supervisor, had also lost large accounts in the last month.

The supervisor asks George where he thought he should look from there. Where does he think the cause of the problem might possibly lie?

George says he has identified three possible steps in the delivery process that may be breaking down. The supervisor asks George to prioritize the three options according to the likelihood of causing the problem.

In the next conference George tells the supervisor that he has researched all three of his options and that he is relatively sure that the breakdown is

occurring with the trucking company contracted with to deliver the supplies to the customers. In addition George says he has discovered after talking with several customers that they had been calling in complaints about late deliveries but George was never notified. He also found out that the same thing was happening to other salespersons. So another problem area was identified in the way incoming calls were being screened.

The supervisor asked George how he planned to handle the problem. George said he intended to call the trucking company to find out the reason for the delays and to talk to the switchboard operator to find out why the calls weren't being sent through to the sales staff.

In the next conference George reports that he has discovered that there was a misunderstanding in the original agreement with the trucking company on their deliveries. The trucking company had mistakenly understood that the shipments were to be held for thirty days before shipping. The switchboard operator said that any calls requesting information about deliveries were being put through to the loading dock. The foreman of the loading dock said he didn't have time to handle petty complaint calls so he had been telling the customers that the supplies were leaving the dock on time and they should therefore be delivered on time.

The supervisor asks George what he planned to do to straighten out the late deliveries and inappropriate handling of customer complaints. George said he intended to talk with the trucking company and clarify the agreement, talk with the switchboard operator about sending all customer calls to the salespersons, and call all his customers, including those he'd lost, to apologize for any late deliveries and promise prompt deliveries in the future.

The supervisor told George that he had done a fine job of finding a solution to the problem and that he would like him to address the sales meeting the next day to tell the other sales staff about the problem and the solutions reached.

You will have to make up your own sequential and incremental listing of activities to fit your employee's situation. However, the initial and later increments might include a specific application of the five-step process that we have already reviewed, as set forth in this series of supervisory conferences.

Conference 1:

"George, next time you sense this difficulty, I want you to get more information on the specifics rather than leaving it at the rumor stage. Get some specifics and check out the sources."

Conference 2:

This time you can extend your request to include a report from George on how he sees this as a problem, how this is a problem for him, and what he wants.

Conference 3:

At this point request that George generate several possible courses of action to deal with the situation and present those to you along with laying out the background information and attempting to specify the central problem.

Conference 4:

In addition to requests to this point, have George prioritize the options he generates according to the greater likelihood of resolving the problem.

Conference 5:

At this point George should be ready to present his choice for a course of action from among the possibilities and to provide a rationale for what he does.

Conference 6:

George will consider the forces that will facilitate or hinder his choice of a course of action and anticipate those forces with an implementation plan.

Conference 7:

Finally, George should plan to come to you, tell you what action he has taken, what choice he made (if it is within the range of his authority and responsibility), and what the outcomes are.

The supervisor increased the amount of specific activity and responsibility George had in the situation. She worked George into a decision-making, problem-solving capability. Consequently, she made it possible to rely on George to do more of his job.

There are cautions to exercise in this process of getting the employee to do it for himself. You will have to guide the employee's developing ability. There is no set rate at which George or anyone can be anticipated to learn the entire process, to become autonomous or fully functional in it. You will have to assess as you go and determine incremental steps that will constitute an objective for the employee, and at times a challenge (within reach and still possible), to provide stimulus and development on the job.

If you work with more than one employee on this process training, you will note distinct individual differences. Each employee has his own pace. One employee may do very well in gathering facts and presenting them and then show little ability to generate options. Another might require additional time to gain confidence with prioritizing and making a choice of options. For these situations, be forewarned that there are these individual differences. Know also that the time line on the incremental growth figure allows you to negotiate and fill in the time of accomplishment for each employee individually.

There is no set pace. A project that might take one employee three weeks to finish might be a six-month project for another. For example, one employee might master the technical information required and the interviewing technique required for conducting interviews under cooperative, collaborative conditions. If the interviewer has to deal with a hostile interviewee, however, he or she may require several months more to overcome fears and be able to elicit data in a hostile interview alone.

SUMMARY

The five-step problem-solving and decision-making process can be taught to employees for their use on the job. Proceeding by small learning increments of activities for each step of the process, each employee's development will be paced according to that individual's ability at each activity. And each employee may have slightly different activities to learn according to the situation the employee encounters on the job. The process is flexible and resilient enough to accommodate these differences.

Learning Module 9

Forget Employee Motivation: Focus on Objectives, Activities, and Results

Many of us tend to attribute motives and intentions to explain the actions of other people. As long as they are peers, our judgments or projections may not affect them or unit productivity directly. But when we become supervisors, we can seriously obstruct, even damage, the supervisor-employee relationship by continuing to attribute intentions and motives to our employees, rather than focusing on their actual performance.

Employees are considerably more capable of speaking for themselves and tending to their own needs than many supervisors give them credit for. Yet we see supervisors investing hours of energy attempting to interpret their employees' actions, intentions, and motives. They want to know "why" an employee does what he does. What's the attraction of knowing "why"?

THE SEARCH FOR CERTAINTY...AND CONTROL

Most of us would like to create a secure, predictable, controllable world. Even though our experience proves out differently, we attempt to establish some absolute certainty to operate by—something that relieves some of our longing for situational control, security, safety.

When a supervisor wants to know "why" an employee does what he does, most often the supervisor is looking for some handle on the employee, some way of knowing how to manipulate, control, or dominate the employee. To know "why" employee X supposedly does something becomes a "certainty principle," a source of control, in the mind of the supervisor. If the supervisor found some primal motive, some "why," it would seem like a bit of magic, the magic we often think we need to bring certainty to a world in which change is the only constant.

After a lifetime of exposure to mystery thrillers—which almost always depend on an elaborate exposition of the characters' motives for resolution of the drama—it is natural to subscribe to the illusion that you can write the script and control how your unit relationships will proceed.

You may even be able to—sometimes—if you have exceptional sensitivity and sure-fire intuition. However, supervising in the real world does not require or consist of such extraordinary skills. The practice of supervising is much more in line with average, everyday abilities. Forget the magic. Develop skills such as feedback and developing a common data base.

WHEN YOU PSYCH OUT EMPLOYEES

When a supervisor searches for an employee's motive or intent—some "why" behind the employee's actions—the supervisor makes two assumptions:

    1. That a major "why," motive, or intent *exists*, and

    2. That a "why," motive, or intent *can be discovered.*

These assumptions are fallacious, and playing them out in supervisory practice can seriously obstruct a supervisor-employee relationship. Here are some of the reasons.

The supervisor's hunt for the employee's motives assumes that there is a direct, linear, sequential chain of identifiable events or indicators that lead back to the initial step, the font of origin, of work performance. In an attempt to discover motives, a supervisor will usually begin with a line of questioning such as "Why does Herb come late to our weekly meetings?" The "why" in the question implies you can track backwards from the action—coming late—to "the" main reason for it.

Here's an example of where that line of questioning leads.

"Why does Herb come late to our weekly meetings?"

Well, he gets to the office in plenty of time, but then he just putters around until he is scrambling to get to the meeting.

"Why does he putter around?"

Because he is very disorganized.

"Why is he disorganized?"

Because he hates to be pinned down to any one thing. He keeps everything going at once.

And why does he hate to be pinned down? Herb's dad was very strict with him and used to punish him when he didn't get his chores done. *And why did Herb's dad treat him strictly?* His dad is from the Old Country and he was concerned about instilling good work habits in Herb. . . . Pretty soon we will be back in Eastern Europe dealing with the Magyar invasion, and then back to the creation of the Universe.

The only reliable responses to "why" questions are a rhetorical "why not?" or a flat "because." You see, questions that ask for a single "why" don't recognize the multiple factors that contribute to, add to, influence employees' performance and results. Some more productive formulations of questions about Herb's coming late to meetings—which are more suited to elicit responses that recognize that reality is not ordered in strict, single, sequential causality—would be:

"What factors contribute to Herb's coming late to weekly meetings?"

This asks for a range of factors—not just one cause.

"What specifically is involved in Herb's not getting to our weekly meetings on time?"

This question invites a narrative description or listing a full range of considerations.

"What is it about Herb's work that he comes late for our meetings?"

This asks for various work-related factors rather than some hidden "motive."

The important point is these sorts of questions emphasize *broad, concurrent, activity-oriented analyses of multiple factors contributing to the situation.* There may be some *major* or *predominant* contributing factor, and you can acknowledge it. But the point is that it is unlikely there is one single cause leading to a person's behavior in a direct, unswerving chain reaction.

THE PROBLEM WITH "FIGURING OUT" YOUR EMPLOYEE

Attempting to discover the "why" behind employee behavior not only tends to oversimplify actual situations, it also obstructs communication between supervisor and employee. If you delve into motive with the employee, you would be assuming he is aware of his own motives. Many people are not at all aware of their motives for doing something—at least not at the time—or they are not aware of all their motives. You would also assume that the employee is aware of other influences on himself—besides his "motives"—that work to shape or color his behavior. Suddenly this would become very complex.

Analyzing, psyching out, and trying to figure out an employee who is an intact, consenting adult contributes nothing to truly understanding that employee in a particular situation . . . supervisors generally do not have competence or credentials in psychoanalysis, nor do employees contract to be psychoanalyzed. Psychoanalysis is not part of the basis of the supervisor-employee relationship. It is not part of your expertise, job qualifications, job description, or supervisory responsibility to try to figure out why an employee performs as he does.

It is also patronizing and intrusive to think that you can discover "motives" and then manipulate conditions and situations to get an employee to act in a certain way. You remove the opportunity for the employee to deal with the consequences of his actions—or inaction—firsthand.

AN ALTERNATIVE TO PSYCHING OUT YOUR EMPLOYEES

Try thinking this way: Job performance is a function of three things—objectives, activities, and results. An objective is what you set forth to achieve or accomplish; it is your target statement. Activities lead toward the objective, the target. Results are the "bottom line," the outcomes from the employee's job-related activity.

To illustrate, the objective in bowling is to knock down the maximum number of pins—a strike! The more effective a bowler, the more pins knocked down, the higher the score, the better the results. The more effective and efficient route for a bowling ball once it passes over the foul line—and is in the "in-play area"—is a curved line or hook point in between the lead pin and the second row of pins. If a bowler rolls the ball down the gutter, he is off track and out of the activity range required to get results. You don't have to look at his "intention" in approaching the foul line or his "motives" for playing the game. You simply need to know that once that ball hits the gutter, it is off track and will not achieve the objective and desired results—pins down and maximum score.

The activities of bowling include such things as one's approach to the foul line, the delivery, and the follow-through. There are additional activities subsumed under them; techniques for delivering the ball, for example, include starting your footwork on the dots, coordinating arm swing and footwork for balance, and using the targets on the alley to guide the trajectory of the ball.

To extend the analogy—as the supervisor of an employee whose job is bowling—you would initially work with that employee to familiarize him with the range of activities that constitute accepted and skilled pin-toppling procedure. You would look for early indicators, early activities that require correction. For example, if the employee begins on the wrong foot or starts from an extreme angle in approaching the foul line, you have an early indicator that his activity is not likely to be effective. Over time, giving feedback about the employee's bowling becomes more difficult, because even though you may have seen the employee's approach to the foul line improve, the employee may also require more refined, subtle guidance. Then it becomes your task to work with the employee to polish the activities that have to be done to get the results—topple more pins, improve the score.

THE DIFFERENCE BETWEEN DEFICIENT
AND DISCREPANT PERFORMANCE

One of the supervisor's main daily activities is dealing with employee deficiencies in job performance. The deficiency in performance may be due to an incomplete grasp of the job itself or some deficient knowledge, skill, or attitude upon which results depend. The employee may be new, needing orientation. Or the employee may have been on the job for some time and is still in the process of learning the tasks and skills required to accomplish the desired results. Dealing with deficient performance involves working employees into their full job responsibility.

Dealing with discrepant employee performance is another major supervisory activity. Discrepant performance usually involves an employee who is more fully functional in his job or who is capable of the full range of job activities required. However, this capable employee is involved in activities that are off track, inconsistent, or at variance with individual or unit objectives—hence nonproductive. Rather than building up a repertoire of skills and abilities as with the deficient employee, the discrepant employee needs to be corrected and rerouted back on a productive, consistent task track.

The deficient employee does not know how to perform. The discrepant employee knows how but is not performing. Both situations require application of appropriate supervisory practices. Both are major concerns for a supervisor—part of getting the job done through others.

In the bowling analogy, a new employee who is deficient in performance might require work on the activities of stepping off, holding the ball, approaching the foul line, and the like—the basics. A seasoned bowler who is engaged in discrepant activities might require more finely tuned adjustments—for example, maintaining balance, eye on the front pins, sighting through the targets on the floor, or more deliberate and relaxed delivery and follow-through.

FOCUS ON OBJECTIVES, ACTIVITIES, AND RESULTS

When you view job performance as a function of objectives, activities, and results, you have a powerful approach to ongoing supervisory and periodic evaluation conferences. Starting from your common data base—specifically, the objective and the results, discussion may then follow on the "activities in pursuit" of the targeted objective or result.

In supervisory conferences you begin the first stage by defining or reviewing the objective. *What* was it you set out to do? The objective is stated in measurable, demonstrable terms to point to the results desired.

Then you review the *results* actually attained—what you accomplished when your activities were completed. This puts the focus on the bottom line, the outcome of the employee's efforts. Finally you can review the *activities* the employee performed in order to achieve the results—how the employee went about pursuing the results.

The objectives-activities-results approach focuses both supervisor and employee on job performance, rather than operates in the realm of underlying motives and intent for what the employee does—or does not do—on the job. A failure to achieve the intended results points attention immediately to the employee's *activities* in order to determine what adjustments will be made to meet the objective and get results.

Now the job of the supervisor is not to probe the employee's innermost thoughts and regress him back to the womb to find a hidden motive. Now you are dealing in the realm of simple fact: whether the employee achieved the results you had agreed to in supervisory conference last week. Either he did or he didn't. If he didn't, it is your responsibility to focus on the activities he did perform to discern what alterations will have to be made by the employee in order to meet the objective.

Once you begin to focus on the activities required to achieve results, you are better prepared for day-to-day employee coaching. If an employee falls short in service delivery, for example, by delaying a presentation twenty minutes while setting up chairs for 2,100, rather than wondeing what goes on in the employee's head, you will look at the activities required to get the results.

This approach works for both the new employee who is deficient in performance and for the longer-term employee who is capable of proficient job performance but is off track or discrepant in performance. However, the emphasis on objectives, activities, or results is different in each case, and the supervisor takes a slightly different tack. For the deficient employee, the emphasis in a supervisory conference would initially be on the range of sequence of activities required to achieve the agreed-upon objective. For the follow-up conference, the supervisor would then focus on both the activities pursued and the extent to which the results were achieved. For the discrepant employee, the initial conference would focus on the targeted results. The follow-up conference would then examine the activities performed in pursuit of the results, with the intention of correcting the action taken to get the results desired.

THE USE OF RESULTS AS LEVERAGE

Early in Part I of this book, we discussed the leverage which reality provides. Focusing on objectives, activities, and results—in contrast to psyching out your employees—provides you with solid facts to work with in supervising. The results that constitute the "bottom line" of job performance are an essential ingredient in the kind of leverage I'm talking about. The results are an indicator of performance. To state it in the extreme, no matter how the activities were carried out, if the results are there you need concern yourself with little else. The results are facts gathered regarding employee output or employee effectiveness. They are a point of reference, a bench mark for future performance.

RESULTS: A STARTING POINT FOR DISCUSSION

When you come into a supervisory conference or an evaluation conference to discuss outcomes that your employee or unit attained, you start from a hard piece of reality—results. If you did not provide adequate support to your employee or unit, then you have some responsibility in the "activity" portion of that job performance, as well as the deficient results.

But when you are dealing with an employee who has a certain amount of autonomy, demonstrated expertise, authority to get the job done, and proper support from you, and the results are not forthcoming—results are a good starting point for dealing with the situation. You did not create, distort, or undermine those results, nor are you responsible for them. The results are just there, evidence of the employees' activities—activities that are deficient or discrepant, or effective and efficient. Results are simply your starting point. There is no particular reason for you to feel guilty about delivering the news—the results and what to do about them.

Supervisors often take the responsibility for results so directly and personally it is difficult for them to deal with employee performance and activities. Once again, you have to allow the employee to take responsibility for his own job performance, although that does not keep you from guiding the employee back on track or toward more effective activities.

DOING WHAT YOU HAVE TO DO TO DO IT!

With the New Employee

When supervising the new employee, much of your work in using the objectives-activities-results approach will consist of knowing what is required to get the job done, laying out some of the possibilities, and letting the employee pick up on one of the alternative routes to getting the results. At the outset, you may well allow for more tolerance, permit some inefficiency, in reaching objectives. Over time, however, you will want to decrease the range of tolerance, so that the job will get accomplished at reduced cost in time, materials, and energy.

With the new employee you will use *activities* as the main focus for getting the results you want. Later on you will relinquish more and more autonomy to the employee and concentrate more on results.

With the Seasoned Employee

Seasoned employees may suggest new or alternative routes to achieving results that you had never considered. You will only need to settle on the outcomes sought. The savvy employee will be able to devise the most expeditious route for himself.

The results will serve as a stable reference point for the seasoned employee. *Once you know where you are heading, there are numerous ways of getting there, numerous combinations of activities.* However, a simple review of activities might result in the employee's self-assessment of what he can do differently to embark on a performance-improvement course. At most, you will have to specify some of the particular activities that appear to be needed for the employee to reach even more effective productivity.

With the Deficient Employee

The performance-deficient employee—whether he is new or has been in the unit for some time—is, in effect, just learning to do job tasks. Objectives set in supervisory conferences are task objectives—the employee has not yet accomplished the task, so the proper activities have not been performed and results are yet to be attained. Then you would focus on the *activities* required for the task: what the employee has to do to do it.

At this stage—with the performance-deficient employee—you could demonstrate several approaches (a range and sequence of activities) to getting results. For an employee in customer relations, for example, you might demonstrate several approaches to airing customer complaints: active listening, establishing an acquaintance before hearing the complaint, or taking an active stance by greeting the customer and advising him of the complaint procedure. The employee would then choose one approach and follow it step-by-step, performing the tasks required for the desired result: complaint aired, conflict resolved, action taken, customer disposed to return to store, *purchase in store made by customer.* The underlined "purchase by customer" is the end result sought, the outcome being that the customer does return to the store or stays to shop that very day, as indicated by charges on the store credit card. Over time, as the employee develops proficiency in the prescribed activities, you would begin to focus more specifically on the fine points of performance, emphasizing a more direct and cost-effective approach and an economy of activity, in addition to bringing in the results.

With the Discrepant Employee

In working with the employee who knows how to perform the activities well, you use a slightly different approach. Your focus with that employee in supervisory conferences is no longer mainly on activities. You can assume the employee is capable. Now you focus on *results,* setting a performance standard with the employee. Your objectives are no longer "first time," thorough task objectives. The employee has done similar tasks. Now you write objectives to achieve specific performance and outcomes.

Your indicators of discrepant performance then come from a drop in production or "results." You draw attention to the employee's performance on that basis. Your purpose in working with the discrepant employee is to determine how the employee can get back on the track and achieve the required results. If you simply establish the importance of "the results" with some employees, they will frequently self-correct their activities and quickly regain the required performance standard. If the employee cannot get himself back on track—and many new employees will not know how—then you reset the task and activities with the employee. Those tasks set up the activities most likely to approximate or achieve the results sought.

THE VALUE OF NONWORK ACTIVITY

An important part of staying "on track" in the matter of job performance is to have a clear idea of what purpose an employee serves. One employee who goes around talking and glad handing with other employees may be seen as a disruption to the job effort, while another employee doing the same thing is seen as a morale booster (see Module 3). Both employees may serve a useful function by talking with employees, airing gripes, and just maintaining a caring, concerned contact on the part of the organization. You will have to judge the effect of this "nonwork" activity by such indicators as whether there is a drop in productivity during the time that employee is doing it, whether there are complaints, and whether that employee is received openly.

Office managers are aware that their secretarial pool just sits around gabbing sometimes and then the place heats up and the secretaries start typing so fast you practically have to hose down the typewriters. As long as your employees get the results set out for them and the work done on time, it should make little difference if they do it by filing their nails four hours and typing four.

We tend to think that unless we are doing something demonstrably productive all the time that we are ineffective or that we could be perceived as lazy. Even though we entertain the fiction that we are working steadily, like a mule plowing forty acres, that is usually not the case. There are breaks, disruptions, getting back to the task, times spent "on hold," and times just for daydreaming. Looking more closely at our own experience, most of us will admit that we need times to be linear, goal-oriented, and productive. We also require time to be more circular, withdrawn, contemplative, and deliberative. While it may look like a case of "sometimes I sit and work, and sometimes I just sit," this constitutes work activity also.

We cannot extend with sufficient thrust if we do not consolidate and gather our forces. Even an assault on Mount Everest takes more time in the conceptual and planning stages than in the actual execution of the climb. Some of this low-profile activity, while less dramatic, is most essential to the life of every organization. Some of that activity is not perceived as essential to the attainment of results. However, the bottom line for the supervisor and the bottom line for assessment can be *whether that employee gets the results sought without extraordinary cost to the organization.*

SUMMARY

Many supervisors operate under the myth that they can figure out "why" employees act as they do and therefore run a better unit. But the search for a single "why" is a magical, fictitious endeavor, with strong drawbacks in the practice of supervision. As an alternative to "psyching out" employees, the objectives-activities-results approach to supervision operates from a very strong data base from which to direct and redirect employee performance on task. It provides a guide for orienting the new employee in learning job tasks as well as for directing the seasoned employee who has become unproductive or inefficient.

The beauty of being able to focus on objectives, activities, and results is that you keep your energy in the reality of job performance without trailing off into personality hassles or arguments about why the employee did what he did. When you set clear, measurable, demonstrable objectives, you need simply establish with the employee what tasks or activities are required to achieve the results. You are only responsible for the outcome.

Learning Module 10

Guiding Activity Changes
on the Job

In Part I, you became familiar with some of the aspects of making a transition in role from employee to supervisor. The change from one role to another involved attention to new responsibilities and resources. In this module you will become familiar with making and guiding changes within your work unit while remaining in your supervisory role. In most cases this will require some adjustment in your activity or the activity of your employees. Basically, you will change the way you act, the way they act, or the interaction between you.

Module 8 considered some bits and pieces of the kind of activity required to make changes on the job. This module takes a more comprehensive approach to "changing course" or "doing things differently," so that you can work effectively even if the employee—or entire unit—is resistant.

KINDS OF CHANGE

The basic kinds of change you will guide are interactional: that is, they affect the interactions you have with employees or employees have with other employees, or they affect the activities dependent on interaction in the unit.

For example, you may have an employee who is very dependent on you. At each juncture in the work day, this individual tugs at you for help. Even when a situation has been faced successfully several times before, he will come to you with a pleading look and ask for help. You comply and "help out" by taking over the task. Once you determine that you will no longer continue playing into the employee's dependence and doing his job for him, you may set forth some behavior change activities and objectives for the employee and call a conference. Your goal is to improve the interaction between you and the employee and to work the employee into his full job responsibility.

Or some of your employees may not be working together well. Petty bickering and backbiting, with each one running to you for a solution, cause you to intervene. You would try to improve the teamwork—to change the interaction between the employees.

An individual employee may be working inefficiently, using up more time and other valuable resources than necessary to do her job. You would intervene to improve work activity.

You may be putting more stress on yourself than is required by the job—accepting more work and taking on more responsibility than is healthy for you or within the scope of your job. You have to intervene in your own accustomed inability to say no.

HOW DO THESE CHANGES COME UP?

"Why now?" the employee will ask. "When this has been going on so long, why are you bringing it to my attention now?" What precipitates making changes on the job?

Often it is just the stress of the situation—the wear and tear on you or on employees—that makes you aware of the need for change. Sometimes the stress manifests itself in reduced productivity within the unit, loss of quality, absenteeism, turnover, and illness. Usually when the stress gets sufficiently high, someone will attempt to change activities to reduce the stress. It usually hurts to make changes.

On other occasions, new information requires a change in operation or a clarification of role responsibility. Training, seminars, management articles, books, and new employees bring in new data to the work unit, and with it more efficient ways to supervise the unit.

RESISTANCE TO CHANGE IN YOURSELF

Curiously, you may be resistant to changes within your unit. You may feel vulnerable in making changes to improve your supervision, assuming that doing so will point up your prior failings or shortcomings. If you just continue as you have, things will get done and no one will be the wiser.

You may even have some vested interest in the status quo. True, you feel stressed in your work and some employees drive you up a wall, but at least you know what to expect. Keep alert to signs that the comfort of and need for predictability in your unit operation override effective outcomes.

One resistance that is difficult to comprehend is the investment some individuals have in maintaining failure. For example, no one in a certain unit has been able to achieve a certain standard of production or service delivery. But then a new employee comes into the unit with suggestions about how to achieve that standard. The new employee may be met with subtle hoots, murmuring, and derision from the seasoned employees and supervisor who have already tried to perform up to standard—and given up.

The issue here is competence: as long as no one else can achieve what I have not been able to achieve, there is no affront to my competence—no one else has done it either. But when someone does achieve that standard, then his or her success stands in contrast to what is now my "failure." So be aware of subtle resistance to change in yourself as well as in your employees.

RESISTANCE TO CHANGE IN EMPLOYEES

Employees may also have an investment in the status quo. Like most people, they look for some continuity in life as a way of meeting their security needs. The more things stay the same, the less apprehension about the future. They are even willing to put up with known stresses in relationships or in the job itself rather than introduce unknown stresses.

Competence, a high value to most employees, is another point of resistance. They assume they know how to do their work, they have an established track record, and many would prefer not to have to learn or do something new or different. Often their ability to perform becomes almost second nature, for in time what were once new tasks become habit—"look Ma, no hands!" Who would want to change that, unless they are bored, endangered, or stressed excessively?

You can make changes on the job easier by being aware of employee concerns about continuity and competence and by giving established skills their due credit when introducing changes.

Remember also that humor and humility are two essential qualities for the supervisor. You may need both in dealing with an employee, and acknowledging your own role in a misdirected project. It takes two, in most cases, to botch up a work relationship. In the work unit, the supervisor is most frequently on one end of that two-part botch up.

HOW TO GUIDE CHANGES

What follows is a step-by-step format for making changes on the job. First is a work sheet, with directions for conducting the conference in which you introduce changes to your employee or unit (Figure 9). A separate work sheet may be made up for each employee or activity for which you wish to effect some changes. Some of the format will be duplicated for each situation.

Using the Work Sheet: Step by Step

No matter where the change you wish to make originated—be it a book, training session, or sudden insight—your first step is to determine what you want done differently—what you want to do differently or what you want someone else to do differently. That may require some anticipation of whether the changes will be possible and just how you will shepherd the changes over the allotted time period with one or more employees. Before your write your statement under "Activity to be done differently," you may want to mentally rehearse the steps necessary for effecting the change.

Part of your homework in preparing to discuss the changes with the unit or with an individual employee is to thoroughly understand what has gone on up to the present—the history. Often the rationale for an

Activity to be done differently:

_____
_____
_____

History (what has gone on "up until now"?)

_____
_____
_____

Special circumstances that contributed, e.g. holiday rush:

_____

How I have played into that activity: _____

_____

What I want to do "from now on"

Long-term goal: _____

Short-term objective: _____

_____

Terms of agreement with employee: _____

_____
_____

Step-by-step approach:

• _____
• _____
• _____

Obstacles to change:

_____

Figure 9. Work Sheet for Making Changes on the Job

employee's acting a certain way, or a unit functioning as it does, has its origin in an earlier episode when it was the appropriate way to handle the tasks at hand. Now things are different.

What is different now is you know something you didn't know before. Sometimes you are forced by circumstances and the pressure of deadlines to make changes. And then there are times when you simply reach some intuitive determination that "things have got to change." Whatever the impetus for wanting things done differently, you can smooth the changes on the job by informing yourself about the background for that particular change you are about to effect.

For the sake of your employee and yourself, provide the history and build a common data base with the employee or unit. You both can then clarify the circumstances that are the background for the change. The history also affords you an opportunity to acknowledge what in fact has been going on and what has to change. Too often a supervisor will pull a quick demand for change without any explanation of what precipitated the change or where different personnel fit into the picture. That lack of explanation can breed suspicion and paranoia among involved employees.

Acknowledging the history of the situation provides the employee with a reality check: "So this is what the supervisor has been experiencing; this is what would change." A quick change without acknowledging what precipitated it may leave the employee feeling detached, alienated, and insecure: "What did I do wrong?" The history provides a sense of continuity with the past. Out of that continuity comes some sense of security for the employee.

Acknowledging the history may also point out your own foibles as a human being who also happens to be supervising. If you expected to do the job perfectly, knowing all there was to know from the very first day, you would have been better off continuing as an employee. When you enter the ranks of management, you come under scrutiny of more than your immediate supervisor. Acknowledging your role in the history of the situation can provide some perspective to your supervisory position. You need not wallow in shortcomings, but your honesty in dealing with them when they affect the operation of the unit or the effectiveness of an employee will build you a greater degree of respect from your employees. Everyone is wrong at some time. Only the more realistic or courageous supervisors acknowledge it and learn from it.

The script suggested for leading into the history begins with "Up until now..." (at which point you describe the circumstances, their evolution, and any other insights you may have about them).

Sometimes this script would be delivered just to the concerned employee, other times to the entire work unit you supervise. Call whomever is concerned in the situation into a private conference, where

10. *Guiding Activity Changes on the Job*   *139*

you can begin the session by arriving at some mutual understanding of the issues and then discuss and reach some agreement about how to proceed.

Even though you may begin your conference with carefully researched notes, the employee may have additional data only that employee can provide. There may be "special circumstances that contributed to the work situation" you are determined to change. At the very least, you do not want to invite or incite employee resistance. At the very most you want employee understanding, agreement, and commitment to make the change with a minimum of intervention or hounding from you. Use the employee as a resource in the conference to find out additional information. Give the employee a chance to elaborate on the circumstances you describe. Be open to the possibility that the employee's data may change your assessment of the situation and even the way you thought you wanted to proceed.

"How have I played into that activity?" invites you to make a clearer delineation of your role in the situation beyond your general acknowledgement in its history. For example, you may be aware that a lot of time is wasted by your employees and also by you in supervising them. You are all more bluster and flurry than productive. You may want to ask their help in keeping you on track and effective in your use of time.

"What I want to do 'from now on' " has two parts: The "long-term goal" sets out in more general terms an overview and the direction in which the change is headed. The supervisor might say, "Tom, in the long run we want to get to the point where you can act as supervisor in my absence." In the second part, the "short-term objective," make a concrete, specific statement of the results you expect. You may have an employee who is indecisive and counterdependent, for example, in which case a short-term objective could be "show interest in pursuing sales leads by making seven phone calls per day to potential customers."

THE FACTOR OF CHOICE

An important consideration for the power you have in making an activity change and guiding it through to completion is the factor of choice in the change.

You are the most powerful when the change you propose is totally at your *discretion—it is your choice*. You need not consult with anyone. The change depends upon what you want.

When you have to *negotiate* the change with an employee or with the entire unit, the accomplishment of the change may hinge upon their agreement. They have a choice to agree and to change the conditions under which they will agree, and then they have the choice to perform. In this case, the agreement one reaches through negotiation may be the most important factor.

The time that you must assert your rights more than your power is when the change you are introducing is neither negotiable nor a result of your discretion, but rather *a given, fixed, contractual matter.* For example, your boss may have been promoted above you and you became supervisor in his place. For months your former boss continues to supercede your delegations to your employees, his old subordinates. Now, you begin to realize the full extent of your supervisory responsibility and wish to wrest that activity from your supervisor. Your approach might go this way:

> "I certainly appreciate your having helped me out by getting my employees to work on projects these past three months. The transition to supervisor has had its surprises, and I was a little overwhelmed at first." (This is your "up until now" statement. Now begins your "from now on" statement.) "Now I am ready to assume full responsibility for dealing with my employees. So, while I appreciate your assistance with them, you will not have to be doing your job and mine too. From now on I will bring up any problems I have with delegation or in clarifying objectives during our supervisory conferences. If you have any specific things you wish to convey to one of my subordinates, I would prefer to give that message to the employee myself so that the unit becomes aware that I am taking full responsibility now for their supervision." (You have also included the short-term objective, conveying the message, along with the long-term issue, taking on full supervisory responsibilities for these employees.)

Agreements will be discussed more in depth in Module 11. However, the "terms of agreement with employee" are relevant for your own record and perception of what transpires in the conference.

Once you have clarified the background data with the employee and set forth your long-term goal and short-term objective, it will be important to note whether the agreement reached constitutes an *acquiescence* by the employee, giving in to the force of your assertion; *acceptance* of the terms, possibly with some reluctance; or *mutually derived agreement,* in which mutual responsibility for specific performance of the terms is implied. The fundamental issue in the agreement is the degree of mutual responsibility taken in the conference.

When it's "dealer's choice," you may get grudging acquiescence or acceptance in recognition of your position and discretion. In a "horse-trading" situation, you may still seem to obtain employee agreement, but it may be given with the intention of undermining the change. If the "power of the contract" is used to pressure change, the employee may see you in the role of enforcer down the line.

The "step-by-step approach" refers to the bite-sized incremental activities you will use to guide the change. These generally are the continuing sequence of short-term objectives. A comprehensive listing of objectives is totally unnecessary if you have the cooperation and initiative of the employee. However, if the employee is resistant or the behavior is entrenched, you may require a map to guide you through the process.

The "obstacles to change" line asks you to anticipate potential resistance from the employee or the unit and to identify any distractions or events that could throw the changes off track or delay them. For example, an attempt to equitably divide the office work among all the secretaries—so that even the angry, difficult one is carrying a full share—may be thrown off when the work load requires some technical expertise the difficult secretary does not have. Or, your attempt to establish a new work plan may be "blown out of the water" by a demanding deadline dropped on your unit. Anticipate what you can prior to starting an activity change process.

The overall rationale for using the work sheet is to have a checklist to guide your supervision of the project. There is a certain amount of homework required of you to begin with. So, the work sheet is designed to help you take the important considerations into mind.

To recap briefly: You have determined that there are some changes required of yourself, an employee, or unit operations. You preset the activities to be changed and then meet with the parties involved in the change. You build a common data base with them, acknowledging the circumstances that have led to the change. Then you advance a plan for effecting the change, over the long and short run. You encourage communication in that meeting so that everyone involved either "gets the word" if there is not much choice in the matter, or you negotiate and reach some agreement involving shared responsibility for the change. No matter what the range of agreement reached, you would then set out to implement the change on the job.

IMPLEMENTING THE CHANGE

The initial conference with the employee or with the unit sets the stage for the changes you wish to effect. What then remains to bring about the changes is the day-to-day implementation. Together with the basic planning, guiding, and controlling functions of classic supervision, there are some particular considerations that hold true in most cases of making changes on the job.

You Will Be Tested at First

Whether you are just back from training, have read some new information, or are simply responding to pressures from your superiors, there is a tendency for employees to test your resolve at the beginning of a change effort. Most of us have been exposed to ill-fated projects for changes on the job that never materialized. Why should your employees really make a change when you might just be responding to a whim? What will your concern be tomorrow? So, expect some degree of cynicism about the change you propose.

There is also the issue of sticking with the established order. The established order says employees at least know how things are, how to relate to you, and what they can or cannot count on for support. Now you want them to carry on differently. You can count on their testing your resolve on this basis, too, before they will go ahead and attempt to make the change and institutionalize the new activities.

Here is an example from family life to illustrate the point.

In a family in which two of the children fight constantly, one or both parents may intervene regularly to break up the fight. One payoff for the kids is the attention they get from their parents; another is the power they exercise in being able to draw their parents in.

The parents intervene to keep one or both of them alive, or so the parents think. Miraculously, these same two children are able to get along without killing each other when left alone. In fact, the parents note that they fight only in the presence of the parents; furthermore, if one were going to kill the other, it could happen any time—even with the parent there.

Coming to this realization—that the kids have this choice in the matter—the parents also realize that the kids can learn to make other choices besides fighting to settle conflicts. So, both parents call a conference involving both children.

Each child is informed, "Up until now your mother or father has broken up the fight, but from now on you two are going to have to be more responsible for each other's welfare. If you have some difficulty, either one of us will be happy to talk it over with you. However, we are not going to jump in when you start fighting. If you want us involved, come to us and we'll talk it over." So the stage is set, the terms presented.

For the first week or two, the noises coming from the children's room sound like World War III. The kids pull out all the stops in an apparent fratricidal attempt to test the parents' resolve. The parents meanwhile have to come to grips with their worst fears, which used to motivate them to step in between the children. When someone's accustomed reward, payoff, or reinforcement— one to which they have become conditioned—is withdrawn, they will initially increase the activity in frequency or intensity in order to obtain the usual response.

In the same way, the children test the parents' resolve harder at first, and then eventually the fights subside over a period of several weeks and the children begin to take on more responsibility for themselves, their own choices and activities—extinguishing the fighting.

There are several additional issues to be aware of in implementing a change on the job.

One issue has to do with your own frame of mind regarding critical incidents. When some people attempt to make a change, they sense that the first challenge to their authority or plan is a critical incident. In their own minds this is a make-or-break situation that they must dominate and control or else lose the objective. Bunk! Hogwash! *There are no critical incidents in supervising!* This is no life or death matter. You will probably get caught up in old accustomed responses several times before you finally get things moving toward the changes you desire on the job.

Ultimately it takes cooperation from all parties to implement the change. But if you have the idea that one step back into the old habitual activity constitutes a defeat for your change objective and you allow that belief to shut down your efforts, it becomes a self-fulfilling prophecy: you *will* be defeated.

There is a prevalent myth that change occurs in one great leap and then levels out. Graphically, one scales a mountain only to find a plateau beyond—no continuing effort is required to sustain the change. The roller coaster scheme illustrated in Figure 10 portrays a more realistic picture of effecting change on the job.

A *continuing* effort is required to effect activity change for yourself or for others in an ongoing system (unless you have some sort of powerful intervention such as mass hypnosis to program employees anew or shock therapy to wipe out memory traces). Few, if any, employees will respond to change when they must make a cold-turkey withdrawal from accustomed ways of behaving.

As the instigator of the change, you will have to **reassert your objective time and time again.** That repetitive cycling is depicted in the up and down slopes in the illustration. Each time you fall back into the old activity is an occasion to learn about how susceptible you are.

What triggers your getting into that pattern? At each point where you identify some other influence or activity that triggers that habitual

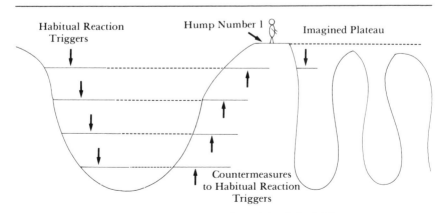

Figure 10. Guiding Changes in Habitual Activities

reaction, you can work out an effective activity to counteract the habit and reprogram yourself toward the activity you desire.

How often will you have to reassert your objective if you continue to discover new triggers to old patterns? *You have to reassert yourself as often as it takes to get the change implemented.*

Draw upon your humor and humility when dealing with an employee who has a tendency to hook you back into the former way of doing things. When you have been hooked, admit it. You may as well know that you will live through this minor show of human weakness. However, once you have acknowledged your retreat into familiar patterns, you need only continue to reassert your objective—let the employee know what will be expected the next time, what counteraction will prevent your getting hooked. Not all countermeasures or counteractivity to old programming need to be discovered after you have been hooked. You can anticipate some.

With an employee who has come to you with a crisis on her hands soon after you discussed her taking more responsibility in decision making, you may feel completely co-opted. It is natural to feel that way, but you are no more defeated than you think you are. Pick yourself up. Call a conference to discuss it. Reassert what is expected and required of the employee and continue where you left off. *Anticipate further situations in which you might get drawn in. Attempt to have that employee take responsibility in advance for averting those foreseeable situations.* You may have to specify activities for the employee.

For activities that are really entrenched, whether personal or personnel items, chart out those activities on a format like Figure 10, which illustrates the process of making changes in established relationships. The items to be listed on the down slope of the "roller-coaster curve" are the activities that influence habitual response, the unthinking responses. The items listed under the up slope of the curve would be the countermeasures, new activities or responses, that will offset or neutralize the activities that "hook" you into the habits. List all the distinct activities that throw you into the habitual response or activity and then develop a countermeasure activity for each one.

Here is an example of how all of this works in a supervisory situation.

DEALING WITH CHICKEN LITTLE

Most supervisors will have at least one sky-is-falling, hysterical, dependent employee during their tenure. This employee has a way of creating crises or escalating crises to a fever pitch. Somehow you find that you are reacting and taking over for the employee—often before you have the facts. You know that you react to the emotion, so that is one counter-measure to develop—relaxation or slowing reaction time under crisis conditions.

Set up a conference with the employee. Acknowledge that you have often become caught up in the excitement of the moment and so you act hastily, often without adequate information. In reacting to the crisis, you have been infringing on the job responsibility of the employee. Then begin your "from now on." Your long-range objective with the employee is that he will take more direct responsibility to cope with those situations. In the short term ask the employee to slow down the action when he starts to detect one of his crises—slow down the action and really study the situation.

So at first the employee speaks in modulated tones and even conveys an accurate picture of the situation. But during the course of conversation, somehow, the employee starts to express a helplessness about coping. Before you know it, you are jumping to the rescue. You've done it again! You've reacted.

So now you know—you are vulnerable to high hysteria and also to abject helplessness. How can you counter the latter tendency? One way is to hand the problem back to the empoyee. You can't work with that employee on his crisis if you take it all on yourself. It would no longer be his crisis. It would be yours. So plan to turn the responsibility back, continually. In a short time you think you have foreseen every possible hitch in your activity change plan. Shortly, your employee will respond more skillfully to problems and will not manufacture crises. You, meanwhile, will not take on the crisis.

You have figured out your countermeasures and have asked the employee to be conscious of how he triggers off that situation. In a few weeks you seem to have overcome your dependent sky-is-falling employee.

Most habitual activities do not change instantly without some costly trauma or remarkable willpower. It takes time to reprogram oneself, to establish new or different activities, new response patterns. On the roller-coaster curve the first big upswing is the initial attempt to offset the old activity and to establish the new activity. This is where you exert major energy in diagnosing habitual activities and anticipating how they might reassert themselves. The countermeasures are devised and put in place. Within a moderate amount of time, with some determination, the person attempting the change may think he has made it—"we're over the hump."

The sense of accomplishment is considerable. The old activity seems supplanted, replaced. There is even an assumption that once there, you have hit a plateau below which you are unlikely to fall again. Wrong! At that point some unforeseen, unanticipated influence triggers the old activity or response in you, and you find yourself back in the very same rescue pattern you thought you had already overcome (with appropriate countermeasures.)

It is 3:15 Friday afternoon. Several employees are about to go on vacation for two weeks. A large order comes into your shipping clerk whom you have attempted to have take more responsibility for orders. The order would require several days to fill even with a full staff. The customer wants shipment as soon as possible and she is a regular customer. Your clerk comes to you panicked about the order. Before you know it you are on the phone calling the customer for clarification— you've done it again! The clerk got you to do his job!

You feel defeated. In your efforts to reduce crises and get the employee to control himself, you thought you had been successful in effecting the change, and now this.

This is the point on Figure 11 marked Pit Number 2, the point where you might feel depressed, misled, defeated and done in. You could just lie there and console yourself or you can realize that this is not a defeat. This is a very fortunate place to be! *This is part of making changes in habitual activities.* There is some useful learning in the fact that you had not anticipated the particular activity that threw you back into your patterned response. There will be other influences and triggers that you will not have anticipated. That is part of the important learning of making changes on the job, especially in entrenched or habitual areas of activity.

You will be lucky if you are brought down off your mythical first plateau, your high spot, fairly soon after attaining that temporary sense of accomplishment. Otherwise, as time goes by, you may begin to believe

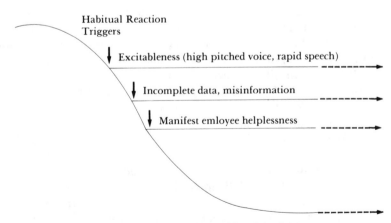

Figure 11. Guiding Changes in Habitual Activities:
The-Sky-Is-Falling Employee

you have really made all the necessary adjustments to accomplish the change, when in fact you have not. If this momentary setback does not come within about six weeks, you tend to get immersed in other activities, to set up other priorities. Your objective fades into the background. Then suddenly you are back into your old habitual response pattern, *and* you may not notice it in time to recoup the gains you have made. Your resolve to work out of the pattern may get shelved rather than reasserted.

You might feel a sense of frustration and disappointment when the response gets triggered again, but consider yourself lucky if you have such a throwback situation early on in your resolve to make changes. For, at that point, you are still primed and determined to make the changes and you are aware. There is still time. You have not lost your initial resolve.

Get out your countermeasure chart and go to work. You already have some countermeasures you can continue to use effectively. You can go on to develop effective countermeasures for each unanticipated trigger that emerges.

In this case you could talk with the employee, using some humility (you got hooked) and discussing some ways to prevent similar occurrences (triggers) in the future. You can also work with yourself to further consider your own snap reactions and overdeveloped sense of responsibility.

You don't have to be overjoyed. But you can welcome any such apparent setbacks with interest and energy and work up the necessary countermeasures. Remember you have to assert your new activities *again and again, as often as it takes.* Soon you will level out at a higher, more effective level of activity.

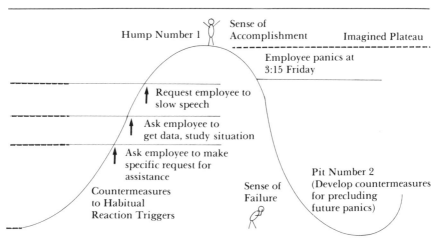

Figure 11 (continued).

SUMMARY

To make changes on the job, remember:

- Employees will be threatened.
- To build in continuity, "up until now..." provides security.
- State a clear expectation or objective, "From now on . . ."
- There are no critical incidents—leave room for learning.
- Give a long-term goal and overview and a short-term specific objective.
- You will be tested most severely at first.
- You will fall back into old patterns numerous times.
- Old pattern triggers are valuable learning points.
- Reassert your intent explicitly again and again.
- As you discover new setbacks, build a better transition base.
- Early setbacks keep you focused on your objective.
- Employ humor and humility in all phases of change.
- Transitions take time; be patient and firm.

Learning Module 11

Agreements:
Supervising Is a Two-Way Street

The traditional organization chart is most often perceived and used as a one-way, drainpipe, top-to-bottom, order-delivering vehicle for the use of higher line authority. Some have even referred to the chart as a sewer system, for what they get out of it. As long as the line of authority is interpreted as one-way, one necessarily is required to exert more power with each move higher in the organization. At the same time, one runs the risk of becoming removed and isolated from the real work of the organization, being cut off from below.

There are some ways in which the traditional top-to-bottom interpretation is unfortunate for personnel at all levels, supervisors and employees alike. But there is no need for you to function from a position of isolation.

START WITH TWO-WAY COMMUNICATION

To begin with, supervision has to be a two-way street if it is to work at all. You cannot simply issue or pass orders from above down to your employees. Each of your supervisory responsibilities may have some particular details that require your support and attention as well as the direct involvement of your employees. In order for you to run a viable operation, you may have to attend to details that only your employees know: time required, other priorities, available materials, probable client response, and the like. Without employee input at the beginning, you operate at a disadvantage throughout your work relationship. Two-way communication is essential.

Two-way communication ought to be depicted on organizational charts with an arrow pointing from employee to supervisor and vice versa. Using arrows like this, instead of connecting personnel on the line of authority with straight lines, would *explicitly* illustrate that not only is communication two-way, but also that subordinates have a responsibility to initiate communication on issues related to their work. I believe this approach would go a long way to eliminate the employee's tight-lipped acquiescence, passivity, and avoidance of supervisors seen in so many supervisory relationships.

Advantages in two-way communication for the supervisor are that you can expect some employee initiative in keeping you informed and that there will be a more realistic and proportional sharing of responsibility throughout the organization. The two-way interchange between adjoining positions also emphasizes the interdependence of positions within the organization, rather than a single concern with one's own position. It also deters turf building (see Module 5).

For your sake as a supervisor, two-way communication provides a way for you and your employees to get your act together. You have complementary roles. And often you have to discuss specifically how you can work together most effectively on particular tasks or toward new objectives. Your work agreement goes beyond preliminary ground rules into who does what. How you reach that agreement will affect employee work performance, unit productivity, and your stress level.

APPROACHING AGREEMENTS

Two-way communication goes beyond a simple responsibility to converse and exchange information. One specific end product of supervisor-employee interaction is agreements reached to perform tasks to accomplish work objectives. Much of what passes for an agreement falls short of the essential ingredients of true agreement, so that the employee is left without adequate support and guidance to get the work done. At the same time, the supervisor takes on the role of enforcer, backstop, or safety net for the employee. Their interactions involve a high degree of drama and tension, with little real effectiveness reflected in results.

Acquiescence

Top-down commands often hit the employee like "tar baby"—"He just don't say nuthin'." Meanwhile, the supervisor thinks that the employee's silence signifies agreement. At the very best, the employee is passively, sometimes helplessly, acquiescing to the command. The employee may not perceive an opening to discuss, question, or make observations, let alone play devil's advocate, bargain, negotiate for support, or refuse to perform. But the absence of two-way communication in reaching what appears to be an agreement results only in acquiescence, a reluctant giving in. The consequences of acquiescence remain to be discovered in the employee's actual performance. The supervisor will have to be on his toes to keep the employee on track and pursuing the objective.

Acceptance

A "perceived agreement" is only slightly better than acquiescence when it comes to real performance and accomplishment of work tasks. A perceived agreement is simply an acceptance by the employee of what he is being told. Acceptance may take the form of "I'll do it," "Sure, I can do it," and other reassurances to the supervisor. The supervisor states the objective, and the employee appears to pick up the objective and be ready to run with it. Once again, two-way communication is missing, though in this case the employee takes a more active role by showing signs of life and responding to the supervisor's request.

The employee's acceptance can be made grudgingly (not perceiving any alternative or choice in the matter) or more or less willingly, ranging up through eager grasping for more to do. However, eagerness by itself does not accomplish objectives. There may be a need to plan and direct the actual accomplishment of various stages of the objective. Eager medical students are not turned loose to perform brain surgery, nor should your employees be allowed to pluck any objective off the shelf to try to accomplish. Be selective in delegation. Selectivity and collaboration in delegating require more careful discrimination about what the employee can actually do, what supports are required, and what assistance you might provide. These also require two-way communication.

Agreement

Real, active two-way agreement on task objectives most naturally contains some understanding of how to proceed. Real agreement also includes and recognizes a shared responsibility in carrying out the objective. Agreement activities are important to accomplishing your work as supervisor.

An agreement is simply an arrangement between parties. In organizational terms, an agreement would seek to establish a complementary match between the organizational mission and the responsibility extended to a unit and the resources required to accomplish unit goals, objectives, action plans, priorities, tasks, and activities. Much of the work of supervisors involves establishing agreements with employees and guiding and directing employee energy through these agreements toward organizational goals.

NEGOTIATING AGREEMENTS

In the module on guiding activity changes on the job (see Module 10), not much was said about getting an *agreement* with employees to carry out the activity change. That module primarily covered situations in which the main leverage rested with you, the supervisor, to effect the changes you desired. The desired changes were, in effect, "nonnegotiable." And there are many nonnegotiable situations in organizational life.

In order for you to supervise effectively, however, many negotiated agreements are essential. Depending on your particular supervisory activity, you may consider yourself the final judge or an equal partner with final authority. Whatever your stance in making agreements in the supervisor-employee relationship, focus on getting the assent of your employees.

There is some "tit for tat" in making agreements, some bargaining and negotiating. You have to be aware of what you want and what you are willing to provide. The basic exchange in making or negotiating an agreement involves a standard trade-off.

Supervisor:
"Your job requires that you . . . "

Employee:
"Doing that task will require the following support: . . . "

Supervisor:
"I will provide these
resources . . . "

Employee:
"It will be done."

The best agreements are explicit, aboveboard, complete and direct expressions by the individual personnel involved. Such agreements may involve goals, objectives, tasks, and plans within the organization. It is particularly important for agreements to be stated in a way that you can know when you "get there"—when the product is completed, the services have been delivered, the promise complied with, or the action taken. If the terms of the agreement are left vague, it may be impossible to assess the performance of either party.

In essence, we are talking about contracting. The word *contracting* conjures up the sense of a legally binding arrangement for which both parties can be held accountable for nonperformance. *Agreement* carries the connotation of interdependence, suggesting the exchange and reliances that typically occur between supervisor and employee.

An agreement is like a contract in that it requires *specificity*, with as much *concrete detail* as is feasible without restricting the actual performance of the agreement. An agreement also requires the *involvement of both parties regarding the terms*, the specific performance aspects, and the *anticipated results*. The more clearly defined the terms of the agreement, the easier it is to guide performance and the more assuring it is for both parties.

Another aspect of an agreement is that it be bilateral with some specific performance required on both sides. An agreement in which an employee merely gives in and states that she will complete a research study by October 15th, with a complete statistical analysis in triplicate, is a unilateral decision. The agreement should commence with some thorough discussion and anticipation of what is required to achieve the purpose of the agreement, to get the desired results.

If you ask an employee to increase productivity by 15 percent and your employee passively gives you an O.K. without further consideration of what is required for such a production hike, you are both in trouble. The employee will probably not achieve the increased output without some delay, renegotiation (the employee's first negotiation), or strain on resources. Review requirements or potential obstacles in advance, to help anticipate what is needed. Then your agreement will be more realistic and complete to begin with. Unless you are out to perform heroics with your personnel or to exploit them—the consequences of which result in high turnover or loss of work time through illness and low morale—plan to act in support of employee activities, to promote their productivity.

Many supervisors fail to realize that they have the responsibility to provide support for employees. That support consists of both feasible planning with attainable, time-framed objectives and support in the way of guidance, encouragement, and resources. Many employees are unaware that providing this support is part of the supervisor's job, so they will attempt to perform their jobs with limited resources and then fall short of objectives for lack of adequate support. What is most notable here is that when agreements are not discussed, negotiated, firmed up, and carried out, the employee, the supervisor, and the organization lose.

So, whether you plan to impose an objective or negotiate one with employees, you have to determine some range of what you want and what support you are willing to provide. The 15 percent hike in productivity may require supports that you alone cannot foresee, and your employee will not learn to consider the requirements of the job as well if you unilaterally make the determinations about what the employee requires. There are two sides to the performance requirements of an agreement. The supervisor requesting the 15 percent hike may have to provide guidance, technical advice, additional clerical support, administrative clearance for access to documents or laboratory materials, a higher budget, or whatever other resources are required to complete the projected agreement.

Supervising is a two-way effort between employee and supervisor: The supervisor relies on the employee for specific performance and feedback, while the supervisor provides those resources and supports required to facilitate employee performance.

A FORMAT FOR MUTUAL AGREEMENT BY SUPERVISOR AND EMPLOYEE

Figure 12 is a format for recording the main elements of agreements you make with your employees. The following sections describe some of the background for using that format, together with some pointers on working through it with your employees.

A *job contract* is the employee's initial agreement with the organization. Though not always stated in the *form* of a contract, the job contract is a legal agreement and has to be updated periodically. If this agreement is not updated so that current activities are reflected at least in the job description, the employee does not have an ongoing accord with the organization that corresponds to what he or she is doing. You also do not have a strong basis for negotiating agreements with the employee if the underlying responsibilities have not been included in the basic working agreement or job contract.

In Part I we emphasized the importance of providing new employees perspectives on the purpose or mission of the organization, the mission of your particular unit, and the importance or difference their jobs make. The usefulness of these perspectives becomes increasingly evident when you begin to work toward agreements. That particular common data base not only promotes understanding but also keeps employees in tune with their contribution to the organization, a morale consideration. Now to make agreements, that prior understanding will be most helpful.

What is the *mission* of your organization? Typically, many employees in any organization do not perceive the role of that organization in the larger scheme of things. Much less, then, do they realize the importance of their unit or their own position in the scheme of the organization.

We will not dwell on the sometimes frustrating attempt to define the "purpose" of your organization at this time. However, the purpose, mission, or function is the reason the organization exists in the first place. With that reason as a basis, the organization then sets out organization goals, more operational statements of results sought through the organization.

Goals are general statements of desired results. The language of goals falls somewhere between the specific, demonstrable terms used in objectives and the more abstract statements of purpose. Goal statements usually begin with verbs like "to increase," "to improve," and "to expand" and end with such objects of the verb as "profitability," "communication," "productivity," "customer satisfaction," or "client service." In order to make the goals of an organization operational, to put them into day-to-day specifications for action and accomplishment, we have objectives.

An *objective* must fit several criteria to qualify as a meaningful supervisory tool. The objective generally is *concise*, a statement of fifteen

---

Goal:

Objective (concise, possible, time-framed, measurable):

Performance provided by employee	Dates	Supports provided by supervisor	Dates
•		•	
•		•	
•		•	
•		•	
•		•	

First Mutual Check Point: Date_____ Time_____ Place_____
Additional Performance and Supports

•		•	
•		•	
•		•	

Second Mutual Check Point: Date_____ Time_____ Place_____
Additional Performance and Supports

| • | | • | |

Final Assessment of Objective:

Attained:

Further Steps for this Objective:

Figure 12. Mutual Agreement by Supervisor and Employee

to twenty words. The objective states an activity or accomplishment that is *possible* (real or ideal). It is time framed for accomplishment, listing either a date for completion or a range of time—between the 15th and 18th of April. Most important, the objective is stated so it is measurable or demonstrable: Someone can tell whether it has been achieved.

To say an objective is "demonstrable" means that someone could come in during your absence as supervisor, pick up your supervisory notes or "mutual agreement form," and from the objective statement determine whether the objective had been achieved. An explicit statement of a work objective is essential to the continuity of work in your unit: Consider the possibility of your reassignment, vacation, illness, or other changes that would give the employee a new supervisor. With explicit objectives, the employee's work can be guided and results achieved, whether you are there or not. That is the way it should be for an organization. To set yourself up as the sole source of information or interpretation on objectives is to create a dependency on your presence to properly carry out activities to accomplish the objectives sought. Objectives provide an organization presence, structure, and continuity that institutionalizes your agreement beyond your individual presence in that particular unit.

To make sure that the objective is demonstrable or measurable, build a check-off method into the statement of the objective so that anyone could indeed measure results accurately. An example would be: "Stacked shipping crates 1-105 through 1-127 in Warehouse H by 1:45 P.M. August 17." Anyone could simultaneously record the time and certify those crates by number in Warehouse H.

The mutual agreement format emphasizes the interdependence of the supervisor-employee relationship for performance. Deficiency in job performance may be due to the supervisor as well as to the employee. The agreement may be scuttled by the supervisor's failing to deliver required resources and support. The agreement may also be scuttled by the employee's falling short in performance even when resources and support are provided.

The negotiation leading to the agreement and the agreement itself ensure both parties are involved in fully plotting what they're setting out to do. Just having an agreement does not guarantee there will be a successful accomplishment of the objective, but it does increase the likelihood. Furthermore, mutual agreement increases the likelihood that employee attention and energy will remain focused on the agreement and its objective.

GUIDING THE AGREEMENT

Both supervisor and employee have the responsibility to keep each other informed on their particular requirements during the term of the agreement. This process of informing begins essentially during the planning and negotiation phases of the agreement. From those discussions both parties should derive a clear picture of what is required of each to accomplish the aims of the agreement. The next responsibility falls on both parties to deliver their contribution to the agreement.

The term (time period) during which an agreement is enacted provides an excellent opportunity for the supervisor-employee relationship to develop and become more effective. Each party's keeping the other informed allows two-way communication practices to be tested and refined. Any requirement to renegotiate some of the details of the agreement provides an opportunity to practice anticipating contingencies, rather than simply responding to crises as they arise. An employee

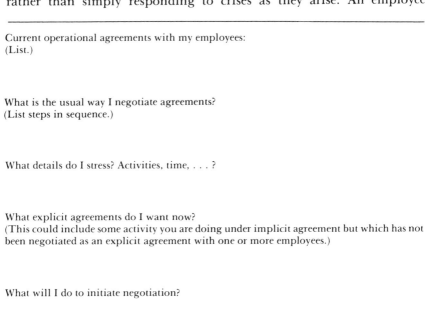

Current operational agreements with my employees:
(List.)

What is the usual way I negotiate agreements?
(List steps in sequence.)

What details do I stress? Activities, time, . . . ?

What explicit agreements do I want now?
(This could include some activity you are doing under implicit agreement but which has not been negotiated as an explicit agreement with one or more employees.)

What will I do to initiate negotiation?

What will I do specifically to ensure the agreements are mutual ones?

Figure 13. What to Do About Agreements

apprised of his or her responsibility under an agreement would keep the supervisor informed throughout—reporting progress as well as any requirements to complete the project. The supervisor would keep the employee informed about any possible changes in organizational approaches or priorities and any conflicting objectives in the unit.

WHERE TO FROM HERE?

Figure 13 provides a convenient format for you to use to check the way you enter into agreements with your employees now and note what you may want to do in the future. Remember, much of the success of an agreement depends on what you do in the early stages—the planning and negotiation that makes the agreement explicit and mutual.

Learning Module 12

The Psychology of Planning

Planning is so commonly discussed in the supervisory management literature that it is easy to dismiss it as an innocuous, though necessary, item on a supervisory check list. But somehow the word *planning* conjures up dread in some of us, dread sufficient to keep us from doing any effective planning ourselves.

A PLAN SHOULD SERVE YOU— YOU DON'T SERVE THE PLAN

Most of us are aware that planning clarifies goals, stimulates communication, elicits alternative methods in accomplishing tasks, and improves data flow. Planning also saves time in the long run—though it may require more time initially to set the practice of planning in place within your unit. Planning distinguishes the important from the urgent, provides options, anticipates the unexpected, averts high pressure crises, and seeks the most simple and economical approach to getting results.

There is no great mystery about the planning process. All it requires is the following:

- Focus on the *purpose* or mission of your plan and organization.
- Review the *background* information.
- Get a thorough reading of available *resources*.
- Set up *objectives*.
- Develop *alternative approaches* to overcome obstacles.
- Set *priorities*.
- *Choose a course of action* from among alternatives.
- *Implement* your plan.
- *Review* and *update* your efforts.

In devising your strategy or procedure you also consider the authority involved, together with various other contingencies for anticipated and unanticipated occurrences.

Note that this common-sense listing of the planning process directly parallels the problem-solving and decision-making process introduced in Module 7. This points up the advantage of knowing the more complete problem-solving/decision-making process well. It can be directly translated and applied to purposes other than strictly "solving problems." If you know the problem-solving process and can implement it, then you already know what you will require for planning.

So the planning process is simple and straightforward. Then why is it that so few of us actually plan?

When you don't plan to plan, planning gets lost in the downward energy spiral of crisis management. Rather than allocating time to anticipating requirements and effectively lining up resources and energy toward the accomplishment of an objective, your time and energy get siphoned off toward meeting emergencies that have arisen because of negligence in planning. It is not unusual for a supervisor to fall into the habit of crisis management, failing time and time again to devote front-end time to planning.

To break out of the crisis-management spiral, it helps to give planning an honest try, an opportunity to be applied and to work. First, you have to decide to plan. Then you either have to begin to plan immediately, or plan a time to plan. Planning has to become an integral part of your work life. (If the word "plan" has lost its meaning for you, simply substitute "decide in advance"!) You have to set aside a regular block of time in which to plan each day. Plan your work and then work your plan.

WHAT GOES INTO IT

Now, to bolster your resolve and encourage the use of planning skills in daily operation, consider some of the psychological factors that come into play in planning. They are applicable to both you and your employees.

What Difference Do I Make?

Knowing how one's job or tasks fit into the team or unit effort, or the organizational purpose, gives us a sense of perspective that makes our job more important. It boosts morale, encourages serious application on the job, and decreases a lackadaisical attitude.

Do I Have the Go-Ahead?

Few of us are motivated to continue to plan "just in case" we have an opportunity. Most of us will participate more fully and enthusiastically in planning either just for ourselves or with the unit if there is clear authority and responsibility set out to do so. Employees will show more initiative if authority for planning and decision making about their work is clearly set forth or delegated to them. At first, the scope of authority can be limited to planning responsibility and then expanded as the employee demonstrates responsibility in handling the smaller tasks. Employees respond to increased latitude in planning and decision making. Make sure they have it.

What's in It for Me?

You may have to devise your own short-term rewards to stimulate yourself to plan. Some individuals derive satisfaction from being able to accomplish tasks and cross items off a list. Still others derive satisfaction from the sense of increased responsibility within the organization, or from interactions with peers, subordinates, or superiors in planning sessions. Greater access to information about the organization is another incentive to planning. In working through the planning process, one steps beyond one's own basic job perspective and considers variables affecting the entire unit or organization. It gives the employee a sense of connectedness with the organization both horizontally and vertically. Not all jobs provide instant payoff, so it helps to make your work as rewarding as possible. Provide your payoff by working out your plan in manageable, bite-sized steps.

Planning Looks Like a Trap

There is a degree of accountability in committing one's plan to paper. If an organization allows you to get by with no defined or stated objectives, then it is most difficult for them to hold you to specific performance. However, it is also difficult for you to anticipate the resources you will need, the time frame in which you can reasonably accomplish the tasks, and the support and interaction upon which you will rely within the organization. You may also take a most cost ineffective approach, where a plan would have allowed someone to review your approach with you and cut corners. In most organizations, the benefits of planning far outweigh the disadvantages.

Having a Plan May Be Instant Frustration

It is true that each one of us could plan out more activities than we could possibly accomplish in a lifetime. Some of those plans might be totally realistic. Yet they will span a time far beyond today, or even this year.

That is one of the reasons it is so important to place plans within a time frame. If you do not, the plan can become an unrelenting goad to you to do it all right now. You can make your plans unbearable and difficult to live with, or you can make them feasible and bearable by plotting them out so that you allot sufficient time to accomplish the tasks and objectives required.

Most plans come about as a result of a desire, an "I want..." statement. To deal with most frustration, you also need to look at the desire from which it springs. Rather than focusing on the "frustration"— a sense of irritability, squirming, or being ill at ease—look at the source of wanting to move toward that goal in the first place. Then either ease up demands on yourself or look for a more effective approach to reaching your goal.

When I'm Not Sure Where I'm Going, Planning is Too Risky

Clear, measureable objectives plotted into a feasible time frame make for a useful plan. However, it is essential also that your plan be flexible and negotiable. As long as you know the general direction, you needn't know the last step. Few individuals can or wish to make all decisions now, and then be held to them later. Build some flexibility into your planning and plan.

The Curse of the Intelligent

One difficulty many intelligent individuals face in planning is that they focus on the end result and tend to ignore the process of getting there. There is a tendency to pressure themselves toward the final task accomplishment and to not derive any satisfaction from reaching short-term intermediate objectives. Consequently, it is excruciatingly painful for them to have a plan, for they do not allow themselves to rest until it is accomplished, nor do they enjoy the process of moving toward accomplishment. For individuals who approach planning this way, having a plan is like hitting your head against the wall because it feels so good when you stop. Build in your own short-term satisfactions by developing a step-by-step detailed plan. Try not to sabotage your satisfaction by thinking you must wait until you reach the end objective to feel a sense of accomplishment. Take bits of satisfaction in accomplishments along the way.

EXISTING PEACEFULLY WITH YOUR PLAN

When you draw up your plan, involve all the people and resources you can foresee will be essential to carrying out the plan. You will not necessarily have a workable plan until you have actively included the essential personnel in the plan.

When you make your objectives clear, measureable and time framed, you have to think operationally and in terms of viable results. You have to do a little imagining to see what it will look like when it is finished. That increases the probability that the end result will happen and the probability that when it happens you will know it.

Work out your plan in sufficient detail so that you do not combine very distinct and sequential steps. The more detail you anticipate and plan for, the easier it will be to deal with unanticipated contingencies.

One contingency we have already mentioned occurs when two equally valid objectives compete with each other for personnel and resources (see Module 7). Initially, it would appear that there is some oversight in the planning that allows the same resources or time-frame to be devoted to competing objectives. In the interest of resolution, you would discuss the situation with all involved parties at the earliest possibility—rather than allow conflict to arise or criticize the planning process itself. Ultimately, this situation would have to be referred to superiors if there is no resolution at lower levels. The case is similar to the goal-goal conflict in the problem-solving model, which requires resolution through priority ranking.

Exercise moderation in committing yourself to a time frame. In most cases you will not know what is required until you get to that point in the plan, so build in some negotiating or wiggle room. The time frame is important to providing some structure with which to work. At the same time, allocating too little time distorts the entire purpose of a plan. You end up serving the plan; the plan does not serve you.

Concentrate on what is realistic to accomplish. Be aware that if you have not done the tasks before, there may be numerous unforeseen adjustments and choices that will have to be made along the way. Absolute goals may keep you from any real accomplishments.

Finally, remember one of the real joys of planning is to work or implement your plan and watch it unfold. There is a strong sense of situational control in knowing that you can anticipate and plan for events to unfold in a predetermined way. At the same time, keep your planning perspective resilient, so that implementation accomplishes the function of the plan and is not merely a rigid adherence to the form of the plan.

Some organizations and individual personnel consider any requirement to plan an affront to their dignity, to their humanness, and a limitation of their choices. Be aware of some of these obstacles to planning within your organization or in your unit. Sometimes you will just have to plan to demonstrate its effectiveness in operation.

SUMMARY

Even though planning is a well established practice in supervision, there is some reluctance on the part of many supervisors to decide in advance what they will do and then to commit that plan to paper. Often the supervisor senses he is entering into an unretractable pact. Suddenly, a supervisory tool, intended to facilitate performance, becomes a deterrent. One must maintain a sense of proportion about planning. Planning is intended to benefit and serve the planner in job effectiveness or efficiency. If it does not prove useful to you, you will need to review your own methods of planning or your perspective on planning.

Learning Module 13

Contingency Planning
and Anticipatory Guidance

Contingency planning is a bit more detailed than most routine planning efforts. It is planning on a higher level of sophistication. In contingency planning you attempt to foresee possible outcomes or anticipate consequences of earlier steps in the plan then decide on particular options, depending upon those outcomes or consequences.

So the purpose of this learning module is to learn to distinguish patterns from the ongoing experience of supervising, to engage in detailed contingency planning to both anticipate and guide unit activities through repetitive or cyclical occurrences, and, finally, to standardize or routinize those aspects of the planning that are effective. But first a bit of background.

ROUTINIZATION

A certain amount of routinization comes from contingency planning. The person who sees his twelve-year tenure as a supervisor as one year times twelve treats each new year, each new cycle, of supervisory duties and incidents as novel and distinct. Contrast the supervisor who sees the same length on the job as twelve years of supervision, who chalks up an experience as new or novel only when it occurs for the first time. When an experience, an activity, or an event repeats itself and is of sufficient importance for the supervisor to notice it or devote some energy to it, some routine dealing may be in order.

Routinizing involves detecting some of the essential repetitive elements in the work cycle or a particular situation. Then one meets those repetitive occurrences with activities or routines planned in advance, which still allow for some flexibility and responsiveness. So one acts neither from a naive position nor a rigid position, but rather systematically responds to routine events as they occur.

Routinization is one way to apply some structure or gain some situational control on seemingly chaotic or random events. Routinization may involve development of step-by-step plans, "how-to" guidelines, or standard operating procedures.

An example from personal life:

All of us have established routines in our personal lives. For example, you probably take the same route to the office every day whether you travel by automobile, bus, subway, or train. There are probably alternate routes to get from your house to the office but you've either checked them out and found them less convenient or perhaps you have randomly picked a route and stuck with it.

The advantage of the routine route is that you can predict what your trip to and from work will be like—you know how long it will take, you know how many stops to expect, and you know what you will likely see on the way. In other words, you could practically run it blindfolded.

OVERSTRUCTURED?

Some supervisors are horrified at the detail and anticipation involved in contingency planning. Their fear is that all spontaneity will be stifled or suppressed by such an extensive behavioral formula. The plan, of course, is not all that extensive. It provides a guideline more than a script. Furthermore, it provides for greater likelihood of spontaneity by swiftly anticipating what is likely to be involved. In some ways contingency planning is like a rehearsal.

Even jazz music requires a steady or routine beat to improvise against. Establishing routines in activities simply recognizes that there are some predictable, repetitive patterns that need not be approached as "novel," unique, or new. The routine captures the essential activity to facilitate organizational activity.

FEEDFORWARD

Doing contingency planning involves, first, learning from your experience, and then applying that learning toward future tasks. In contingency planning, information on task performance moves beyond just being feedback. It is used in the analysis of present and potential situations, becoming "feedforward" for the future. *Feedforward* is a studied anticipation of the future, based on your experience and your ability to learn from that experience and to apply it.

CONTINGENCY PRESSURES

Even when each person knows his job and is fully capable of performing it, there are still going to be some intervening factors or influences that will interfere with the smooth functioning of an organization. They are worth noting and paying attention to if your work flow is seriously disrupted so you can plan for more fluid work performance in the future.

External Pressures

You may be part of an industry that is a current focus of public scrutiny and have to guard your activities carefully, lest you come under the fire of the media. The government may be increasing the demands on your work site for health and safety precautions. Consumers may boycott your company's product for some political cause. If you work for an organization that is dependent upon the Congress for its funding, you may well get tied up in the fallout of some amendments arousing controversy on Capitol Hill. The union may have an overzealous shop steward in your work area, whose mission in life is to get that union established.

Whatever the pressures from the outside, pay attention to them and to their ramifications for your operation. The ramifications could simply be financial. Then again, they could be mandates on the composition of the work force you are required to hire, regulations and strict guidelines on whom you can fire for what reasons or whom you can ask to perform extra duties under what circumstances, or shortages due to trade boycotts or international tensions. It is important to know these external influences so that you can relieve yourself of some of the responsibility for what goes on within your unit—there are lots of things you have no control over, but you can expect to know what you might do when they occur.

Internal Pressures

New Pressures

There will always be some pressures generated from within an organization that cannot be foreseen. This set of pressures includes everything from the health of employees and their love lives to the results of rapid growth and unskilled personnel, temporary remodeling, industrial accidents, and other unexpected occurrences. In good planning there is time set aside specifically to deal with such unpredictable events. That time is not always fixed at 9:15, Tuesday morning, but it is helpful in the course of a month to plan two or more hours to deal with the unforeseen.

In the real world you never know what is going to be coming at you, so be resilient and as prepared as you can, even if it just means being ready for the possibility that something can get off track.

A Repetitive Cycle Is No Longer a Novelty or Surprise

Cyclical internal pressures are the ones that allow for more precise anticipation. Anyone who has lived through several yearly cycles in an organization will probably begin to recognize some recurrent phenomena. These phenomena may be the biannual reorganization, spring turnover, the new parking policy which is introduced and ignored, the once-a-year rumors and trauma about personnel cutbacks, the March budget freezes, more guarded behavior in meetings after the Christmas office party, or the new chief's coming on strong in the first meetings and then being absorbed into the bureaucratic way of doing things. These things all happen. Some employees are just more aware that they occur in cycles than others. They learn from their awareness to plan for such eventualities, rather than to be taken unaware by them.

ANTICIPATORY GUIDANCE—THROUGH THE UNFORESEENS

One thing you can do to become more aware and to be able to anticipate what will happen again and again in the organization is to use a skill called "anticipatory guidance." For the supervisor, anticipatory guidance is a more inclusive and extensive activity than strict contingency planning. That is true partly because anticipatory guidance entails some specific activities that are not normally associated with straight contingency planning. In any case, given the full explanation of the use of anticipatory guidance as a planning tool here, you may use the terms interchangeably—keeping in mind that anticipatory guidance is a larger, more comprehensive definition for contingency planning.

Anticipatory guidance is a planning skill, a skill for discovering patterns and cycles within a system or institution in order to predict and plan for a cyclical "given" of that institutional cycle or a predictable element in a particular task for that system. It employs a "feedforward" method, an aspect of contingency planning leading to routinization or the development of standard operating procedures for dealing with repeated situations.

During the Munich Olympics, terrorist activity came as a surprise. However, in the following Montreal Olympics, there were well-rehearsed contingency plans for the possible recurrence of a Munich-type terrorist activity. Once an event has occurred, even though it was not foreseen the first time, it would be negligent, irresponsible, and naive not to anticipate and prepare for the possibility that it could occur again.

Many traffic signs, especially warning signs, have been placed on roads due to an experience with accidents at the spot. "Slow—10 mph on Curve" and "Slippery When Wet" warning signs are the responsibility of the highway department for the driver's safety. One can be held negligent under the law for allowing dangerous or hazardous conditions to exist on his property. Why then are there no such safeguards when the hazards are interpersonal or intra-organizational?

Possibly, no one has stopped long enough to look at it from this perspective, to do the necessary background study and documentation. There are also questions about looking out for number one (me first) and about not being your brother's keeper. However, there is also the responsibility for running a smooth, efficient, functional operation, to reduce stress for yourself and your employees.

For some of us, the question of whether we want to anticipate and guide within our units on the job may turn as much on our philosophy of life as on our perception of supervisory responsibility. If, for example, I believe that it is a dog-eat-dog world and that meeting challenges—no matter how ill prepared I might be—is "good for my character," then it would make sense not to concern myself with employee stress and crisis reduction on the job. Now if your focus is on the results for your unit, irrespective of the "character development" of your employees, you are more likely to focus your energies and the energies of your employees on accomplishment of work tasks. When that requires smoothing out some kinks in the work of your unit, that is the place to begin.

Few people choose to recognize and plan for cyclical contingencies in their organizations. For some, supervising is not a cumulative experience of years of learning; it is a totally brand-new year after year with no carry over from the last. Contingency planning relies on learning from your previous experience.

Anyone who has thrown a party more than once learns to keep a towel where the crowd congregates. The towel is there for *when* someone spills a drink, not *if* someone spills a drink. Likewise, if your focus as a supervisor is on results, then your focus will be on facilitating the foreseeable tasks of your employees.

In no case is anticipatory guidance or contingency planning meant to preclude challenging employees or stretching them through work assignments. It simply means that in whatever you do, you would plan to the extent that you consider predictables—things known to have occurred under like circumstances in the past, things that cannot be considered chance or unlikely occurrences under similar conditions in the future.

DEVELOPING A CONTINGENCY PLAN

Detecting Cyclical Stress Points

If "it" hasn't happened yet, either here or anywhere else, it may be difficult to develop a complete contingency plan for it. You would have to rely on your imagination to foresee the unforeseen. The number of possibilities could be infinite. So it is more useful initially to review what has actually occurred in the past and what is likely or probable to occur again.

For example, when you take a business trip by plane you may pack a carry-on bag just in case your baggage is delayed. There is also a remote possibility that your plane would be hijacked to Cuba, but you wouldn't carry your passport just in case. You make arrangements for possible contingencies, but only those that have a reasonable chance of occurring.

Figure 14 is a format you can use to review your organizational experience to see what is likely or probable to occur again. You will be looking to uncover or discover cyclical or recurrent stresses within your organization. You will do this by reviewing the time, the conditions, and other variables associated with previous organizational experiences.

In English common law, "every dog gets one bite" before the owner is held negligent, hence responsible for damages. The stressful situations you want to detect are the ones that have already bitten your operation. It is time to plan how you will deal with them should they recur.

---

1. Review the past fiscal or calendar year (or go back as many years as you remember clearly). Sketch out, month by month, a list of incidents—especially unanticipated, disruptive stress points or dysfunctional, time-consuming situations—that you or your unit had to deal with, that could occur again, and that you want to anticipate and guide next time.

January: •

            •

            •

            •

February: •

            •

            •

            •

Figure 14. Detecting Cyclical Stress Points to Develop a Contingency Plan

March: •
  •
  •
  •

April: •
  •
  •
  •

May: •
  •
  •
  •

June: •
  •
  •
  •

July: •
  •
  •
  •

August: •
  •
  •
  •

September: •
  •
  •
  •

October: •
  •
  •
  •

Figure 14 (continued).

November: •

                 •

                 •

                 •

December: •

                 •

                 •

                 •

2. Review your notes and check your own experience to determine whether these incidents are recurrent, or are likely to recur in the future. Is there any notable repeated pattern over the yearly cycle you have traced?

POSSIBLE PATTERN	**LIKELY DATES OF REOCCURRENCE**

3. Now arrange the events leading up to these disruptive stress points. Is there a predictable sequence of events?

POSSIBLE SEQUENCE IN STRESS PATTERN	*PERSONNEL INVOLVED*
1.
2.
3.
4.
5.
6.
7.
8.
9.

Figure 14 (continued).

4. Specify the particular disruptive activity below and beside it, note the costs to the organization. What were the outcomes of that incident?

ACTIVITY	*COSTS*	*OUTCOME*

5. What intervention steps might forestall such a recurrence of disruptive stressful activity within your unit in the future? What preventive measures can you delineate in anticipation of such a recurrence?

- _____
- _____
- _____
- _____
- _____

6. What standard operating procedures or routines might you develop to deal with these contingencies?

_____
_____
_____
_____
_____

If possible, work on this activity with others from your organization. You will have additional perspectives on the *generally discernible patterns* in the organization over the yearly cycle, together with the meaning that other employees attribute to these recurrent patterns.

7. What skills would you acquire for yourself and other employees in order to better cope with such disruptive recurrences in the future?

_____
_____
_____
_____
_____
_____

Figure 14 (continued).

Learning Module 14

Performance Appraisal in the Evaluation Conference and Personnel Actions

This module deals with the regular evaluation conference in which you appraise employee performance over the past performance period (usually a full year). I prefer to use the term *evaluation* rather than *performance appraisal*, although the latter term is rapidly becoming more common. *Evaluation* carries the connotation that a broader band of concerns and activities may be dealt with in the conference than strick task performance. However, I have made it sufficiently clear throughout this module that the supervisor's *main* responsibility is evaluating or appraising job performance in that periodic conference.

The first part of the module elaborates the main considerations for the supervisor in preparing for the evaluation conference. The last part describes the various personnel actions that may result from an evaluation conference, together with some ways for dealing with your feelings, particularly if the action is termination.

THE EVALUATION CONFERENCE

The clearest statement to remember about evaluation is that you are appraising job performance, not a person. You are evaluating the performance of an employee who has a specific charge and contract to perform certain tasks and activities.

The evaluation conference generally follows the culmination of tasks over a period of time, usually a year, unless someone is on probationary status and has a shorter performance period.

The evaluation conference should hold no major surprises—particularly for the employee. Specific deficiencies and capabilities would ideally be noted all along in supervisory conferences, which are mini-evaluation conferences, and in the day-to-day coaching that makes up the real life of supervising. At times, though, evaluation conferences have been seen as a time to "sock it to 'em," the result of a large build-up of animosity or frustration, so that employee and supervisor alike may have some apprehension about the conference. With even the subtlest hint of "put down" activity in an evaluation conference, employees will see it as a no-win situation, and just attempt to get past it, to survive.

The evaluation conference can be an immensely supportive time. It can also be a demonstration of supervisory fairness. The focus of the conference can be upon goals set down early in the performance period, including such difficult-to-delineate individual goals as "improve working with the team." By now, you should be able to refer to specific activities or the fulfillment of specific objectives that would support, demonstrate, or give evidence that the designated "improvement" had taken place. Focusing on overall improvement indicates that some attention has been paid to this aspect of employee development (your supervisory responsibility) throughout the year, rather than attending solely to crisis situations and minute deficiencies.

Direct feedback regarding accomplishments and improvement (affirming feedback) as well as deficiencies (corrective feedback) needs to occur if the employee is to benefit from the evaluation conference. That will require some advance preparation by the supervisor to review long-term goals, note specific gains, assess continuing deficiencies, specify corrections in activity, and always keep the focus on job performance rather than on "personality," character, or attitudes.

Job performance is not the only legitimate basis for dealing with an employee in the evaluation conference, however. *Effects on team productivity and morale* are equally important considerations, as are the employee's *contacts with the customers, the community, clients, or other sources of revenue and support for the organization.* All of these are major considerations that properly enter into supervisory and evaluation conferences and may form the basis for a personnel action.

HOW TO DO IT

There are three things you generally line up when making your judgments for an evaluation conference: the position description, employee job performance as noted in your supervisory conference notes, and your expectations. Ideally, your expectations have already come out early enough in the relationship so that they will not be a surprise at this stage. If not, they should be part of planning for next year, not part of assessing the past year.

In terms of the judgments you make and discuss with your employees, be aware of general criteria and specific factors upon which all employees in a similar position will be rated. This offers some comparable objectivity to the process and ensures some fairness.

Emphasize the positive. Dwell more on strengths and specific activities to correct deficiencies, rather than concentrating on shortcomings and deficiencies. Let past failures go. Each of us needs the possibility of failing in order to learn from those mistakes (missed-takes). But do not overlook or bypass recurrent failures or patterns of activity that jeopardize productivity.

Watch out for your own reputation and attitude. The inclination to be tough, even though other supervisors are lenient or even soft on ratings, may be fine as long as your reputation is known and considered along with everything else when considering promotions. However, your employees belong to an organization, not just to your unit. When you leave or they leave, that rating is your legacy that gets carried on and considered along with other more lenient ratings for personnel actions. It is possible that your tough rating will neither spur improvement nor work to the future benefit of the employee. Know what you expect to gain from your evaluation. Know what you and the organization are likely to gain from it.

Be aware that recent incidents can color your view of overall performance. Take a full review of the whole year, not just the past month. Concentrate your observations on the activities that indicate real job-related improvement or development.

Rating all employees alike, whether all high or all low, is a rejection of the evaluation system. You will establish little credibility by simply reacting to the requirement to evaluate. Nor can you just employ personal likes and dislikes. The basis is still job performance.

When you do not take care in evaluation—you miss developing a skill, you mock your relationship with your employees, and you leave your employees no record or resource based on their performance for future promotions, rewards, or transfer.

In preparing your ratings, you may want to compare the performance of employees in similar jobs or consider the employee's performance against some usual level of performance achieved given the length of time on the job. You can often distinguish important differences in performance by comparing employees side-by-side or rating them in terms of historical patterns in similar jobs. However, it is a major failing to compare employees to each other in the conference itself. This not only generates intra-unit competitiveness, but may also seriously flaw any cooperative work relationship or team morale that has developed. More than that, it is a serious breach of confidentiality. The purpose of doing such comparisons at all is to give you added perspective on performance achievements and deficiencies. Since you are to work with each individual employee for that employee's development and performance, you violate your relationship with one employee by invoking the performance of another employee as a basis for comparison. You also invite future comparisons.

The best standard to rate against is the objective performance standard. Rate demonstrated performance and results rather than depend on certain characteristics or attributes or impressions.

LIKE IT OR NOT

The evaluation conference can underscore whatever strengths or weaknesses there are in the ongoing supervisor-subordinate relationship. With it can come discomfort felt by both parties. However, the evaluation conference is a supervisory responsibility, and when it is done appropriately it can be a great boost to the employee, a resource you can offer him.

In focusing on job performance in the conference, be as specific as possible about what is being done well, what specifically needs improvement, and how improvement can be accomplished.

Evaluation conferences may point up specific unit needs for training or individual needs. These might also be organizational needs. So, record them and forward them to the personnel or training office to help identify an organizational need and reinforce support for your unit needs.

Evaluation conferences are seen as a lead-in to personnel actions— raises, tenure, permanent status, promotions, demotions, transfers, and firings. Your ratings on the evaluation form are more permanent than your ongoing supervisory conference notes. The evaluation conference is *the summation of performance for a set period of time, not a running commentary.* Employees should attach importance to evaluation for their future in the organization. It is your responsibility to recognize the importance of your preparation and follow-through on the conference.

PERSPECTIVES ON PERSONNEL ACTIONS

Raises

Any time you have limited resources or incentives for your employees and little real distinction in performance, awards of any kind are going to seem discriminatory. "How come he got a raise and I didn't?" Establish a clear system for awarding these organizational incentives because they are almost always limited. Awarding a raise to someone in the unit without some clear basis in service or performance may be counterproductive and bad for morale, so at least be clear in your ratings, expectations, and conference discussion to help avert disappointment or disruption when some employees get raises and others don't.

Demotions

A demotion may be a career saver when someone is in over his or her level of capability. Rather than register a complete failure in performance, the employee can be demoted to a position he can handle.

Demotions also work for employees who have become disabled or who for some other reason cannot maintain the prior performance or activity level required—for example, the hours someone works can be reduced or job responsibility can be decreased. Demotion in pay scale or to part-time status can be a compassionate way of keeping someone on the payroll who does not qualify for retirement or disability but has an established record with the company and can still perform, though at a lesser level.

Demotions can also be used in cases where performance is just plain deficient. The demotion can be temporary, with reversal of the action dependent on some change in performance by the employee.

Promotions

Use your power to promote advisedly, based on merit. Nothing will kill morale faster than the practice of promoting individuals out of a unit because they never performed but could not be dealt with effectively to improve performance. A promotion should be seen as a rewarding personnel action. As a supervisor, discuss your employees' career plans with them. An ill-advised, untimely promotion or a promotion into the wrong position can deaden an otherwise promising career.

Transfer

In order to forestall dealing with a firing, many supervisors will attempt to transfer out (or promote!) unproductive or disruptive employees. Too often a firing requires so much energy and paperwork that a supervisor will attempt just to get the employee out of his unit. Unfortunately, the employee stays in the organization—and often at a higher, more responsible position—supervising and affecting more employees than before. No one knows exactly how he got there, but he is even more entrenched and obstructive to the organization than before. I recommend against transferring employees whose performance in your unit is deficient unless the transfer position is a clear match for the employee's competence.

Outplacement

Placing the employee in another organization is a current practice in some organizations to lessen the impact of termination on higher level employees. However, even though the professional outplacement personnel may deal smoothly with the employee's grief, anger, and insecurity about the move, other organizations may perceive outplacement as a dumping activity.

Firing

One approach before simply firing the performance-deficient employee is to lay out a series of options that he clearly will choose based upon his performance. To do this, you will have to set feasible, reasonable objectives for improvement in performance with the employee. The result of accomplishing the initial performance improvement objectives would be to pursue a further objective of continuing improvement toward total job responsibility. Deficient performance would drop him into further negotiation about how to get himself back into the job, or one step closer to a clear choice (by his action or inaction) to opt out of the organization. Using this approach makes termination more clearly the employee's choice and option than a "force out" on your part (see Module 15).

Because most supervisors do not know whether they have done *the very best job possible* (no one ever knows that), there is usually some soul searching and apprehension about firing. Not only can the union raise a ruckus, but there are also lawsuits, grievance procedures, and the immediate effect of reduced employee productivity and morale.

What usually happens when firing is a detailed personnel action is the supervisor has to accept the fact that there are rules to be followed. This may necessitate getting briefed by personnel specialists or study the manual on how to carry out this personnel action. The termination procedures in some organizations, for example, require a concerted effort to bring the employee up to an adequate performance level. This might be a ninety-day probationary period, preceded by supervisory conferences to set out a reasonable development plan, and a documented agreement setting forth the goals of the probationary period. However, at the end of this period, if there is no noticeable improvement or other indicators to merit continuation of the employee in his position, then steps are taken to terminate. (Module 15 covers procedures to correct performance, through probation and termination, in more detail.)

DEALING WITH SECOND THOUGHTS

Few people can fire an employee and just forget it. They feel some concern for the employee. There are some second thoughts: "Did I do all I could? Is it my fault?" Consider this: Some employees clearly choose to be fired by becoming unproductive or failing to correct their performance. While they don't really want the job, they also experience some difficulty or fear in leaving the position. So they effectively choose to have someone else make the termination decision. That makes termination a homicide (you did it to me) rather than a suicide (I did it to myself). And the employee does not take direct responsibility from the start. That may be part of why you feel so responsible—the position you are placed in.

Once you have made the determination to sever the employee from the organization, there are two main considerations:

1. How to disengage the employee at the least cost (emotion, finance, or morale) to the organization and the individual.
2. How to heal the organization and deal with your own feelings about executing the termination.

In response to the first consideration, get the employee off the premises as soon as possible. Very few employees can continue on in a position when they have been fired and not spread some dissension among other personnel. They either do it through bitter complaining or through a helpless victimized stance that arouses their colleagues' pity. If you don't get them out quickly, they can poison an entire unit.

Even if you move a terminated employee out quickly, you may have to deal with some anger and insecurity among the employee's colleagues in the unit. When an employee is not productive, most other employees usually know it anyway. Some may put up a protest out a friendship to that employee or out of a sense of defensiveness about their own job security, but deep down they will be glad that you took the action.

Part of the second consideration in a firing is how the other employees will close ranks and continue to work. If you clarify the procedure that was followed—and that will continue to be followed—employees will see they have plenty of recourse, opportunities to correct their performance, should they be called in for similar deficiencies in performance.

Avoid kangaroo court atmospheres in which the ex-employee is discussed and vilified without being there to present a defense. However, if there has been some misinformation spread, especially if spread by the fired employee, then candid (though not confidential) information can and should be presented to clarify the circumstances. Go over the procedure that was followed, giving it in a data-sharing format rather than as a blow-by-blow scenario.

For yourself, make sure that you keep your superiors informed, follow personnel procedures closely, and document your interactions with the employee. You may have some fears of retribution (someone is going to get you or make you pay for this). Once you have done all that you know to do, you will have to accept the limits of your power to change that employee's performance. That was the employee's task.

You may also feel some anger toward the terminated employee for not improving performance, for "making" you fire him. Try thinking about it this way: the employee chose to terminate his employment. If you legitimately attempted to develop and support the employee, you did what you were required to do. When the employee was not fulfilling his specific job responsibility, that responsibility still had to be filled. Now that he is out, you will find someone else to take over his responsibilities.

You may also be angry with the terminated employee for not matching your attempts to help him improve performance. But if you legitimately, and in a skilled way, attempted to develop and support the employee through a specific performance improvement plan, you did what you were required to do.

Now it is left up to you to deal with your feelings. You can feel just as rotten about it as you want to. Or you can realize that terminating employees who choose not to correct performance deficiencies is simply part of your job. You have job slots that must be filled with individuals who will perform the specific duties outlined for them. If an employee continues to fall short in performing these duties, then those duties are not accomplished, to the detriment of the organization—or you or someone else in the unit makes up for the employee's deficiency. Over time, rescue work gets tedious. Your employees deserve the right to focus on the work and tasks *they* were hired to do. You have to keep their responsibilities clear for them and keep them clear of being encumbered by performance-deficient employees.

SUMMARY

Performance appraisal for the periodic evaluation conference goes on throughout the supervisory cycle and throughout the year for each employee. You safeguard your own ability to conduct that conference by following the regimen of regular supervisory conferences, documentation, and employee support throughout the year. Personnel actions are then taken more as foregone conclusions rather than surprise decisions with ill-fated consequences for you.

Learning Module 15

Shaping Up or Shipping Out
the Employee

This learning module is about the procedural aspects of three supervisory operations:

- Supervising the probationary period for new employees.
- Intervening to correct performance.
- Firing or terminating employees.

PROBATION FOR NEW EMPLOYEES

Many supervisors have viewed the probationary period for a new employee as a mild annoyance, too short to check out the employee, or simply a technicality. As a result, supervisors do not take charge of the probationary period, but rather feel victimized or helpless in dealing with "that employee at that time" when there are so many other things to do.

So, how do you check out an employee? How do you tell whether he will learn and do the job? Among the press of daily responsibilities, what criteria can you establish for that time period so that you can make a solid decision?

Many supervisors have learned to their dismay that probation is an important time for further screening and selecting appropriate employees for the unit. They really thought hiring was it. One O.K. is enough. They let a few employees slip through, rubber stamped them "acceptable" for permanent employment, and now are left to deal with them. How those supervisors would like another probationary period now for those employees with the pass/fail choice at the end! Do yourself a favor and plan your probationary period with your new employees. Either way, you and the organization have to live with the consequences of your decision.

Similiar supervisory practices come into any probationary period, although there are special considerations when the employee is new to the organization.

The new employee generally has a probation period of about three months before a decision is made to give that employee permanent status in the organization. Of major importance in that period of time is a determination of what you perceived in the employment interview to be that employee's potential deficits. During the probationary period, you will want to work the employee into the job as fully as possible and help the employee reach full capacity. You will also want to provide the employee with a sufficient challenge on the job to allow that employee to stretch and test his own capability.

Emphasis on the need for shared responsibility with employees begins in the hiring interview, and the necessity for shared responsibility extends through the probationary period. Again, the employee needs to take some choice in the matter of whether he really wants the job, now that he has been hired. He can't always be expected to fully know whether he wants the job when first brought on board. Rather than making the probationary period something to live through, like an extended selection and trial period, the employee can also be counted on to provide his own judgment about his future in that job. He could do his career a great disservice by staying on in a position he does not enjoy or find stimulating. He needs to recognize that possibility early, rather than bluffing his way through and not allowing himself or you, as his supervisor, to explore other career opportunities.

During the probationary period, challenge the employee with some selected, job-related task—one that allows the employee to gain some trust or confidence to accomplish all his job requirements, to act more autonomously, and to carry out a specific assignment on his own. The task ought to be important to the organization. At the same time you will not overburden this new employee with disproportionate responsibility by asking him to do something, such as preparing the budget, that does not allow a margin for error.

If the employee takes the challenge and performs adequately, his performance is a strong indicator of his capacity to do the job, evidence for extending employment beyond the probationary period.

The employee's meeting this sort of challenge is also perceived by others in the unit as that employee's "pulling his weight" or "earning his stripes." For the employee, accepting the challenge and performing responsibly serve as an initiation rite into the unit. So, it is important for you to select or structure some task that will not buckle and frustrate the employee but one that he can undertake and accomplish with more than routine application of his knowledge and skill.

To arrive at the end of a probationary period without having gathered sufficient evidence of the employee's actual performance to make a clear-cut decision is to do yourself, the employee, and the organization a disservice. If you do, you could try for an extension of the probationary period, to gather additional data for the decision to place the employee in permanent status or to terminate him. However, you may be required to make a decision, one way or the other. You may be able to depend on your own intuition about the person's potential and initiative and base your decision to continue employment just on that. I don't recommend it. Unless your intuition is accurate 100 percent of the time—or you are so efficient or underworked that you can carry another job responsibility for someone who does not do his job—you will begin to view the end of probation as an important decision point, the point at which you take the action to place the employee on permanent status or to terminate his employment, based on your observation of actual performance of his job-required activities.

Take the probationary period seriously. Employees you select will not necessarily last because you chose them. You may be investing too much work in developing them when better selection in the first place would forestall such heroics on your part. Letting them go clears the way for better selection next time.

INTERVENTIONS TO CORRECT PERFORMANCE

As a supervisor you have a responsibility to provide guidance and some reasonable means for the employee to establish himself—both during the initial probationary period for new employees and during special probationary periods set up to correct performance after the employee has gained permanent status. The second kind of probation period—to correct performance—can go on and on and may be quite difficult to deal with. Here are some of the main considerations.

Early Indicators Loom Larger with Time

Very few problematic situations on the job arise overnight. They usually evolve over a period of weeks, even months. When you get to the point you sense some situation requires your intervention, you can usually look back in the supervisory relationship and re-discover early indicators, early warning signals that were there all along. Now here you are months—or years—later in a stall pattern with an employee, having to face it all.

Supervisor Paralysis

Some supervisors have a great deal of difficulty in overcoming the inertia of their inaction, their initial decisions not to act up until now. The situation builds up while you reconfirm your worst fears, while you ignore it or wish it would go away. But it doesn't. And you're no dummy. You know what is going on. You simply haven't done anything just yet. Now you have to act.

Supervisors often feel guilty about making an intervention when they have watched the situation build over time. They fear being criticized for their inactivity. "Why didn't you tell me sooner? I would have changed if you had only said something. How was I to know?" or "I don't see what is so different about what I am doing now,"—all dreaded words from employees. Supervisors don't want to be perceived as picking on an employee, either, so they tend to let things slide a little longer. Oh, how you wish that situation would go away!

Intervention Criteria

No matter what the situation, you have to attend to the *timing* of your intervention, the *manner* in which you make your intervention, and the *confidentiality* of the intervention. Timing and manner are matters of discretion, while confidentiality entails respect for the individual's privacy. All these considerations will impact on your relationship with the employee, so you have to find the balance.

Know how you are likely to react to ongoing build-ups of deficient performance. If you tend to build up resentment until you are ready to explode all over the @#$%¢ employee, you should intervene *early* or learn to get your hostility under control.

When you do start to get indicators of a problem or conflict, there may be numerous variables to take into consideration. Knowing when and how to intervene can seem to be a delicate operation. And well it might. For the manner in which you carry out the intervention can facilitate or obstruct further smooth working with the employee. But, unless an employee is particularly "touchy," I advise a direct approach.

BEFORE INTERVENING

To begin with, the more clear you are about what constitutes *adequate job performance*, the more likely you are to be able to diagnose or detect early warning indicators of poor or deficient performance. If you have the "field of play" (the range of task-appropriate activities) marked off in your mind, then you will know when an employee is out of bounds in his activities or when he has his foot on the chalk mark.

Most of us have pretty good crap detectors. We can tell when "things are not right," when we are being conned or led on. The employee who leaps tall buildings in job performance one day is not likely to have to relearn his job the next day. *Yet, some employees claim they can't do what they just did.* Now, there is such a thing as beginner's luck, and only time will tell whether the employee can apply a particular skill over and over again. On the other hand, an employee who can perform a task at will, up to standard, can be considered to have his competence established.

Usually the only reason a proficient employee would not be able to continue already established performance is for lack of practice over a period of time, some organic difficulty such as brain damage or toxic substances or illness, or trauma caused by exteme shock or emotional upset. Otherwise you and the organization should be able to rely on the employee's being able to perform. Then you simply have to retask the employee during times of discrepancies.

First, Intervene "Off the Record"

Initially, most employee interventions are best carried off *informally* and *off the record*, when dealing with suspected or perceived problems. You could be documenting or keeping notes all this time, but those notes should be informal, for your consideration only. Any formal recording of the activities or incidents leading to an early intervention could reflect ill on you or on the employee if there were no basis in fact or if there were an easily correctable situation.

Once you place your observations on file, proceedings begin to have a formal, less retractable air. Make sure that your intervention is based on performance-related activities. Also, follow the documentation procedures required in your organization. Before beginning formal action, develop some alternatives or corrective activities to work on with your employee—something that he can carry out correctly and effectively to remove the cause for intervention.

MAKING THE INTERVENTION

Build a common data base with your discrepant employee. Take time to spell out your concerns. If you saw him at his desk appearing to be napping in the middle of the afternoon when there was a rush order to get out, you might bring it to his attention right away and ask about his health. You may find that the employee has a slipped disk and that his pain pills make him drowsy. Without the pills and a short nap, he could not function at all on the job.

Suppose you are in a conference and find you are meeting direct denial of everything you have observed directly and noted. Long lunches and the odor of alcohol on your employee's breath may have you suspecting a drinking problem interfering with an employee's job performance. Even in the face of denial, you have to confront firmly and not back off unless you receive some reasonable explanation.

Now, if you should find someone asleep at his desk once, and there are no other pressing requirements or immediate ramifications for the unit right now, why not let him sleep? How many of us have sat at our desks just dying for a quick fifteen-minute nap but wouldn't take one because someone might see us? If, on the other hand, you repeatedly find this employee deficient in performance and sleeping also, then you would bring it to his attention. Considering all the relaxation and meditative techniques being practiced widely, it is not safe to assume that someone is not performing just because his eyes are closed.

You can deal with perceived problems both directly and indirectly. Indirectly, you could call a meeting of the unit and talk about the general need for improved performance. However, specific references to particulars (sleeping, for example) in a group setting could result in more embarrassment for some individual employees than would a direct confrontation with you alone. General statements to the unit, when specific individuals are indicated, can invite distrust because of the indirectness of your approach.

Pinpoint Your Interventions

If your concern is with certain individuals, sit down with them and find out what is going on. The leader of a rock band who comes to work tired and listless is allowing his outside activities to affect his work performance. But there may be other considerations you may not know about. For example, he may be going through a divorce and requires additional income to finance the lawyer and to pay child support.

You can't really make a definitive judgment without talking with the employee. The employee should have the opportunity to speak for himself.

Rather than building a case like a lawyer going into court with your employee, voice your concerns and ask for some clarity on things you do not understand (that's right, *do not understand*) about the employee's activities. Give the employee an opportunity to clear up your confusion.

Be aware that as you delay an intervention, there is a point at which you are no longer withholding acting for lack of data, but you are withholding for lack of initiative or for a time for intervening. When you finally have sufficient cause from your side to intervene, you may tend to assume that any further discrepancy in performance is intentional. After all, you know about it; it is obvious to you; the employee must be doing it on purpose; and your attributing malice to the employee will certainly come across in your approach to the employee. Act as soon as you reasonably can.

There is also sometimes a tendency to isolate or avoid direct contact with the employee if you are busily substantiating your observations of discrepant performance. However, you can lose perspective when you concentrate more on the intervention and how well you are going to do it than on your supervisory duties of guiding employee performance. You may also lose sight of the performance outcome for the employee and the relationship with the employee.

You have a continuing responsibility to participate in two-way job related communication with your employee. So spend less time hovering and observing and more time communicating with your employee. The format in Figure 15 is offered as a guide for those situations when you want to prepare for an intervention.

FIRING/TERMINATING THE EMPLOYEE

There are employees who will go through the initial probationary period with flying colors and then suddenly burn out or become a walking disaster area on the job. Whatever the sequence of circumstances, there are some employees who have been through probation, later required supervisory interventions to correct performance, and never quite got up to an acceptable production level. Meanwhile, you have continued to be supportive.

In cases like that, spot interventions are no longer a useful means to deal with the employee. So you begin to set up consequences for various performance levels. Through establishing performance consequences, you continue to engage the employee to share responsibility for the choice of continuing on the job or of terminating his employment. This approach may occur under the aegis of an official probationary period imposed to correct performance, or it may occur in the normal flow of supervisory conferences.

Serving Notice

When termination begins to loom more probable as a consequence of continued unproductive employee activity, then that possibility needs to be stated to the employee and documented. In fact, you will want to document the basis for your actions and your observations throughout this process. Part of your documentation will include sending follow-up memos to the employee after conferences or to record observations. You also need to record supervisory conferences in detail. Get it all in writing.

What do you consider to be the most difficult supervisory situation for you at the present time, i.e., one involving an employee? "Most difficult" will be different for each supervisor: difficulties could include morale, hygiene, absenteeism, fallen productivity, obnoxious activities, tardiness, depression, explosive temper, dependent activities, resistance, meddling, and so on.

Once you have determined which employee situation you want to work on, begin to gather and organize some further data about that employee situation.

Describe the employee's current job responsibility:

What is the basis upon which the employee was first hired?

Can you update or make current the employee's original job description?

What results are expected, required, contracted for with this employee?

•

•

•

•

To what extent have those results been made explicit with this employee, i.e., written out, worked into objectives, or spelled out in terms of specific tasks and activities?

•

•

•

What is the degree of control that this employee exercises or is capable of exercising over these work outputs? (Someone in a highly interdependent work situation may depend on others.)

What specific tasks and activities are required of this employee in order to get the assigned results?

How does the employee perceive "his" difficulty? (Ask him!)

Once you have agreed upon some specific deficiencies, or tasks to be accomplished, how can you anticipate and prevent further shortfalls in performance by this employee?

Figure 15. A Guide for Preparing a Supervisory Intervention

Now, the way you get the employee to take responsibility for choosing in or out, continuation or termination, is to specify a range of performance consequences that are time framed and dependent upon specific activities. Up until a set cut-off date, the employee can still qualify for continued employment by achieving certain performance quotas or standards. At each point along the way the employee can still regain his position by attaining a specific performance level. However, failure to perform adequately will have specified consequences for the employee, which will be clearly spelled out in the "performance-consequences" statement. During the time period allowed for remedial work for the employee, the supervisor will continue to guide, to provide support and encouragement to the employee to bring him back on line. Once several time-framed choice points are passed or a certain performance level is lost (your option), the employee may be beyond recall. In effect, the employee—either by his inaction or his deficient or discrepant performance—chooses a line of consequences that leads ultimately to termination.

Here's an example of how it would look for a three-month period with the performance level communicated in a prior conference between supervisor and employee.

Performance-Consequences Statement

1. If employee succeeds in reaching and maintaining an average production level of 15 gastors per week for one month, he will be returned to full employment status for as long as he maintains that average. Any future decline in production would place the employee again on this performance level regimen.

2. The employee has a three-month period, beginning April 1 and ending July 1, to produce up to the 15-gastor-a-week average over a month period, without altering the state of probation for termination considerations. However, by not accomplishing the 15-per-week average by July 1, the employee will be choosing to vacate his position through continued deficient production.

3. If the employee produces less than an average of 10 defect-free gastors per week over the period of a month in the given time period, the employee by his lack of productivity chooses to vacate his position.

Statements 1 and 2 above may be sufficient for your employee situation. Your employee will then have three months within which to establish his production average and regain employment.

However, if your unit can no longer afford defective products or simply must boost production, you can establish a minimum average that your employee must maintain even while on probation or be terminated immediately. The employee then frees up the job position for someone else to attempt that production level. There would be no continuing trial period if the employee falls below that standard.

Statement 1 has an addenda statement that includes maintaining a level of performance once probation has ended and the employee has achieved the fifteen-gastor-a-week level. The continuing production level helps to ensure that the employee will not just slump once probation is over or the pressure of that time period is over. You thus avert a situation where the employee meets the challenge of the quota set during probation then promptly slacks off to preprobation production levels, thereby setting off the entire process as if it had never occurred.

SUMMARY

Through your use of the performance-consequences approach advocated here, the employee continues to share responsibility with you and the organization for his continued presence in the job position. Shared responsibility between supervisor and employee through the supervisory cycle, from hiring through termination, has been emphasized throughout this book. The employee has to be engaged as an active participant in those parts of the supervisory cycle that affect him, his job performance, and productivity. The performance-consequence regimen provides a method of involving the employee in taking responsibility for his termination of the job position through maintaining performance standards that must be met over a set time period and then maintained in the future.

Learning Module 16

Personal Realities in Supervising

This module is about some of the personal realities of supervising—because supervisors are people, too, and much of what they do and the choices they make originate from personal needs, wants, and preferences. Throughout this book, I have emphasized appropriate, effective, classically correct supervisory practices to use in working with your employees. At the same time I realize that in the "real world" personal factors enter the work place. This module points up some of the down-to-earth issues on the personal side of the supervisor-employee relationship—from choosing to work together through the decision to work apart or terminate employment. I offer some ways of incorporating some of these personal considerations into your supervisory practice so as to reduce stress and harmful outcomes for you, the employee, the unit, and the organization.

CHOOSING TO WORK TOGETHER: FOLLOWING FEELINGS

In Part I we made the point that you need not necessarily *like* someone in order to work with them, you only have to be compatible in working with them—so where does personal choice enter into the working relationship?

Consider the words of the supervisor who, after interviewing and comparing the qualifications of various job applicants, came down to some more immediately and personally sensed criteria. "I feel I can really work with two of them, and the other three would be hit or miss," he said. The selection process was narrowing to some personal gut reactions—liking and willingness. Our choices are often prompted by some interpersonal attraction, and some intangible sense about people plays into much of what we do. Rather than wait for a scientific analysis, we make some decisions based partly on this kind of hunch.

Over time you will learn more about your hunches as you test them against the consequences of your decisions. Meanwhile, take note of these decisions and your basis for them. Your decisions and their consequences will constitute some of the growing wealth of experience and wisdom you bring to bear on future decisions.

Is It "Who You Know, Not What"?

Personal preferences will enter into your decisions to fill unit positions. We tend to choose people we like or feel good about, even sometimes when experience has shown these reactions to be disastrous criteria for work relationships.

Preferences and feelings emerge from numerous sources, from experience, prejudice, similarity, projections, and out of one's own stage in the life cycle. Kindred spirits seek one another. For example, most people like to teach. And many young people want a mentor, someone to serve as a role model and to show them the ropes. That will suit some supervisors just fine. In fact, some will prefer an inexperienced employee over an experienced one, an understudy over a star.

Supervisors meet personal needs in choosing employees (and in transferring or terminating them). The main point here is that even though care is taken in setting up organizational procedures to assure objectivity and fairness in the competition for positions and promotions, personal feelings, attractions, and preferences will often be the actual critiera for some choices. And those "soft" criteria are hard to document.

You won't find "soft" criteria in the personnel policies or in the selection-procedures manual, and supervisors rarely mention them as a formal rationale for a selection decision. The use of these criteria is just one of the political realities of organizational life, one that has probably affected you already in many ways. Just be aware of this reality as you hire and supervise. Work, policy, and regulations still count. But learn to recognize also the influence personal feelings have in your choices and decisions.

TENTATIVENESS IN WORKING TOGETHER

In certain parts of the world there is such a high infant mortality rate that parents seem almost indifferent toward their newborn infants. Because sometimes as few as one in four children survive past age five, parents tend to hold back any emotional investment in their new child until the danger period passes. In organizations where there is a trial period for new employees, or a probationary period for discrepant employees, the supervisory relationship may carry a similar sense of suspension of investment. It is difficult to deal directly and effectively when the relationship is in "limbo."

Each of us likes to make an investment of time and energy that pays off. If you are dealing with someone whose future with the organization is tenuous, it may be more difficult to provide your part of the support and guidance required to help the employee out. The tendency to hold back just a little is usually there, and that may create more hesitancy on the part of the employee to do his or her best. You tend to stimulate each other in a rising spiral if there is the right mix of energy, skill, and activity. However, a mix of hesitation, doubt, deficiency, and passivity creates a downward spiral of energy and job performance.

The investment I am talking about is not necessarily a plan for employee development during the probationary period, which arises out of supervisory conferences. I mean an investment of a more personal nature, one that concerns *your willingness* to be present more frequently, to provide feedback and encouragement. If you consider the employee a loss, then your lack of willingness is a foregone conclusion. Not much of your inner reaction can be documented. But it can make the difference between the employee's staying on, if he has the willingness and capability, and the employee's being terminated or transferred.

You may want to take a wait-and-see attitude. But if you wait for the employee to "really demonstrate" that he wants the job, you may wait a long time. You will have to gauge your own interventions and determine whether you are making a good-faith effort with the employee. The employee is not like the stray dog that followed you home when you were a kid. Then all you had to do was get your parents' approval to keep him. Now you must take a more active overall role—investing guidance and support—so that you can "keep" the employee. The decision and the required action are yours to effect, as long as the employee follows a program of improving performance. No one is looking over your shoulder parentally, poised to take the decision away from you. At the same time, you will have a continuing relationship with this employee if he stays. You have to consider the consequences of "keeping him." Like the stray dog that has to be fed, this employee is going to be part of your ongoing responsibility—for support, guidance, and getting results.

You will also have to accept the limits of your ability to "change" the employee. Changes on the job in the interest of unit functioning and performance involve changes in *activities*, not in the employee himself. And the employee has the choice to work in and toward those activities or not to.

CHOOSING TO WORK APART
(THINGS YOUR MANUAL NEVER TOLD YOU!)

One of the solutions most frequently heard from supervisors discussing employees who are not performing well is, "I'll fire the blank-blank-blank!" That, of course, is the statement of an aroused, frustrated, and often untrained supervisor who does not know what recourses he or she has for helping the employee become productive.

On the other hand, consider this personal reality: *there are some people with whom you will just not work.* For whatever reason, you have already made up your mind to fire, separate, or transfer. "It's me or him!" The only thing that remains is the opportunity for you to do so. I am not going to preach from behind the established guidelines and pronounce this reality despicable. It just happens to be the way it is sometimes. However, you can accomplish the personnel action in an inefficient or despicable manner. That I will preach about, a bit.

Whatever you choose to do, you already know to look at the likely consequences. The main point is to know what you are doing. If you are really out to get someone (and it happens in the best of organizations, with the firmest personnel policies and guidelines) *know what you are doing!* Most of your colleagues and the target employee will know what you are doing anyway. After a while, in any organization, one learns to read the writing on the wall. As soon as a few test predictions come true, your employees will be placing bets on your actions. You, too, may as well be aware of what you are doing.

If you squint your eyes and become mean and determined about getting rid of the employee, you may be doing yourself as well as the employee a disservice. If you are in a situation in which your choice is being guided by personal antipathy rather than work deficiency, look at your options. If your objective is to "work apart" from the employee, then you can neutralize your animosity. There is no reason to limit the employee's options outside your unit. Engage in an active pursuit of options for the employee. At least here you can adopt a professional supervisory stance by helping that employee secure the best career alternative outside your unit.

Whenever possible, minimize the impact of your personal feelings on your supervisory duties. On those occasions when you simply cannot manage to do so, take responsibility for your feelings and work toward a resolution that does the least damage to you, your employee, and the unit.

Turkey Trots

Another basis for easing someone out is poor work performance. Although deficient performance can be readily documented, some organizations do not provide ready recourse—that is, reasonable firing procedures—to help you expedite removing the "turkey" from your unit or the organization. So you are left to your own devices, and that can set you up for a guilt trip and even for recriminations from management.

Most supervisors do not want an irretrievably deficient employee to remain in their unit. The lazy way of handling the situation is to simply let it go on while you take out your frustrations on the employee in little aggravating ways—giving him the worst assignments, checking up on him constantly, making disparaging remarks to other employees. In other words, making the employee so uncomfortable he'll want to leave. We all recognize that as an immature way of treating someone. But equally important, it is not easy to neutralize someone by just putting them off in a corner. Nor is it easy to avoid getting caught in the guilt that accompanies treating someone poorly. So the next move is to put them out.

You will then have to deal with any negative feelings surrounding your own decision as far as the recommendation you provide, any promotion you might give for the transfer, the nudging you engage in. If you oversell the employee, you have the employee's new supervisor to deal with. On the other hand, if you are overly candid, there might not be any takers. You have to moderate your sales pitch or chance making real enemies—plus the potential for retaliation within the organization increases when you deal someone a "bad card."

In a way it is like trying to unload an automobile that's proved to be a lemon. You keep investing in it, hoping it will operate efficiently, but it keeps needing repairs. Even as you unload it, there is still the thinnest shred of hope that it will operate well. But there is also a grave doubt overall. And the grave doubt can shroud you as you unload it. Sad in the case of a used car as well as a used employee. Buyer beware—supervisor beware!

If you modulate the way you "advertise" the employee for a different position and let the employee handle getting the new position, you may even gain some sympathy from the new supervisor for "what you have put up with."

Termination for Due Cause

There are cases of deficient employee performance that clearly merit termination. You may even have the documentation and organizational procedures and support to back you up. So you proceed. But there will probably be some lingering feelings for you to deal with.

"Survivor" syndrome gnaws at people who have lived through airplane crashes in which others have died. They see death as a punishment and sense that they have only temporarily been spared this punishment. This can set up a tension within themselves about when their turn will come. When you pull the strings or put through the personnel action forms to initiate a termination, there is a sense of connectedness, a there-but-for-the-grace-of-God-go-I empathy or identification. We get a sense of our own mortality and limited control over our own lives.

Another possible reverberation in the personal reality of terminating an employee—even when substantiated by repeated performance deficiency and unwillingness to improve—is very similar to the guide associated with having someone close commit suicide. It is easy to punish oneself with self-recriminations: "Surely I could have done more . . . ." Lest you punish yourself the same way when you terminate an employee, remember, first of all, some employees are just flat in the wrong job. They don't want it. It isn't them. But there they are. They chose in. Now how do they get out gracefully?

Too few employees acknowledge their unfortunate choice and correct it with the excellent choice of terminating in that position. Too many hang around, doing themselves and everyone else a disservice by their inactivity. And a poor supervisor will carry them along with gritted teeth.

Other malsuited employees will foul out. They will commit so many notable, extraordinary, and exceptional errors that red flags will go up and they will be ousted. It's a dramatic way to go, and it requires some determination to self-program their demise this way. Other times those gross errors come as major blips in an otherwise normal job performance profile, but they all add up to "justifiable" termination.

Finally, the cautious passive employee may not draw attention by extraordinary acts or bad performance, but by inactivity: With a deadline at 4 o'clock, you walk in at 2:15 to find the employee asleep, head on his desk. There may be an accumulation of little misdeeds (suicides), but you are the one who has to keep track, then make the decision. Which is the straw that breaks your back? When do enough misdeeds stack up to due cause for termination or firing?

The worst part of firing the passive, inactive, undramatic employee is that you are being used. You are being required to read the signals and call deficient performance to the employee's attention. You end up having to make a decision to fire based on bits and pieces of poor performance—worse, based on that employee's covert or implicit decision to get fired—but all the responsibility is on you. It is likely that a supervisor would feel some outrage at being used in this way. One would like to kick the employee's tail "to get him to take responsibility for himself." And, indeed, if you do not have a clear idea of the tasks or range of activities that you supervise for that particular employee, you may involve yourself much more from a personal or parental basis.

If you are going to supervise, you are probably going to continually confront your own outrage that some employees do not take more direct responsibility for themselves. Most of us avoid taking responsibility as long as we can find someone else to foist it off on. There may be some ways in which you are subtly taking on responsibility for employees. You will continue to confront some of these issues as long as you deal with individuals, whether as employees, superiors, or peers.

But the disgust in the case of the employee who would not perform and draws a termination action from you gouges you from two sides: the employee's reluctance to act and so suiciding out of the job position, plus your unwilling complicity to "pull the trigger," which becomes necessary after deficits accumulate. If you dramatize the situation in personal terms, you can depress yourself. If you keep it in terms of job responsibility, tasks performed, and so on, you should be able to maintain your peace of mind.

SUMMARY

This module has emphasized some of the "feeling side" of supervising. It recognizes that, irrespective of the most tightly drawn personnel policies and practices, the factors of personal attraction, wants, and needs tend to enter into supervisory choices, activities, and interactions with employees. You have seen some of the down-to-earth issues on the personal side of the supervisor-employee relationship—from choosing to work together through the realization of choosing to work apart or terminate employment. If you gain nothing else from this module, my hope is that you recognize and take responsibility for your own feelings and activities as you supervise, rather than denying them as inappropriate. Know what you do and choose what you do wisely.

Status Deprivation: Dealing with the Passed Over, Downgraded, Underemployed, Undercompensated, or "Bumped" Employee

There are many sources of job dissatisfaction. So many, in fact, supervisors sometimes feel they do little else than deal with those employee dissatisfactions that can linger and disrupt unit morale and productivity.

For new and experienced supervisors alike, the most disconcerting expressions of employee dissatisfaction often have some direct connection with a change (usually a loss) of status. Since "status" is the equivalent of self-worth or self-respect for many employees, employee dissatisfaction around issues of status can be particularly intense and complex. You have to be aware of some of the more subtle as well as the more obvious signals of change in status, for status loss is not always readily apparent to the supervisor or other observers. Some of the more typical occasions that involve status loss are when an employee has been passed over for promotion, an employee is hired into a position that does not employ his full capabilities, an employee is not compensated for additional work, or an employee is downgraded. This module lays out a series of supervisory activities which seem to be best summarized under the term *status deprivation*. If you haven't experienced it directly, you probably will have employees who will.

WHAT MAKES FOR STATUS ON THE JOB?

Ask your employees what constitutes status on the job to them. Their responses will give you some idea of what they value on the job, what serve as incentives for them. You could also turn this information into a check list of indicators to help spot when and under what circumstances your employees may feel deprived of status.

Status deprivation typically occurs when an individual has already attained what he defines as a high position or status and then loses it or when an individual has set his expectations on surpassing a specific level of status at a particular time and yet finds himself at the same status once the particular time for advancement has passed.

What usually follows an actual or perceived deprivation of status is that the employee goes through some of the phases of the process of loss and grieving described in Part I. What also follows with some employees is a more serious manifestation of status deprivation—they either quit or seriously curtail their job performance. In addition, an employee experiencing status deprivation might be openly hostile toward authority or toward those reputedly responsible for his lower status position. There is usually blame placed: "someone" is holding him back. Generally, having someone in the unit who is going through this process will affect the morale of the unit. If the individual makes this behavior a chosen or persistent way of dealing with you or with the organization, some action has to be taken.

WHAT HAPPENS—AND WHAT TO DO

Unless you are in the midst of some stressful and difficult work within your unit, it is best to give the grieving employee some time to work through the process of loss resulting from perceived status deprivation. You can even be supportive if you know what he is going through. However, after about six weeks—assuming that the employee's expectations were reasonable or the competition for promotion was a close and hard-fought battle, it is time for the employee to resume facing the responsibilities of his current job.

Here are some points to consider in working with the employee experiencing status deprivation.

Still Responsible

The employee is still responsible for the fulfillment of the job performance requirements of his present position. While there might be some slack taken up by other members of the unit while an employee is grieving his loss, there is a point beyond which understanding and compassion are being stretched at the expense of the morale and energy of the unit. In addition, there is a reasonable and prudent time period within which most personnel should have worked through their grief.

Taking Responsibility for Being at the Work Site

In some cases, status-deprived employees have shown such despondency and depression at the work site that supervisors have considered themselves responsible and allowed them to sit and ruminate. However, there are some particulars which most supervisors do not consider.

That employee, no matter how despondent, somehow got dressed this morning. He also got his body to the work site and found his way to his desk or work station. Now, that either took some pretty capable and strong hands to guide him through the process—or he made all those choices by himself. Now he stands or sits there and acts as though he can't do anything. How did he get here in the first place? There are some bits of reality he is contradicting just by being here in the first place.

You Make Your Own Reality

On occasion more than one employee may be disappointed at being passed over for promotion. One may adjust to the loss within a relatively short time with a shrug of the shoulders and an acceptance of the decision. The other may assign much more meaning to the fact he was not selected. At some point he has to realize that he has constructed his own meaning out of the situation.

Some employees experiencing status deprivation in this way tend to box themselves into the situation by believing that the organization or certain individuals insulted or demeaned them. "Because he got the promotion and I didn't, I'm feeling insulted." The employee is so despondent over his loss that he begins to assign to the work site the power to degrade him, just by virtue of his being there. Inside his head the conversation goes something like "The fact I am here is an indignity. Sitting here in a job I should have already surpassed is an insult to me. This place and this organization are both insulting to me." So he makes the work site an unbearable and degrading place for him to be. Fortunately, he can also remove the stigma from his being there, but he has to come to terms with the facts he is there by choice and he has made his continuation on that job a kind of punishment for himself.

I'm Going to Make You All Suffer

Some employees are so angry about their situation that they are determined to self-destruct and to take the unit or organization down with them. Often their rage leaves them very shortsighted and self-defeating. As a supervisor, you may have to face that employee with the likely consequences of his behavior.

Incidentally, most employees know what minimum performance level is required and they may just maintain it and leave you knowing that they will do no more. The following may apply to them too.

Career Consequences

An employee raging over status deprivation may not care to admit he is being difficult or destructive. But he may listen to the probable consequences for his career, or the decreased likelihood of getting that promotion the next time one comes open. He needs to take responsibility for his own behavior now, and also put himself in perspective with regard to his career. "If you continue at your present low level of performance, and continue to bad mouth the manager and lower unit morale, your next performance report will decrease your chances of getting a promotion," is one approach the supervisor could take.

An employee who is still bent on taking the organization down with him as revenge for being slighted may also have to be faced with possible termination. "If you choose to continue on without performing your job functions, then you are effectively deciding that you will not fulfill your contractual responsibility to the organization. We need someone to fill those functions, so we will have to let you go and hire someone who will perform those functions." In that way, the employee may begin to concentrate on the consequences of his current activities rather than on the revenge he can wreak on the organization.

When *You* Got the Promotion

If one of the conditions of *your* promotion was that others were competing for the same position, you may have to deal with this type of situation as a new supervisor at a more highly charged level. You got the job that someone else was counting on. Now he wants to get you.

For some employees, it will be difficult to continue on in the unit where not getting the promotion to your job feels like a daily slap in the face. So, one thing you can do with them, besides understanding what they are putting themselves through, is to work with them to help them get either promoted or transferred. Try a line of reasoning like this: "While you are still in this unit, let's work together so that you can increase your chances of getting promoted. Just because you were passed over once, does not mean that that was a final judgment. Let's work even more closely so that you are assured that every aspect of your career is developing as fully as possible on this job."

REALITY MAY BE A CLEANSER

Many persons passed over for promotion, when they fully expected to be chosen, have been the unfortunate victims of "kind" evaluations throughout their careers. They should be indignant that they were never told about their deficiencies and were not given the chance to make the necessary adjustments or corrections. However, the reality up to now is that the record shows they did "just fine" or "satisfactory" or some other innocuous term. Now this person is sitting in front of you, indignant at being passed over for a position he thought he deserved and no one else ever thought he stood a chance for. The record reads one way, but common knowledge in the organization says this employee is a loner, someone who could not work effectively with a group of employees. Do you tell him?

The supervisor holds the key to how much job-related, off-the-record information will be dealt with and corrected. At the very least, if the unwritten comments about this employee within the organization have some merit, the employee should acknowledge some part of them when told. If the comments do not fit, then he ought to have the right of rebuttal and explanation. He would get neither opportunity if he does not know what is being said about him. To withhold such information is also detrimental to his career development and could conceivably be held as a point of contention in a grievance against the supervisor or the organization.

Frequently an employee reacts to being leveled with by recognizing and appreciating the supervisor's candor, even though he may not like what he hears at the time. As the supervisor you need to remember that you did not make all those original observations, and saying does not make it so. Even if your observations are accurate, the fact that you make the statements is simply a reflection of the employee's activities, not a controlling factor. It is the employee who is the source of the observation. And observations are just that. What is important is whether they are useful in improving the job-related activities of the employee, or in providing the employee with a more accurate perspective to understand how he is viewed within the organization.

It is entirely possible that an employee will choose to transfer out of a unit or organization after getting clear feedback. That should be his prerogative, rather than suffer a blocked career. An individual may have a difficult time changing in the midst of other employees who were not accepting of his old behavior. The information that his career within the unit or organization is at a dead end provides the employee with options he might not consider otherwise and gives him a basis for choice.

If promotion is not likely for this employee regardless of any conceivable effort by him, it may remove a lot of stress for him to know that. Some individuals may not have sufficient skill developed to handle a promotion. They may be semiliterate or simply lack crucial interpersonal skills, yet they plug away year after year and expect to land a promotion. You are not being fair to the employee—or to the ongoing interests of your unit—if you allow him to work with the motivation that arises from the illusion that he will eventually be tapped for promotion. He would probably work as well and with less stress to just receive support for his current work with the recognition that his current position was as high as he could possibly go in the unit or organization.

SUMMARY

Some points to remember in dealing with an employee undergoing status deprivation are the following:

- Allow time for the employee to deal with his own loss or grieving process—sometimes about six weeks.
- Confront the employee only if there is an asserted stance to maintain his despondent state or to harm the organization or if he is sabotaging the operation.
- The employee is still responsible for his job performance even though you may tolerate some short-term deficiencies.
- The employee chooses to continue coming to work but has a responsibility that exceeds just showing up: job performance at former production or output levels can be expected and recorded in supervisory reports, unless there are mitigating circumstances.

Learning Module 18

Dealing with the Violent Employee: You Have Rights To Exercise

Some of the more difficult issues for most personnel to deal with, especially when they are in the subordinate position, revolve around rights! For some reason, in attempts to "do the right thing" and "follow all the rules," there is sometimes a tendency to tolerate too much on the job. Once this tolerance gets established in the work place, practiced and reinforced through the acquiescence and complacency of other personnel, it becomes more difficult to dislodge.

In some operations it is not unusual to find more than petty bickering going on between personnel at various levels, and some bickering leads to more than idle threats. There may even be some direct confrontation. For example, one employee confronts another with an ice pick and threatens to gouge his eyes out. Meanwhile, the supervisor of these employees may wonder what action to take under such unusual circumstances. The higher he goes for a response to find out what action is allowable or advised, the more distant he gets from the initial threat. Often administration will consider the situation in all coolness and recommend that nothing be done. "Let's wait and see." Meanwhile, the threatened employee is waiting.

If a threat of that nature occurred out on the street, it would result in arrest for assault with a deadly weapon. Some supervisors have attempted to deal with such conduct through the personnel manual, when in fact the employee's action is a flagrant and open violation of the law. This is no fraternity bash where "boys will be boys," and felonies are reduced to misdemeanors and misdemeanors reduced to a warning. Here individuals' lives are at stake, and there are laws to protect citizens.

Yet, somehow in-house authority takes precedence and there is a failure to invoke one's rights as a citizen. There is a loss of perspective. It is almost as if what goes on on the job falls under a whole different set of rules, which have to be dealt with in-house (in the family) and not by civil authorities. Yet some activities are beyond the responsibility of the supervisor. To say it another way, the supervisor cannot be responsible for the activities of the violent employee. The violent employee puts himself beyond the in-house capability of the organization when his actions are criminal.

There will be operations in which the surrounding community and organization culture will tolerate a wider range of activity than is normal in the rest of society. As a supervisor, you will have to determine what that range of tolerance is, so that your intervention is not perceived as officious or meddlesome. Meanwhile, you have a job to do, and there is no reason that you should subject yourself to any abuse in your position as supervisor. Nor is there any reason that you should allow one member of your unit to intimidate other employees who are then reluctant to report the intimidator.

When you or one of your employees is seriously threatened with physical violence by an employee in your organization, it is your business to determine your course of action. The legal route is the one you have paid for with your taxes, the protection that is set up for such occasions.

Sheltering an employee who engages in violent or bizarre activities within an organization can be a disservice to the employee, to his colleagues, and to the organization. While the organization withstands the tensions and results of his deviance, the employee is not being put in touch with community resources set up specifically to deal with such activities, nor is the employee placed in a position to have to deal with the consequences of his own actions. It is not the responsibility of the supervisor to indulge criminal or dangerous behavior, nor is it the responsibility of the supervisor to rehabilitate the employee single-handedly. Community resources exist for that purpose. It is the supervisor's responsibility to provide the employee with information on these resources or to refer him to someone who can provide that information.

Employees have the right to work in a safe environment. In some cases, when one employee invokes violence or a threat of violence to intimidate another, it is an either/or situation. *Either* the employee is dangerous to others and to himself, in which case he should not be continuing on the job without treatment (which could come from an in-house counselor or from outside resources), *or* the employee is just bluffing and represents no real immediate threat.

If the employee is just bluffing, his conduct is still threatening and disruptive, and that employee should be confronted with appropriate services to determine his fitness for duty. He should also face the consequences of his activities. If he is capable of continuing on the job, his referral for diagnosis and for services recognizes that his activities are not tolerated and do have consequences for him. He then has to own up to and deal with those consequences.

Some supervisors hesitate to act, fearing retaliation from the disruptive or violent employee. This only compounds the problem, with you and other employees intimidated. If the employee threat is substantial enough to seek outside intervention, it has to be affecting production in your unit or team morale. If the threat is not substantial, you should discuss his conduct with him in a private conference.

Most communities maintain counseling services and alcohol-detoxification and drug-abuse treatment centers. Familiarize yourself with your organization's procedures for dealing with employees who have such problems affecting job performance and with the resources in your community. Remember:

● You do not give up any of your rights when you contract for employment or become a supervisor with an organization. If anything, your rights should become more specific.

● You retain your rights to protection under federal, state, and local laws, even while you follow the particular policies and regulations of your organization.

● You continue to have responsibility for yourself even while you are an employee of an organization.

● Any action you take while a member of an organization may reflect on that organization's interface with the community or on team morale within the organization. It is appropriate to inform and involve other responsible personnel of the organization when considering a particular civil or criminal charge against another employee. However, discretion and the stress of the situation may require that immediate action be taken without consultation.

● You have rights as a supervisor and as an employee!

Learning Module 19

Some More Human Touches

Up to now, I have attempted to spell out effective ways of working with your employees using appropriate, recognized, classically correct supervisory procedures. I continue to endorse those procedures and recommend you use them. At the same time, I realize that the "real world" of many organizations lacks a certain humanness, so in this module I suggest and endorse some additions to your practices to improve the climate and results of your supervision.

Celebrating, giving affirming feedback, and developing supportive relationships are each distinct and important "personal" contributions supervisors can make to the morale and productivity of a work unit, even an entire organization. When you engage in these activities, you add a strong morale boost to individuals and teams, with broader impact likely—most of it highly profitable and very inexpensive!

CELEBRATING—WHEN THINGS GO WELL

The gold watch at the end of thirty years of service need not be the only mileage marker to celebrate in an organization. Nor does the birthday party have to be the only reason that the unit can get together for a less formal session. Plan to recognize other achievements and to celebrate when things go well in your unit.

Celebration marks an event—a project completion, a passage, an accomplishment—with public recognition. It is important to reinforce teamwork. It brings closure to a major effort, caps the achievement of a goal. By marking the achievement by convening participants and making special acknowledgements, you signal the termination of that particular work thrust. It helps people to complete that phase of their work, to create their own payoffs for other participants through recapping their efforts (also stories) to mark the finale of that particular group composed for that objective. Once closure is achieved, they can then move on.

Celebration is a time to enjoy. After all, the job has been done. Something must have fallen into place! What went well? Rather than having to be constantly task-oriented, moving, pushing, achievement-bound, we also need to have a time to admire our accomplishments, to share our satisfactions with others, especially those with whom we worked. "Smell the roses" before moving on: note your own strengths and the strengths of your employees. Be aware of your and your employees' very human need to mark important moments in organizational life.

You won't find much in the personnel manuals about celebrating. It is something you do because it makes sense and it works. If it is not done at the work place, small groups go off on their own to celebrate. You lose the team sense, the interaction of the situation. It's a little like not getting everyone's glass clinked when someone makes a toast. You experience the impulse to stretch a little farther and touch that last glass until everyone is connected.

When groups splinter and take their energy away from the group—say, to go out to a tavern after work—you are missing an opportunity for group celebration and closure, failing to catch the energy that could be directed toward an internal celebration, toward a sense of team unity and team accomplishment. You leave the sense that you are "all work and no play." Celebrating is time to take care of team maintenance needs, rather than just pushing on to the next project. It is an important moment for the supervisor, especially the supervisor who would lead.

Determine when you can next celebrate with your unit. Some organizations have banquets, pot luck lunches, picnics, take over an amusement park for employees and families, have a night out at the ball park. However, the more personal approach sets out a time to celebrate to correspond with some achievement of the unit, or of some individual employee within it.

AFFIRMING FEEDBACK: ALSO A SUPERVISORY RESPONSIBILITY

Affirming feedback promotes supervisor-employee support and employee development (see Module 3). As a supervisory responsibility, affirming feedback buttresses the ongoing work of the unit and provides recognition and incentive for individual accomplishments and contributions to the unit's functioning. Affirming feedback is also a nice thing to do, a way to add a touch of humanness to the work environment.

In an organizational setting, suspicion sometimes accompanies affirming feedback, particularly when the feedback is not perceived as being particularly "job-related." The recipient wonders, "What's her angle?" "What's he buttering me up for?" "When is the axe going to fall?" and the like. If there is little history of giving affirming feedback in your unit, your employees might experience some difficulty in receiving it at first—they might feel suspicious or have some sense that the feedback is "out of order."

Quite often, affirming feedback is more difficult for the supervisor to provide than corrective feedback. Recipients will tend to act embarrassed, look away, change the subject, thank you profusely, and then deny that they really deserve the recognition. You begin to realize what it is like to "give" when someone refuses to "receive." Shoving it down their throats would distort the major point in giving the feedback. Maybe you see a lot of yourself in the employee who acts embarrassed, so you might not proceed with the affirming feedback you had intended to provide—and a lot never gets said.

AN EXERCISE: STROKES FOR ALL YOUR FOLKS!

This is an exercise that has been used effectively among employees and supervisors to set up a situation where *only affirming feedback is allowed.*

The ground rules are that the giver seeks out the recipient. Givers are allowed to state their feedback using their own words. However, since they all work together, the suggested instructions give examples of statements that put feedback in a work-related context. The recipient is not allowed to say anything after receiving the feedback—not "thank you," not anything. To ensure that the recipient hears and retains what the giver is saying, the recipient is encouraged to write down the feedback.

Once a giver has finished with his feedback to a recipient, I suggest that he move on to the next person he wants to give feedback to—or he can sit quietly and think up affirmative feedback he wants to give to another. To have the giver stay with the recipient of his feedback puts pressure on the recipient to reciprocate, to say, "You too." The giver, then, is not heard because the recipient feels the need to start thinking up some equally potent, corresponding feedback. Ideally the givers move on, and the recipients just write.

Here are the particulars on doing the exercise with your employees.

Instructions[1]

Objective

To provide an opportunity for offering greetings, compliments, and support to co-workers during a time of celebration.

Time Required

With ten or more participants, allow thirty minutes to one hour. If fewer, judge the time by the level of involvement. I recommend you conduct it late in the day or prior to a planned celebration.

Materials

1. Copies of the (a) giver-role and (b) receiver-role handouts for all participants,
2. Pencil and paper for each participant, and
3. Refreshments to continue the celebration.

Supervisor's Introduction to Employees

"I want us to take some time to think about how we have been working together lately. Specifically, I want you to think about what other individuals in this room have done to help, support, or facilitate your work or morale in the past (month, year, project, etc.).

"We will deal only with compliments in this exercise. Criticism and corrections are not appropriate, only compliments.

"This is a one-to-one exercise. You will have privacy to prepare and participate. I am handing out some directions to help you prepare."

Note: Hand out copies of the giver role and receiver role to all participants.

Supervisor's Instructions to Employees

"There are three activities for this exercise: preparation of compliments, giving compliments, and receiving compliments. All of us will first prepare compliments, as noted on the role sheets. You'll do this part of the exercise by yourself. Prepare as many compliments as you can in the time available. You'll have about five minutes to prepare. Now find a place in the room to be by yourself, for privacy. Read your roles and begin preparing. Any questions?"

Note: Give them one or two minutes to distribute chairs to a private place and five minutes to write their compliments.

After about seven minutes continue with the following:

Further Instructions to Employees

"Now start moving around and find people to compliment. Place the chairs in a private place so that when you give your compliment you can be undisturbed. Start now to deliver your compliments to someone in the room. If you have to wait to deliver your compliment because your person is already talking, use the time to see those who are not engaged and think about what compliments you can give them."

Note: Employees may be shy at first. That's O.K. Simply encourage them to begin when they are ready. Encourage everyone to take notes of the compliments given to them. (This gives everyone a tangible gift that they can keep for future reference. It also provides an activity for those persons who have some difficulty receiving a compliment.)

Within ten to fifteen minutes the pace and energy level will pick up in the room as enthusiasm and familiarity with the activity increases. You may have to move around the room and make sure employees are writing down compliments and not disclaiming them.

You may participate as a giver and receiver also. Give the exercise a chance to get started before you become involved. Once the energy level picks up you can monitor the exercise in between your giving or receiving.

Call an end to the exercise when you think it is appropriate (thirty to sixty minutes).

SUPPORTIVE RELATING: A GIFT ANYONE CAN PROVIDE

The possibilities for celebrating and providing affirming feedback underscore the continuing usefulness of developing supportive relationships in organizations. Whether support consists of a smile, a pat on the back, affirming feedback, inclusion in specific activities, or a celebration, the initiation of supportive relationships is not limited to supervisors in an organization. Support can begin anywhere, at any level.

Employees and lower-level supervisors tend to expect that support within the organization "should" originate from the top. Meanwhile, higher-ups seldom have any contact with subordinates that does not involve official business. Subordinates most often come in to complain, make a request, or deal with a particular business agenda. (Subordinates believer superiors should initiate and provide strokes in addition to responding to requests and complaints.) So where do the higher level managers and supervisors get their strokes, their pats on the back?

It is easy for employees to say, "Well, they are paid more. Besides they are the bigwigs around here. They should be providing the support and encouragement. Why should I provide it? I'm just a _____" (spelled "underling"). **Wrong!** Support does not depend on position or status or salary.

Support consists of recognition from another individual given in an affirming, rewarding manner. Whether you are giving support to your

Handout for Employees[2]

As Giver

Too often we have people in our organization with the "Charlie-Brown syndrome" of going to the mailbox for valentines and finding none there. Now is a good time to change this. All those you work with daily have probably done something during the last several months that has been helpful to you. Here's an opportunity to tell them about their help. List as many compliments for as many people as time allows.[a] Make your compliments as simple as:

"When you did _____, you helped me to _____."

"I feel supported when you . . . "

"I like it when you . . . "

"Your contribution of _____ helped me (this project)."

"You are important to me (to this unit) because . . . "

"I appreciate _____ ."

Go to the persons you choose as they become available. With both you and the receiver seated in chairs, placed in a private place, compliment them. When you talk to the person, be as specific and detailed as you can.

---

[a] Some of the people you want to compliment may not be here right now. So, when you have a moment during this exercise, prepare additional compliments for people you can compliment later.

As Receiver

You will need paper and a pencil to record the compliments you receive. This is to ensure that you hear what is said to you and accept it as a gift. If you are not clear about what you are hearing, ask for clarification. Do not return compliments at this time. Remember, the only way someone can be a giver is for you to receive their gift, without giving right back. So, really receive it and just accept it. (A profuse thank-you is like giving the compliment back. During this exercise, simply accept a compliment without giving one back.)

---

subordinates or superiors, if you want to make it personal, you can always say something like, "I like . . . " or "That _____ means something to me." If you want to make it more job-related, specify the situation or the activity you appreciate, and let that person know that how he or she handled it helped you. Let people know how they are important to you. Let them know what difference they make to you, what specifically they do. Even the pesky, irritable, daily complainer may make some valuable contributions to the organization. Recognize what they are. Tell him. Let him know that you are aware of them in a particular way.

Up to now, we have talked mostly about the support that comes in celebration and affirming-feedback situations. Now consider ways to develop support for yourself and others so that it becomes a part of your ongoing work relationships—in addition to the celebrations and formal occasions for affirming feedback.

You may already have supportive work interactions with certain colleagues. There may be an older or more experienced person in the organization who has been something of a mentor to you. You can count on certain employees, and they can count on you. Other employees may have similar supportive relationships in place. But that's not all there is! There are numerous possibilities to expand your support network just by listening. Supportive relating can originate through increased under-standing or empathy or awareness.

You may discover that different employees tend to view the world quite differently. While you think that more careful inspections should be conducted, they couldn't care less. They want their boats on the lake this weekend. Their incentives exist off the job, and the less they can do while still drawing a paycheck, the better they seem to like it.

You will possibly find support on the job among your like-minded colleagues. At the same time, don't write off your weekend boater. He may just be reflecting his own frustration at having cared at one time and not having had any support for his concerns then. Now you expect him to reopen his hopes? Most people care. You simply have to find the spark and respect their position.

Some organizations intentionally foster supportive relationships through company policies, priorities, and benefits. Even so, employees will interpret what is being promoted quite differently and react accord-ingly. Some employees will go along with the organization's interests in establishing supportive relationships because they believe in them. Others go along because their main concern is to keep their jobs and security, go with the tide and survive. Another group of employees will question certain practices and not readily accept every policy decision that is handed down.

You will discover through your search for more supportive ongoing relationships who is more concerned with immediate security and who is interested in improving support or discovering new possibilities. Be careful not to promote a "we-they" split in the unit or organization. Supportive relationships are easier to promote and more likely to permeate the organization if you consciously avoid getting into a definable clique: you need to operate with the services of all your employees. Keep the conversation open, but find a warm place for yourself in the organization. We all want to have some sense of belonging based on attraction, liking, or acceptance. Develop your own support system throughout the organization. While your supervisor and employees may fulfill an official support role, you may have to search further for the more genuine and personal ties you want.

PART III

SUPERVISING IN THE HUMAN DIMENSION

DRAMATIC VERSUS EFFECTIVE SUPERVISION

Do you want to be effective or dramatic? As a supervisor you have the opportunity to play into the various soap-opera scenarios that develop within groups of people who work together. Before you jump into drama, consider some of the longer-term influences that enter into and support organizational soap operas. Here are some of them.

Critical Incidents

We have touched on critical incidents in our section on "Guiding Activity Changes on the Job" (Module 10). However, it is important to note how ingrained the idea of the critical incident is in the mind of each of us.

It is Tuesday morning, 9:45 A.M. For the past month you have been stewing because you consider yourself underpaid for the work you do. You are about to walk into your boss's office to talk about a raise. You have been working up your courage for the past two weeks, rehearsing what you will say, trying to keep your anger from blurting out, antici-pating how your boss will react. Now you are ready. You announce yourself to his secretary and are told to go into his office. The boss greets you and then suddenly is interrupted by the phone. As the phone conversation is long distance, you realize that the boss is in conflict with a customer and that he is getting progressively more testy. This is obviously not the time to discuss salary, so you excuse yourself with some gestures and leave silently.

But you had been working up to this for weeks. You even made this morning your deadline. Now what can you do? If you have made today a "critical incident" through your own decisions about its being "now or never," then you have missed your chance. But you have also set up today as a deadline totally by yourself. You can therefore also re-negotiate with yourself and pick or choose a better time in the future. You make that choice.

How often people select a time or situation they invest with a "do-or-die" significance for themselves! If they dread doing the deed, setting the deadline serves to force them. It can also work against them, because one cannot always anticipate and choose the best time to act simply by setting up a given date as a deadline. To pass up this critical date then amounts to missing your chance and a further opportunity to avoid doing what you want. Stay flexible.

Sometimes others will help you to create a critical incident. I may get an order that a certain product "absolutely, positively" must be sent out by 5 P.M. tonight in order to arrive at the destination by 8 A.M. tomorrow. I then take on that responsibility and set this product as top priority for the unit. But it becomes more than just a priority. I also make my continued survival in this organization dependent upon my getting the package out tonight. If I do not get it out, I have conjured up tortures and catastrophes in my own mind, visions of what is sure to happen to me if this deadline is not met. Surely I, and even some intimate associates, will be eliminated through my misdeeds or failures. It might be all right if just I were held to blame, but when I start to take others with me, then my survival becomes even more important. The "package by 5" becomes a critical incident. Getting the package out will prevent (in my mind) some deadly mushroom-shaped cloud from blasting me off the earth.

Suddenly at 4:45 P.M. there is a call from the customer. He wants to change the order and add some refinements to the specifications. Now he wants it next Wednesday. The crisis is over. You sit back and ease off the tension. But the incident was only as critical or life sustaining as you made it in your own mind.

Fear Is the Motivator

How many times have you been involved in a "flap" at the office? Everyone runs around sounding like the sky is falling. While scurrying around to get the flap nailed down, most everyone is busy conjuring up an image of catastrophe and his own demise if this crisis is not met and dealt with. Curiously, this phenomenon can be observed over and over again, no matter how many times any individual—or an entire organization—meets and deals successfully with a crisis.

Almost from birth, most of us are exposed to fairy tales and to moralistic messages that use fear as clout. From them, each of us learns to make life an attempt to survive, to see danger coming before it gets here so that we can deal with it and survive through it. Rather than operating from an exciting sense of discovery and resilience to deal with what comes, to guide some of it, we end up with a general defensiveness and dread of change.

Fictions about the criticalness of incidents are sustained through a variety of experiences in our lives. In history class many of us had to designate the "turning point" of World Wars I and II. This fictitious "moment" in time was supposed to be the moment, the battle, or the event that marked a change in the fortunes of war and brought the defeat of the Axis powers. The turning-point mentality doesn't end with a history class. On Monday night football, the annoncers play a guessing game to determine "the" play that turns "the" tide or "the" momentum from one team to the other, bringing the inevitable conclusion of victory.

The turning-point mentality carries its own self-fulfilling prophecy. For if you think that there is a particular opportunity to do something and you then pass up that opportunity (as in asking for the raise), you have made that moment a critical incident beyond which you see no further opportunities. You have already given up. Your mind super-imposes its own meaning on reality and then reinforces that interpretation of reality: you can say to yourself, "You see, it *was* critical, because you haven't found another opportunity to ask for a raise."

Critical incidents have to be dealt with by each one of us in our own minds first. Critical incidents are in the same league as "shoulds," "whys," "absolutelys," "musts." They impose a false sense of reality. Like the "shoulds" and "whys," critical incidents are framed by simplistic cause-and-effect thinking (If A, then B. Why? Because A)—they represent a search for absolute explanations, for certainty, as if the universe were set up that way. But you can renegotiate your own approach to critical incidents if you insist on having them in the first place. Just take responsibility for the control you exercise in creating them and main-taining them.

Catastrophizing

What makes critical incidents pivotal in our thinking are the catastrophes we set up to be the result of that imagined incident. For most of us, the worst catastrophes that could happen to us on the job are that we would look inept, crazy, or stupid. The imagined result of appearing that way is that we would be let go (with or without ridicule) and find ourselves out on the street. Consequently, without a job, we would be rejected by our families, who in turn would also be destitute and starving in the street.

In most cases of critical-incident thinking and the catastrophizing that attends it, there is some imagined issue of survival, either physical survival or survival of one's self-esteem. Sometimes the catastrophe is imagined as a fate worse than death. And you can't get much worse than that!

The Survival Mentality: Pervasive and Potent

Many of us grew up either during the depression, a war, or some major "conflict." Whatever the major preoccupation, it helped to reinforce some popular beliefs that life is a struggle. It even presented catastrophe as imminent and requiring eternal vigilance by every individual. Life is perceived as a continuing struggle for survival.

The fact that in spite of inflation and the energy crunch, we have a strong economy has done little to allay fears. The fact that we have met the basic needs for most members of the society and that none of us would lack for food, shelter, or clothing for long—even in a major natural disaster—is pretty much overlooked. Since the game is survival and the investment and activities we are engaged in are survival oriented, there seems to be little chance of looking beyond all the superstitious activities and tension that accompany the primary occupation of surviving.

The survival mentality dies hard, and it requires very little bad news to put survival back in place as a primary concern. Besides, no matter what we are doing, no matter how inefficiently, we see we are still alive, hence, surviving. And that reinforces whatever superstitious survival activity we have been engaged in.

Tension, vigilance, and incentive are part of survival. When we have the basics for survival, we raise our standards for a survival level of life, even though that level has little to do with survival itself, but rather with preference or achievement level. Survival, then, is no longer just bread and a place to lay our heads. Survival today is a three-bedroom house with a two-car garage (one station wagon or van per house) and money for college educations and summer vacations. In our mind's eye we have determined that "we cannot live without" those comforts or conveniences, that life would not be worth living without them.

How do we break out of this cycle of rising survival levels and tensions? How do we work out of our own self-devised soap operas in organizations and off the job? First we have to come to grips with some of our daily realities and the meaning we impose on that reality.

First off, you have to look at the survival mentality and recognize it for the anachronism it is. Sure, there are survival concerns about radiation, nuclear holocaust, crime in the streets, and other dangers in contemporary life. There will always be some dangers of this type. Some dangers are also beyond your individual ability to cope, but few of them will be imminent or chronic. We can neither trigger these dangers, nor can we prevent them to any great degree. We can kick our shins in our helplessness, fret, and worry endlessly, or we can recognize our helplessness and go on with our lives.

HOW DO YOU DEFINE SURVIVAL?

Look at how you have created a survival level for yourself, the necessities you have determined you and your family absolutely must have and cannot live without. Get a grasp on that level of material possessions and what it means to you. Then get a sense of what material level is realistic and essential for a dignified continuation of your life.

Look also at the way in which you have built up to this "survival level"—the achievement orientation in which other people determined the essential goals and payoffs of keeping up with your classmates or TV characters, doing like Daddy and Uncle George and the Heisman trophy winner. Look also at the survival characters in the media who helped you prepare and become vigilant—Mighty Mouse to the rescue, John Wayne in war movies, the grasshopper and the ants, and other such learnings. Look also at the time spent playing "war," when you practiced operating under combat conditions so that when you really got into a war you would know how to survive.

You may have some experiences that are more meaningful to you personally than those sketched out above. The point is that "survival" is a massive motivator, so much so that it is an undue source of tension and an obstruction to organizational effectiveness. Recognize the survival mentality in yourself and in your dealings within the organization.

There are also some side effects of the survival mentality—understanding them can help you work more effectively with your employees and your superiors.

In early Sealab experiments to check out human adaptability to living in a small confined space under different atmospheric pressures over time, one method used to keep occupants alert was to plant some intentional malfunctions in the unit. That would send personnel scrambling to fix it. The drive to survive was engaged by creating the malfunction. Perhaps, on occasion, you cannot pull out of a drowsy state while driving, but a sudden emergency will get your adrenalin flowing and suddenly you are very alert.

Someone who values this type of fear-bound motivation will be interested in maintaining the survival mentality among his employees. He will always want some buttons to push. Fear is too familiar and too manipulable a motivator for some of us to let go. However, some of the side effects that would have to be attended to include psychosomatic illness in employees kept under stress, turnover, and employee absenteeism.

HANDLING DRAMATIC ACTIVITIES

There are better soap operas going on in many work sites than you see daily on TV between noon and 3 P.M.—only the writers, producers, and participants in the work site soaps are each one of us: "Will George finish his next task before the deadline and so avoid a confrontation with the boss?" "Can Edith withstand the boss's advances and still get a promotion?" "Should I let Jenny slack off work when her husband gets thrown in the drunk tank and her son calls from juvenile detention?"

One result of getting into soap opera in the work place is that much energy gets spent on following out and acting out the dramatic scripts. Rather than just asking George how he is coming along and whether he needs any help, a "dramatic" supervisor will labor long hours working out contingency plans for "if" George doesn't make it this time or "if" he does, he might not next time. By the time George has done a five-hour project, the supervisor has thought about George and the project some twenty hours. Since supervision involves the channeling of human energy toward operational activities and tasks, it is important to know how that energy gets expended within your unit.

Trying Isn't Doing!

Supervisors aren't the only ones playing out dramas in the work place. Employees do also, and they use certain statements that signal dramatic rather than effective channeling of energy. For example, "But, I tried." For the savvy supervisor, "I tried" is insufficient as an excuse for not doing the required work. "I tried" usually means "I expended energy in the direction of the objective." It also means "Get off my back! You can't fault me because at least I headed in the right direction." The reply of course is, "Yes, but you didn't do it."

Result, outcome, and production are what an organization is in business to get/do/produce. Trying is fine for the layman who is attempting some activity change or learning. We all know that personal changes are not always quick or clear. However, for a member of an organization in which members are interdependent upon each other for the outcomes, production, or results, "trying" affects more than that employee's personal life. He is personnel. And personnel directly impinge upon the other personnel of an organization. So from that standpoint, trying is not only not doing, but also *trying is not enough.* Personnel have to get together, to fill in for each other's deficiencies, to support and supplement each other's efforts, to provide some facility for mutual problem solving and goal achievement. Trying is a symptom of the entire soap opera on the work site.

There are some ways of dealing with "trying" personnel.

● Find out whether the objective is realistic, clear, and attainable.

● Find out what the employee specifically did as part of the "trying" activity—the range of activities, the level of effort.

● Find out what the employee thinks accounted for the short-comings in not attaining results.

● Determine the major difficulty that was not overcome.

● Determine what support is required to accomplish the attempted objective. Who? When? How?

The basic way to handle dramatic behavior or activities is to get at it from several approaches. *Be specific.* What was attempted? What worked? What remains to be done? Then get down to a more fundamental incentive for that individual. *What does that person want?* If trying and not getting results is as far as that person wants to go, there may be a real desire to reinforce his own sense of inadequacy and helplessness.

If one is truly attempting to get results and falls short, there ought to be some spark there to continue on and get the results. That is where asking what the person wants should elicit some continuing attempts to reach the objective. Then you have something solid to work with. Whining and complaining about falling short gives one little to work with and misses the job-related point, which is that the results have not been reached.

You Can Get from "Trying" to "Doing"

Focus on activities. Get the focus on *what has to be done to do it.* That focus avoids personally attacking particular activities and sets out the requirements, the requisite and sometimes sequential tasks, which have to be done in order to get the results. For example, you have to incubate an egg to get a chicken and feed a chick to develop a hen, which can then lay another egg. Concentrating on the things that have to be done, or that precede anything further happening, can pull one off the ineffectual dramatic track and onto the effective track.

WORKING EFFECTIVELY IN THE HUMAN DIMENSION

Before you read further, take a look at where you are right now. In order for you to get to the nearest door, you will most likely have to take several steps. That is what you have to do to get there. Of course, you could crawl, have someone lift you, or jump; but the main point is that you are where you are, and the door is more than one step away. In order for you to get there from where you are, you will have to step and step again, until you reach the door.

Working in the human dimension requires an awareness, an acknowledgement, and an acceptance of your real limits as a human being. Even though the longest journey begins with one step, you have to gauge those steps to be in proportion to the steps you can take day after day. If you have overextended, then you are off balance and your journey already requires some correction for equilibrium or stabilizing.

One way many of us create stress for ourselves is to overextend our demands beyond our physical capabilities. For example, as I walk down the street to a meeting several blocks away, I note that traveling at my current pace, I will be five to eight minutes late for the meeting. Of course, it would have been useful to consider this difficulty prior to leaving the office, maybe leaving five to ten minutes earlier. But, here I am now, on my way to the meeting. I could hail a cab if one were available. Even so, I might be held up at a couple of red lights, and end up arriving about the same time I would if I continued walking. I could break into a run. That would cut down my travel time, but I would probably require several minutes to calm down and wipe off the perspiration, and I would probably be less presentable and more disruptive to the meeting by arriving almost on time than by arriving late and calm.

The way I treat myself while walking down that street will say a lot about the way I treat myself in supervising—and how you treat yourself. If you demand that you be walking faster or that you already be at the meeting when you are fully two blocks away, you are denying the realities of the situation—ignoring the limitations of your physical being.

Getting back to where you are sitting right now, you could demand of yourself that you get to the door in one stride or that you already be there. And you are not there. Therefore, you set up a stressful situation between what you demand of yourself and your present reality. You are in your chair and not at the door, but your position is not attributable to "poor character" or some sort of mental deficiency that affects your survival. No, it is just happenstance that the door is where you are going and that the chair is where you are sitting. You can make that situation as stressful as you will, or you can accept the reality and work within it.

Accepting your reality would involve walking over to the door. In other words, doing what you have to do to get there—acting somewhat in moderation and keeping within reasonable and prudent limits.

HEROICS!

All too often organizational or unit objectives take on the flavor of some heroic feat rather than point to some attainable, reasonable outcome. A sense of the dramatic invades some planning sessions so that an undue sense of stress is set up. "We are going to take Hill 462!" says the Captain. And the soldiers look at their position and equipment and wonder how that can be done. Then, suddenly, three F-14s appear over the mountains and come in bombing and strafing, knocking out some of the major gun emplacements. Stirred by this unexpected assistance, the group charges up the hill, knocking out the other gun emplacements with grenades and capturing the hill within two hours.

That is all well and good for war stories. But what about the work-a-day world where most of us live? How does one deal with real-world objectives and morale? You must know what your role is and what your responsibilities are and where your unit fits into the scheme of things. What can you actually do? And how does that fit into what is required of this job? If you go for heroics, you can put yourself and your employees under tremendous stress.

At times supervisors will take on tasks for their units that say more about their individual ambition to curry favor with their superiors than their sense of appropriate work or capability in their unit. Unwise as this ploy may be, some supervisors get the work out. They may even establish a reputation for doing the impossible. They can wring that little extra out of their employees, "get blood out of a turnip." And what do you see when you look at the early health records of the members of that unit: hypertension, peptic ulcer, gastritis, heart attack? Does anyone check the high turnover due to transfers out and not necessarily in the form of promotions?

Generally a supervisor will consider his employees' and his own capabilities before taking on a major objective. For the supervisor seeking drama, there will be little attention paid to the real interests, concern, or capacities of his subordinates. His focus is on results, with little concern how he gets them. Just do it. Don't tell me how you will do it, just do it! And employees attempt to fulfill the demand.

Demand: Deny

If I demand of myself and that demand actually exceeds my own capabilities, then I am denying my own reality, my present capacity. I am operating outside of the human dimension. To continue to work outside of one's limits creates continuing stress. You have to ignore the messages coming from your own body in considering the possibility of doing what is being demanded. To keep demands in the human dimension, close to one's limits, does not preclude challenging oneself, stretching into new growth and development, discovering new capacities. Working within your own dimension does preclude stressing your system in an unhealthy way so that actual cell structure is damaged through abuse, excess, exhaustion, or internally created tension.

So often people despise themselves for what they cannot do, so much so that they heap abuse on themselves for their own shortcomings. Since we are all human, and therefore not perfect in all ways, that leaves a lot of room for self-abuse on the job and off. Perfectionism is just one of the demands that supervisors place on themselves and possibly on their unit. There are others.

PERFECTIONISM IS AN INHUMAN DEMAND

A perfectionist supervisor can create a living hell for himself and for his employees. The work that is turned out may be neat as a pin, but you may be paying dearly with the personnel for that "neatness." That trade-off for the perfectionistic demand will come out later in lowered productivity during the supervisor's absence, turnover, and absenteeism. Each of us is sufficiently perfectionistic in some ways that we may be creating some difficulties for ourselves, even while we come across to others as easygoing and laid back.

"I Never Ask More of You Than I Ask of Myself"

Watch out for this one! This supervisor will outcommit, outsuffer, outobligate you any day. It doesn't make any difference that your job description says forty hours per week. He has never punched out. He lives at the work site. This supervisor's workaholic mentality can be a real setup for the nonassertive employee. Disguised under the banner of loyalty to the organization, the trap for employees is their time is extorted by the supervisor-martyr's implicit demand to match him sacrifice for sacrifice.

"My Door Is Always Open"

Nonspecific words such as *always* and *never*, when used as leverage, are a license to steal. The supervisor obligates himself and allows employees to indulge themselves on his time and space. He establishes no limits or boundaries. Rather he erases his boundaries. He provides the employee with carte blanche use of his time. This makes it very difficult for both supervisor and employee. First of all, the policy of having one's door "always" open implies that the supervisor has no structure to his day, no particular needs or requirements for private time, for time to be undisturbed. It also leaves the subordinates with the idea that they require and deserve instant recourse for many or any problems. So, employees may not even have to think about a situation, just take it to the oracle beyond the open door.

Employees and supervisors need limits and boundaries to their space as well as some structure to their time. You can schedule your availability and still retain your ability to function openly with employees without inviting constant or spontaneous intrusion.

Indulge: Obligate

The openness in the my-door-is-always-open supervisor should seem a little suspect. The individual who indulges others, from whatever position in the organization, usually has some amount of obligation in mind in providing the indulgence. Most any time that an individual sets up a stationary operating policy, rather than a flexible structure with room for responsiveness as the situation requires, there is an angle or hidden agenda that is getting played to. And this hidden agenda serves to drain off some of the human energy so vital to accomplishing tasks.

For example, if I tell you that my door is always open, then I am always available to provide support or some other resource, it may also follow that along with that backup or support, I expect you to come through for me and sometimes to "go the extra mile." The extra mile gets spelled out as we go along. Having provided more than is expected or usual, and further underlining what I am doing with the open-door-policy pronouncement, I will also obligate or expect more than is usual by way of performance or personal loyalty.

"Extra efforts" in supervisory activities are used as leverage by the manipulative supervisor to get subordinate performance. This makes unit production more dependent upon the supervisor's ill-founded actions than upon clear job descriptions, objectives, and allocation of resources to the tasks. It detracts from the real practice of supervising.

These Kamikaze or self-sacrificing moves by supervisors to gain leverage over their units or to make a good showing for the local emperors may take their toll on the supervisor as well as on the unit. Unfortunately, many persons who took the work ethic, achievement, and competition very seriously have since had to experience at least one stroke or heart attack or other debilitating illness ("my heart attack") in order to leave behind some of the tension. Some of the employees who responded to their supervisor's earlier drive in business adopt their tension-producing approaches. Some drop out, while others have their own debilitating illnesses just like the boss.

It is more useful to use appropriate supervisory techniques to get the job done, rather than self-deprivation, guilt, and other self-debasing and self-abusing methods to establish control and credibility with your subordinates. Supervisors with good practices *use* those practices rather than personal struggle and sacrifice.

Someone whose door is open at specific times also has time to himself with a modicum of privacy to plan, to meet with other personnel without interruption, to follow out his plan, to think things through, and to have definite appointments to meet with subordinates, should they require it. At the same time, the subordinate who realizes that every issue or decision is not a critical incident can begin to exercise some discrimination and discretion in what can be handled alone and in what appropriately should be brought to the attention of his or her supervisor. By structuring such contacts, the supervisor provides the employee with a more efficient and effective method for interacting. Both the supervisor and the employee know and establish their role responsibilities and boundaries for working together. Know and establish your limits.

DON'T "SHOULD" ON YOURSELF

Much of the source of self-defeat and self-destruction in the course of supervising derives from our great desire for certainty and control. The use of "shoulds" in speech or thoughts plays into the fiction that there is certainty in supervising or in life. "Shoulds" provoke stress and strain in us, for they often are diametrically opposed to the realities of the situation we actually face. The only time that we can use "should" correctly is when we are referring to some specific performance that is part of a contractual arrangement. Then one can say that an employee "should" have done "X." Otherwise you are just expressing a wish, preference, requirement, conjecture, or demand.

Cherchez le Should

Shoulds speak to the way we think the world, others, or ourselves ought to be or act. Shoulds are a powerful force in our lives and experience. Using "should" outside a contractual context presumes certain fixed relationships and absolutes in the universe, thereby temporarily providing us with a false sense of security. For though we may want an employee to perform a certain way, to get certain results, we have no guarantee it will happen.

Sometimes shoulds give us just enough sense of control to make us think we actually have some power in what others do. When the organization, our unit, or even we ourselves do not follow the dictates of the way we know it should be, we can stand back in judgment with our standards held intact, knowing how it really ought to be if only it fit our model. "Should" is a word that allows us to maintain our infantile dream of being all powerful in a world that does not yield to our wishes and preferences, and does not even necessarily yield to our most prodigious efforts. Should buffers us from dealing directly and responsively with circumstances the way they are dealt with by "reasonable and prudent others." Our shoulds distort reality and prey on our own performance, on our employees and our relationships with them, on the unit, and on the organization.

Types of Shoulds

The stress-provoking shoulds can be grouped into three categories: those directed at oneself, at others, or at the context in which things happen. The statements may be made overtly or covertly. Here's what these three kinds of shoulds are saying in essence.

1. "*I should . . . .*" This is a demand on yourself. It is a statement that you are obliged or have no other choice than to act in a prescribed way. For example, you could tell yourself that you should have known that Max would not meet his report deadline before the Tuesday meeting. What you are telling yourself is that you require of yourself that you have some godlike omniscience, that you be able to predict the future. The payoff for being able to perform these superhuman feats of recognition, and possibly gain universal acceptance. "Universal acceptance" means that you would no longer have to struggle for acceptance from others, but rather would gain worthiness and universal esteem from others. People strive for universal acceptance in many ways, so there is little surprise that it would follow you into supervising. In any case, when you put a should on yourself, you are telling yourself what personally imposed or surmised requirements you place on yourself to qualify for your particular brand of universal acceptance, esteem, and worthiness.

2. "*You should. . . .*" This is a demand of other people. The immediate payoff of demanding from others performances that are different from what they actually are doing or have done is that you can feel superior and also "justifiably" hostile toward them for not following your formula or script for them to make a predictable, a certain, or a perfect world. If I tell you that you should read this part of the book in 35 minutes, then I have set a standard for you to meet. You will incur my indignance, and possibly wrath, by not conforming to my godlike demands. That also puts me in a position of personal worth based on my superior stance and requirements of others. Taking this position, I can also claim helplessness and disclaim responsibility when others do not follow my standards.

3. *"The organization (world) should . . . ."* I can stimulate much outrage that the world is not fair. Things are going on that I was raised to think would not happen because they are "bad" or "wrong"—or inefficient, unproductive, and so on—and they continue to go on. Now, at the level of moral indignation, I can truly stand above it all and ordain how the world or organization would be if only I were in charge. Of course, how can I possibly be held responsible or be expected to involve myself in the horrendous mess that is going on now outside my control or outside my requirements for the organization!

Realistic Shoulds

We have already mentioned that only contractual shoulds are enforceable. Only when someone has explicitly signed up for a particular activity in exchange for some payoff, only when someone is accountable for specific performance, can it be said that he "should" do it.

Contractual shoulds are enforceable. So, the particular person who has taken on responsibility for performing an activity can be made to discharge that duty or can be penalized for failure to perform. Only within the parameters of this type of legal arrangement can one correctly use "should," and then only due to the contract that backs it up.

The should in most of our lives comes from our own attempts to hold on to things we cannot control. Shoulds provide for self-righteous posturing *against others* who do not meet our standards for conduct, *against the world* in general for not living up to our childish expectations of the way things are "supposed" to be, and *against ourselves* for not being as perfect as we would have us be in the best of all worlds. Hence I can feel *hostile* at "them," *outraged* at the world, or *inadequate* within myself for falling short of a perfection that would surely get me universal recognition and acceptance. Out of the sense of hurt at my own short-comings, helplessness over the shortcomings of others, and outrage at the injustices of the world, one can evoke anger most of the time.

BECAUSE YOU ARE HUMAN, NOT PERFECT

When you have responsibility for the employee's production—or development—it is difficult to know when you have done enough, when it is truly the responsibility of the employee to make the gains. So, the sense of helplessness follows directly. You are not that employee. You have to accept your limitations and give that employee responsibility for doing the activities required of his job. Some of us do not have that kind of patience. We leap in and take over. Our tolerance is limited and we have definite ideas about how and when it simply "must be done," usually when we think it "should" be done.

As a supervisor, a major way to avoid "shoulding" on yourself will be to determine when you have done enough. That is one of those balances you have to determine for yourself, in your own situation.

From time to time, you will no doubt feel concerns about having fulfilled your responsibility, especially in cases of probation, reprimand, performance evaluations, and firings. Agreements will be one way to moderately assure that you have done your part.

Another (and perhaps the fiercest) should that supervisors have to contend with is self-imposed demands. Even when you have done all that you could anticipate and worked out agreements with the employee, you may still have some lingering self-recriminations. "I should have known better." "I should be able to pick up on signals earlier when the employee is floundering." "So what if he messed up again, I should have _____ " (known, foreseen, anticipated, acted, figured it out). Put in your favorite words to put yourself down. When all is said and done, all you can really gain from that situation is some learning for the next time a similar thing happens. You can give yourself interminable grief about it, demanding that you know what you did not know, demanding that you be more a god than a human being.

DEALING WITH YOUR SHOULDS

When you should on yourself, it will be useful to know how to ease up. Here are the two major ways:

Dispute: Where's the Evidence?

First off, you can openly dispute the particular demands that you put on yourself or impose on others or that others may put on you. Where is the evidence that you should or they should have done what is demanded? Is there some absolute law, some indisputable determinant in the universe that removes your freedom to choose, to act, and to deal with consequences? Generally, by disputing the particular demand, by being specific about the particular mandate being put on you, you can demonstrate that there is no hard evidence that you—or others—are obliged to act in that specific way.

Increase Effective Activity

Second, you can begin to act more effectively if you prefer to be more effective. Certainly you can prefer that something occur, that results be achieved. But to simply demand it is to impose an unreality to the situation. Or you can work with your employees to impart more skills so that they can work more effectively. Rather than demand of the past what it cannot yield up, work more effectively for present and future payoffs.

The world just is what it is. The continually evolving bottom line of experience (results) will reaffirm that there is no predictable, guaranteed, or absolute situation that will naturally prevail for us—or for anyone. You have to make of it what you will with effective activity. In other words, you are dealt certain circumstances. Some of them you can influence. Others you are left to deal with as best you can. Much of your learning to be more effective will be from the mistakes you make in those situations.

The best way to deal with these realities you should on is to face them, to assess what you can and want to do, and then to act as effectively as possible to get those results. Wishing, denying, or ignoring does nothing to effect those circumstances in the direction you want to move them. Acting will. You have to recognize your limitations and the uncertainty of outcomes, even processes, given other influences that are unforeseeable or beyond your control.

Dr. Albert Ellis has developed and evolved a comprehensive methodology for dealing with shoulds and other "unreal" activities that afflict most of us in our private lives and that follow us into our supervisory activities. Much of this material has been adapted from Dr. Ellis' work. Here is a message from Dr. Ellis[3] to remember as you supervise. Place it someplace where you can remind yourself.

I
WILL NOT
"SHOULD"
ON
MYSELF,
ON
OTHERS,
OR
ON
THE WORLD
TODAY!

---

[3]Adapted from *A New Guide to Rational Living*, by Albert Ellis and Robert Harper. North Hollywood, CA: Wilshire Book Company, 1975. Used by permission.

Postscript

You no doubt already know whether you are doing your job within the range of human possibility. If so, you need only stay tuned to your own perceptions and feelings about various situations as they arise from now on.

On the other hand, you may be doing yourself in with your excessive self-demand to be the perfect supervisor or the fair and supportive supervisor for every employee. However, once you have learned and acknowledged your own personal limits and have learned what makes up the main work of supervising, you will be able to determine whether your job scope is realistic and whether you can maintain your own human dimension to the work required on the job. If not, then there are several possibilities: job responsibilities have to be redistributed, or you will have to learn some more effective skills for handling the supervisory work.

By this time you probably have increased your awareness of the supervisor's job and the supervisor-employee relationship. You can recognize the multiple points of leverage available to assist you in supervising and your rights, responsibilities, and resources. You know which supports are already in place and those available to you in the future.

So now the job is yours to do. You have the continuing support of your own supervisor plus plenty of learning, which will surface in your dealings with your employees. Good luck, and keep your data base common.

ACKNOWLEDGEMENTS

I wish to acknowledge several individuals whose support, assistance, and encouragement brought this book into print. Larry N. Davis, my editor and colleague, first suggested the book, along with Ray Bard. Lee Neidermann and Linde Finn read the draft and made suggestions. Peggy Brannigan typed the original draft. Sherry Sprague brokered phone calls. Leslie Stephen suggested revisions. Mary Kitzmiller and Rebecca Taff rushed the book to completion. Michael and JoAnn Duffy, Frank and Rama Briganti, Bruce and Peggy Kruger, Melvin O. Hinson, Jr., Ruben Arminana, Nick and Barbara Grant, and Liz Lamond were my support group throughout. And thousands of participants in supervisory training sessions taught me.

ABOUT THE AUTHOR

Paul Radde, Ph.D., is president and founder of Thrival Systems®, a management-consulting firm located in Arlington, Virginia. Paul is particularly involved in executive development, stress management, and professional burnout as well as other OD and HRD areas. His most recent work has been with the World Bank, the U.S. Congressional staff, the Goddard Space Flight Center, the Federal Executive Seminar Center, the Navy-Air Force Joint Cruise Missile Project, the Georgetown University Law School deans, and the U.S. Department of Labor.

Paul received his doctorate in counseling and community psychology from the University of Texas at Austin and, in addition to his international consulting practice, maintains a private practice of psychotherapy in the Washington, D.C., metropolitan area. He has trained thousands of supervisors and prospective supervisors in supervisory-management principles and practices. He is also the author of *The Supervision Decision!*